LIGHT FOR TODAY

365

DAILY DEVOTIONS
FROM THE
LIGHTHOUSE

LAUREN GREEN

BroadStreet
PUBLISHING

BroadStreet Publishing® Group, LLC
Savage, Minnesota, USA
BroadStreetPublishing.com

Light for Today: 365 Daily Devotions from the Lighthouse
Copyright © 2024 Lauren Green

9781424567287 (faux leather)
9781424567294 (ebook)

Devotions inspired by Lauren Green's *Lighthouse Faith: God as a Living Reality in a World Immersed in Fog* published by Thomas Nelson, a division of HarperCollins Christian Publishing, Inc.

Stock or custom editions of BroadStreet Publishing titles may be purchased in bulk for educational, business, ministry, fundraising, or sales promotional use. For information, please email orders@broadstreetpublishing.com.

Cover and interior by Garborg Design Works | garborgdesign.com

Printed in China

24 25 26 27 28 5 4 3 2 1

To the One whose amazing grace guides me.
To the blessed Trinity:
the One who sees me,
the Lamb who was slain,
and the Advocate who intercedes.
To God alone be glory!

INTRODUCTION

Soon after the publication of my book *Lighthouse Faith*, I birthed the daily devotionals found in this book. The conception and fruition of *Lighthouse Faith* took the better part of ten years or more, and after its release, there grew in me an even greater need to be close to God. I hadn't realized how much he had guided me through the process of researching, interviewing, writing, and editing. And it fostered a closeness to the Creator whose image we all bear. I also realized that I needed to be that close to him continually, not just during a big project but also in the slow, moment-by-moment journey of life.

As I continued the daily routine of reading Scripture, praying, and reading theological treatises and other devotionals, thoughts would come to me, by God's grace, revealing the wisdom and deeper meanings of words or verses and how they should or could impact daily living. I began to expand on some of those thoughts in a daily writing called "Thoughts for the Day," which appeared on my Facebook page for friends and family to read. Those thoughts now become the heart and soul of this book, *Light for Today*.

You see, as most of us tacitly sense, life has an ebb and flow. The constant rhythm of waking, working, eating, and sleeping flow naturally and seamlessly through our relationships, and they hold power over us to mold us, challenge us, and strengthen us. But our most important relationship, with the one who created us, we often leave hidden or even forgotten by our daily tasks and our journeying through life's twists and turns. We forget, if we ever even thought about it, to read Scripture, to cultivate in our lives the incredible wisdom of God's Word, which is ironic because "the same mind running the universe expresses itself in the Bible."[1]

Lighthouse Faith took on that challenge of seeing God as the Light that is always present, guiding us, beckoning us to follow him. His light is like that of a lighthouse, shining its beacon in a foggy world filled with half-truths, missed truths, or even lies.

But there's more. The shape of the lighthouse is like the structure of the Ten Commandments, God's holy law. The first commandment, "I am the LORD your God…you shall have no other gods before Me" (Exodus 20:2–3), reminds us that God is the Light of the World. All other laws depend on us putting God first. It's a truth that brings order and clarity and, ironically, freedom. When God's truth and presence is our life's firm foundation, we cannot be swayed by the various winds of culture or even our own emotions that threaten to weigh us down.

Jesus reaffirms the first commandment's radiant luminosity in the New Testament when he says, "I am the light of the world. He who follows Me shall not walk in darkness, but have the light of life" (John 8:12).

Living up to our purpose in life, glorifying our maker in all that we do and say is not an easy task in today's me-focused world, dominated by a culture that is not centered on God or his objective truth. It takes concerted effort. As Oswald Chambers has said, "We can see God in exceptional things, but it requires the culture of spiritual discipline to see God in every detail."[2]

But God is faithful. Every day, nay, every moment of every day, a word of his power holds us up, "for in Him we live and move and have our being" (Acts 17:28). And that is, hopefully, what these daily writings can help you see.

Some of the readings are about people in my life or experiences I have had in the past or things I've observed as a journalist. Many of the devotionals are stories from the Bible. You see, every life—your life, my life—is a story expressing the inexplicable need for God's wisdom. So often we fall short of God's design for our lives. But God is patient through our stumbles. His light is always present.

I pray that these bits of daily light will help illuminate your life and bring you closer to Jesus, the Light of the World.

THE DIVINITY OF TIME

Your kingdom is an everlasting kingdom,
and Your dominion endures throughout all generations.

PSALM 145:13

The start of a new year is a good opportunity to remember that time is also part of God's created order. He established time, designed it, keeps it. To say, "Thank you, Lord, for this day," is to express gratitude not just for the now but also for all the days that have brought us this far, the ups and downs, the hopes, the dreams, both fulfilled and unrequited.

In liturgical time, today is the Eighth Day of Christmas. It's funny that as a culture, we move on from Christmas quickly to the hoopla surrounding the start of a New Year, when in fact, it's Christmas that holds the greatest hope we have. When our spiritual calculations are off and focused on the wrong things, we'll never find the true joy we so desperately need and want. It's like in the movie *Raiders of the Lost Ark*, when the swashbuckling archeologist Indiana Jones and his friend realize their competitor has the wrong map coordinates, and so they both say enthusiastically, "They're digging in the wrong place!"

And that means they'll never find what they're looking for. The joy of this New Year and throughout the year is in Christ. He is the Light shining in the darkness. You'll always find your heart's desire when you seek the King first.

To God alone be glory!

PERFECT LOVE

There is no fear in love;
but perfect love casts out fear,
because fear involves torment.
But he who fears has not been made perfect in love.

1 JOHN 4:18

A married couple thought it would be great if their new little kitten had a companion. As luck would have it, a dear friend who was a vet had a rescue kitten about the same age. At first sight, the two kittens did not get along well. And that's putting it mildly! There was lots of hissing, growling, and hackle raising. The couple had to keep the kittens separated at all times so they didn't kill each other. The couple both had battle scars from trying to separate the warring kittens in their campaign.

But a couple of days later something changed as the animals' hatred for each other turned to curiosity. Fierce fighting turned to wrestling. Then they started eating together. Within a few days, they began grooming each other. Then it was certain: the once mortal enemies were best buds. What happened to change hate to love?

The couple believed it was because the kittens no longer feared each other. With ample comfort and their humans' love, they no longer feared the other's presence. It's the same with us and our heavenly Father. To understand what his presence means in our lives, his love guaranteed by Jesus' sacrifice on the cross, is to know a love that not only brings contentment but that also transcends all understanding.

To God alone be glory!

CAIN'S SIN

The LORD said to Cain, "Where is Abel your brother?"
He said, "I do not know. Am I my brother's keeper?"
GENESIS 4:9

God's query to Cain was a rhetorical question. God knew where Abel was, but he was giving Cain the opportunity to confess and repent. Cain's reply was meant to hide an evil deed, the first murder recorded in the Bible. It was also an attempt to convince himself—the evil doer—that he did nothing wrong. But as in all cases of sin, God already knew what Cain had done. Cain had killed his brother.

God was trying to help Cain, whom he loved, to admit what he had done and to ask for forgiveness so that true healing could begin. It was a little like a soul cleanser. Instead of being wrathful and smiting Cain, God wanted Cain to feel remorse about what he had done, wanted him to hurt from the sin he had committed. But Cain only felt pain about what it was going to cost him.

How we are so still like Cain today, even as we understand this amazing concept called grace. We, on this side of the cross, post crucifixion and resurrection of Jesus Christ, have far more understanding of grace than Cain ever could. But still, we are so like our ancient ancestor. We see it in the man who stops having affairs only when his wife threatens to leave him or the woman who cries before a judge for shoplifting because she's being sentenced to jail time. We understand how sin breaks God's law. But grace can help us understand how it breaks God's heart.

To God alone be glory!

Trauma Transformed to Treasure

You see, at just the right time, when we were still powerless,
Christ died for the ungodly.
ROMANS 5:6 NIV

A woman recalls a childhood injustice when her first-grade teacher made the entire class stay after school because some of the boys were badly misbehaving. At six years of age, she had no concept of time. What was probably all of five minutes seemed an eternity. Her child's mind imagined it was like a life sentence in prison. She thought she would never see her mother or her home again. She began to cry…a lot! She remembers how a classmate called her a crybaby. She felt weak and helpless, wrongly punished, and wrongly mocked.

That moment had a profound impact on her for several years of her elementary school days. As the end of each school day neared, she felt the trauma again. Her throat tightened. The tears came. For years she worked to bury her feelings, fearing being called "crybaby" yet again. But then as a young adult, she began to realize the great benefit of having been through the heartbreak. It gave her the ability to empathize and comfort others. She knows now that what she had been burying was a treasure trove of God's gift to her.

Sometimes the worst thing that can happen to us could end up being one of the best. That is what the cross teaches us. How could the tragedy of God in the flesh dying on a cross, unjustly sentenced, cruelly mocked, amount to anything good? And yet we know it is the climax of human history that cosmically changed the world and defeated our ultimate enemy, death itself.

To God alone be glory!

Twelfth Night All Year

Being divinely warned in a dream that they should not return to Herod,
they departed for their own country another way.
MATTHEW 2:12

A glorious Twelfth Night! It seems a long time since Christmas. The tree is down, or it's looking like it should be. Traditionally, this is the time when the church says the wise men reached the newly born baby Jesus and his parents, Mary and Joseph. They brought gifts of gold, frankincense, and myrrh. However, some scholars believe the magi arrived even later—by two years.

Regardless, Twelfth Night gives us an opportunity to reflect on how we can keep Christmas in our hearts the rest of the year. After the snows melt and the spring rains come, the image of the tiny babe born in a manger helps us remember Jesus' humanity and that his birth means he is just like us in so many ways: vulnerable, breakable, loveable. But unlike us, he is God. And because he lives, we can face whatever is ahead this year and beyond.

To God alone be glory!

God's Word, a Weapon

*Jesus was led up by the Spirit into the wilderness
to be tempted by the devil.*
MATTHEW 4:1

We can learn so much from the account of Jesus in the wilderness. But one of the most striking things is how to resist temptations. They often come when we are weakest. Jesus was hungry and tired. He was tempted first by the very thing his body was craving: food. The devil offered bread to Jesus. When Jesus could easily have questioned God's love during forty days of utter silence, the devil promised safety and security. Jesus also could have questioned God's wisdom in letting him suffer. The devil promised wealth and power. But at what cost? Compromising Christ's relationship with God.

What's compelling about the exchange is that the devil uses Scripture to tempt Jesus. But Jesus knows that Satan has twisted its meaning. The devil believes in God and even knows God's Word. And if he's not afraid to quote Scripture to the Son of God, he's certainly not afraid to use it on us. If the Bible offered only solace and comfort, then occasionally reading it would be fine. But if the Holy Scriptures are truly the Sword of the Spirit, a spiritual weapon, then they have power to thwart the devil's schemes.

The Bible is not an occasional talisman against inclement conditions that pop up in our life but the actual life blood of God's wisdom. God's Word is "a lamp to my feet and a light to my path" (Psalm 119:105).

To God alone be glory!

The Power of Simple Trust

Blessed is the one who trusts in the LORD,
whose confidence is in him.
JEREMIAH 17:7 NIV

The best resolutions are the simple ones, like, "I will trust in the Lord." In its simplicity, it is truly powerful. To see our ultimate fulfillment in serving the risen Savior, we must complete all our other pursuits peacefully and joyfully as we must do all things for God's glory. Disappointment will not crush us but make us stronger. A bad report will only help us learn to find better solutions to problems. And those problems will only become pathways to greater solutions.

By trusting God, you invertedly teach others around you without even using words. You are the gospel in action for family, friends, coworkers, neighbors. All are changed through an encounter with God's holy gospel of grace and truth. Along with a resolution to trust is a mindset to help transform a hurting and confused world by being an example of the gospel of Jesus Christ and the grace by which you have been saved.

To God alone be glory!

Thankful as a Way of Being

Rejoice always, pray without ceasing, in everything give thanks;
for this is the will of God in Christ Jesus for you.
1 Thessalonians 5:16–18

If we're honest with ourselves, this verse is easier read than done. But make no mistake. It's a verse for practical living. This is how we are victorious in the world, overcoming its trials and challenges. To be thankful is to be joyful. And when you have harnessed the power of prayer, you have gained the most effective weapon of spiritual warfare.

Lost a relationship? Be joyful that Jesus is still the love of your life. Lost your job? Be grateful that Jesus became poor so we could inherit riches beyond comparison. Suffering the loss of a loved one? Ask the Lord Jesus Christ to comfort you and weep with you, to hold on to you and help you through it.

Meet every challenge in life with the practical tools of spiritual strength: pray, give thanks, be joyful. It's the trifecta of a spiritual battle hard fought and won. God will never leave us or forsake us. "The Lord is gracious and compassionate, slow to anger and rich in love" (Psalm 145:8 NIV).

To God alone be glory!

CREATED FROM LOVE

I am persuaded that neither death nor life, nor angels nor principalities nor powers, nor things present nor things to come, nor height nor depth, nor any other created thing, shall be able to separate us from the love of God which is in Christ Jesus our Lord.

ROMANS 8:38–39

God created the world by his love. His love is the foundation of everything that we see. It is also the foundation of who we are. All of us are shaped by love and molded by circumstances that are a combination of others' love, an amalgam of our parents, siblings, extended family, and friends.

But because love is so foundational, we are also shaped and molded by the absence of or the distortion of love. That is why we must look to Jesus Christ as the ultimate relationship. He can love us the way we should be loved. Parents are not perfect, but Jesus Christ is. Siblings are sinful, but Jesus Christ never sinned. Spouses sometimes lie and cheat, but Jesus Christ is your true spouse. He is truth and gracious generosity and love.

He is the Word made flesh, and he made his dwelling among us. Override the world's distortions of love by loving Jesus Christ first. All your other loves will benefit from the greatest love of all.

To God alone be glory!

God's Tank Warfare

"The turning away of the simple will slay them, and the complacency of fools will destroy them; but whoever listens to me will dwell safely, and will be secure, without fear of evil."

PROVERBS 1:32–33

An episode of a documentary series on World War II focused on tank techniques. Military tanks are a perfect analogy for how God deals with us. The program showed how tanks are big and bold and can cause a lot of damage, but they can't maneuver well. One strategy for combat tank warfare is to build trenches. This accomplishes one of two things: either the tank will plow into a trench, get stuck, and become vulnerable to enemy assault; or the tank will go around the trench and onto a more desired path, which is God's real purpose for us.

In war an enemy builds a trench to destroy. But when God builds a trench or puts up a roadblock, it's to save us. If we all look back on our lives, we see so many times when we cried out to God in anger. Maybe it was the pain of a relationship coming to an end or an opportunity we felt we deserved that passed us by or just general malaise and frustration over life's circumstances.

But if we see these contradictions as trenches, small and large, in God's divine tank warfare, we can see his firm but loving hand directing us toward a better path, leading to him and his wisdom.

To God alone be glory!

Be Joyful!

You will show me the path of life;
in Your presence is fullness of joy;
at Your right hand are pleasures forevermore.

PSALM 16:11

A funny thing about joy is that the more you express it, the more joyful you become. Joy is like a vivacious virus; once it gets into your system, it never leaves. Even if you don't feel its effects, it's still there. It can remain dormant but never disappear.

Faith in Jesus Christ is a lifetime gift of joy. You don't go out and get it. You receive it. Like a great pastor wrote, "Joy is not a requirement of Christian discipleship, it is a consequence."[3] And like any virus, you can infect others with its power and effects. Being joyful is our special condition as Christians. It's not about forgetting the problems of life but rather being able to see past them to find solutions.

Jesus Christ "for the joy that was set before Him endured the cross" (Hebrews 12:2). He is our example of joy in the midst of hardship. Be a thermostat of joy and set the temperature wherever you go.

To God alone be glory!

LIVING BY EXAMPLE

I will meditate on Your precepts,
and contemplate Your ways.
PSALM 119:15

A middle-aged woman looked back on having to take city buses in her teens. She used to see a lot of interesting characters. But one in particular had a big influence on her. It was a young woman. She was fairly pretty and always had a glow about her. And she always wore a smile. She carried in her lap a well-worn Bible, and she would read a few words then close her eyes as if to memorize what she'd just read. Then she would smile as if she'd just ingested a savory meal. Her eyes would light up.

Back then, the teen used to feel so sorry for the young woman because, being strongly influenced by the liturgy of a secular world, she thought the young woman a little crazy. But the other young woman possessed a positive spirit and a contentment that the teen craved and to some extent probably envied. Today, she thinks about that young woman with only admiration and thankfulness. It was because of her that the teen finally learned how to look upon God's Word. Now, as a grown woman, she lets Scripture fill her entire being. She daily tastes the savory and sweet meal that nourished that young woman and kept her aglow.

It just goes to show that you never know who may be looking at you at any time. And what you do or say can bring a big change in someone else's life, even years later.

To God alone be glory!

Growing in Patience

Be…rejoicing in hope, patient in tribulation,
continuing steadfastly in prayer.
Romans 12:10, 12

Many times, we pray for patience; maybe it's through a difficult circumstance or to deal with difficult people. But patience is one of those qualities that we learn through trials. It does not come via a magic wand. God will not wave his hand and instantly bestow patience on us. He will put more obstacles in our path so that we grow patience as we would a muscle. And we can only strengthen that muscle as we encounter difficult people or situations.

In the end, we must learn to have a sort of "passion for patience." As one theologian said, "We will not learn it by swallowing our sense of outrage on the one hand or, on the other, excusing all wickedness as neurosis. We will do it by offering up our anger to God, who trains us in creative love."[4]

Embracing the prospect of patience also means seeing Christ on the cross, patiently accepting his tortuous death in order to give us life. Be patient with others, for God's patient love has granted us eternity with him.

To God alone be glory!

The Essence of Faith

Faith is the substance of things hoped for,
the evidence of things not seen.
HEBREWS 11:1

While *evidence* is a scientific term based on what we can observe, *hope* is nothing of the sort. It is not a physical presence. Only God could combine such disparate things to describe faith. But hope has its polar opposite, which can be dangerous for us. As Thornton Wilder said, "Hope is a projection of the imagination; so is despair." Hope and despair are opposite reactions to suffering. It is not easy to hope in the midst of pain. So what's the solution?

We can live in hope by training our hearts and minds in the good times to trust in the living God, just like any athlete training for a big race or competition. Try running a marathon without ever having run even two blocks. The stress on those untrained legs will break you and make your lungs feel like they're burning up. Instead, you have to start slowly, building up your stamina, and keeping yourself healthy. The same is true if you want to remain strong at times when your faith is challenged. As Edward Mote's old hymn says, our hope is built on "nothing less than Jesus' blood and righteousness." It is on Christ the solid rock we stand. That is our evidence!

To God alone be glory!

We've Come This Far by Faith

We walk by faith,
not by sight.
2 Corinthians 5:7

A woman once related to me how, over one holiday season, she experienced much pain along with joy. Right before Thanksgiving, one of her dearest aunts passed away. Two days after Christmas, another beloved aunt died. Her "beloved aunties," as she says, were elderly, and their passing was not unexpected. But she remembered how they helped shape her life.

It was one aunt, her mother's sister, who came to her rescue at school when morning kindergarten had been canceled. The school couldn't reach her mom, so they told the child they had called "Mrs. Johnson." The child, at such a tender age, was fearful of this Mrs. Johnson until, to her delight and joy, in walked her wonderful auntie! And it was another aunt who coined the woman's childhood nickname. It was also the voice of this aunt she remembers one evening singing a gospel hymn around the piano, "We've Come This Far by Faith."

For both of these special women, it was a faith built on the foundation of strife and hardship but also joy and hope. They never lost their belief that God would see them through whatever life handed them. The woman says she is so grateful for so much richness of faith her aunts brought into her life; a bountiful harvest of trusting in God's Holy Word. He'll never fail you.

To God alone be glory!

God's Window into Your Soul

[Jacob] was afraid and said, "How awesome is this place!
This is none other than the house of God,
and this is the gate of heaven!"

GENESIS 28:17

One woman told me that God spoke to her through her passion—music. A revelation came to her through music, when God spoke to her in a way that only a musician would understand. There was no doubt that God was making his presence known by using something she knew so well. It's a reminder that everyone has a gateway, a door, a cracked window through which God comes into their lives and radically changes their understanding of who God is.

Instead of seeking God as an intellectual or academic pursuit you join in once a week as part of organized religion, you can let God transform your whole life and become the center around which your whole life revolves. God becomes the environment through which you perceive your life. He meets you where you are.

For Jacob, it was a stairway that opened the way to heaven. For a musician, the notes on a page. For you, it can be something totally different, such as a bike ride or a backyard garden. What matters is that wherever you open yourself to receiving him, God will be there. The gate of heaven is always nearby.

To God alone be glory!

The Power of a Name

She conceived again and bore a son, and said, "Now I will praise the LORD."
Therefore she called his name Judah. Then she stopped bearing.
GENESIS 29:35

Leah named her fourth son Judah. The first three she named out of her grief over the fact that her husband Jacob did not love her. For he was in love with Leah's sister, Rachel. But it seems by the time her fourth child arrived, Leah had given up trying to make Jacob love her and instead praised God for his love for her.

Judah, what a name! It means "praise." It was Leah's fourth son through which the tribe of Judah gets its name. The tribe that generations later gave birth to King David, Solomon, and numerous great prophets also gave us Jesus, God's Son and the Messiah.

In the New Testament, Jesus is called the Lion of Judah. Oh, the things God can do! We can be reassured that whatever we feel and whatever we go through, we can confidently give it over to God. He will make something good come from anything. Praise him! Leah did. And look what happened.

To God alone be glory!

God Knows Us

O Lord, You have searched me and known me.
You know my sitting down and my rising up;
You understand my thought afar off.
You comprehend my path and my lying down,
and are acquainted with all my ways.

PSALM 139:1–3

Physical challenges just seem to accompany us as we get older. It's part of the natural path of aging. Doctor visits and perhaps even hospital stays are not uncommon parts of the landscape of life. The funny part is that we never really give our bodies much thought when we're young. But as we age, the body breaks down, and we become more acutely aware of it. Knees and hips are prone to arthritis. Hands, too, become less dexterous.

We become intimately aware of our body through its pain. But then we should also remember that God knows our pain better than we do. And here's a thought: Do we know God more than we know our pain? J. I. Packer wrote something that is so helpful through the physical challenges. He said those who know God "never brood on might-have-beens; they never think of the things they have missed, only of what they have gained."[5]

We may have pain, but the Bible promises that the love of God is far more powerful. He knows us. And life, even with its pain and suffering, gives us this wonderful opportunity to know God more intimately.

To God alone be glory!

God's Power Overcomes Our Challenges

Your testimonies I have taken as a heritage forever,
for they are the rejoicing of my heart.

PSALM 119:111

People who live in a cold weather climate know that snow is slippery. And after a sizable snowfall, if you want to get into your driveway without getting stuck, you'd better enter at a good clip. If you go too slow, the tires will spin, and your car will slide.

During winters, the entry to a certain alley way would get so rutted with snow and ice that huge grooves formed an odd bobsled track. Veterans of the neighborhood obstacle instructed novice drivers how to get into the alley without getting stuck. You had to speed up prior to entering the alley and let the car's momentum get you through. The weight of the car in motion overcame the slickness of the ice.

The law of ice and snow relates to the law of God's power to overcome any of our challenges in life. Brooding over problems is like getting stuck in an ice and snow rut. The solution is always to bring the problem to God. Not only does he have the answer, but we can also have faith that he is greater than the weight of the problem. He turned the greatest problem, the death of his Son, into the greatest triumph: his resurrection and our redemption. There's no rut too big for God. Trust him!

To God alone be glory!

The God of Love and Justice

Babylon, the glory of kingdoms, the beauty of the Chaldeans' pride,
will be as when God overthrew Sodom and Gomorrah.

Isaiah 13:19

We sometimes forget that although God is the source of love, mercy, and patience, he is also a God of justice. That works fine if we only think of the obvious sins, like murder, stealing, or adultery. But many good things can become sins, like idolizing a successful career or a loving relationship. It's hard to recognize when they've crossed over into the "dark side," so to speak.

Take aspiration versus ambition. They have many of the same qualities but lead to very different goals. As Eugene Peterson said, "Ambition is aspiration gone crazy. Aspiration is channeled, creative energy that moves us to grow in Christ, shaping goals in the Spirit. Ambition takes these same energies for growth and development and uses them to make something tawdry and cheap."[6]

Ambition recognizes no higher authority but its own desires. Aspiration desires to serve, not be served. Only a loving God, who knows our hearts and minds, understands how to judge the difference and lead us to understanding it as well.

To God alone be glory!

Do Only God's Will

Be sober, be vigilant; because your adversary the devil walks about like a roaring lion, seeking whom he may devour.

1 Peter 5:8

At any moment of the day, we should ask ourselves, *Am I doing God's will, following my own will, or being a tool of the devil?* This is the problem with sin-based creatures like us. Taking our eyes off the Source of Life is like taking our eyes off the road while driving. Many times, nothing bad happens. But then sometimes, terrible things do transpire, and we say to ourselves, *How could that happen? I only looked away for a second!* That's why they're called *accidents.* They are the unintended consequences of not being alert to the conditions around us.

Failed marriages, discord in the home, dishonest gain, and other unwanted outcomes all come from taking our eyes off the source of hope and happiness. The Bible is our driver's manual on the road of life. It's number one edict: keep your eyes on Jesus, God's Word made flesh. He has ultimate knowledge of the road conditions. Trust in that.

To God alone be glory!

Cultivating a Heart for God

"The heart is deceitful above all things,
and desperately wicked;
who can know it?"
JEREMIAH 17:9

In the 1970s, a song by Morris Albert called "Feelings" became a big hit. The lyrics spoke of being consumed by heartbreak in the aftermath of a broken relationship. While it's easy to be consumed by feelings, from a biblical perspective, it's not a wise thing to do. Certainly, from God's point of view, it's a terrible idea! His Word says, "Those who trust in their own wits are fools; but those who walk in wisdom come through safely" (Proverbs 28:26 NRSVA).

Feelings are important. They can protect against predators and make us wary of dangers. But they can also lead us astray unless they're accompanied by hard facts. The truth is, "Feelings don't run the show. There is a reality deeper than our feelings." And God wants us to "live by that."[7] God wants us to live by the reality that his Son, Jesus, suffered and died on the cross to defeat the evil that constantly bombards us. And evil knows that the best way to attack us is through our feelings.

God is greater than anything we may feel. He is the ultimate source of wisdom and knowledge. And no feeling can change that.

To God alone be glory!

A Refuge for You

Trust in Him at all times, you people;
pour out your heart before Him;
God is a refuge for us.
PSALM 62:8

A brilliant piano teacher in New York City helps his students understand how to interpret the music of the masters, like one of the famous romantic composers Brahms. Or the powerhouse of the classical era Beethoven. In one lesson, the teacher explained to a student the difference between playing the two composers' works. Beethoven was like telling a story about something that happened to someone else. But with Brahms, you're telling the story about yourself. That totally changes how the musician performs a piece. A certain emotional distance exists when the story is about someone else. But when it's about you, the emotions are raw. There's no hiding.

This is how Psalm 62:8 can affect us. Substitute your name for "you people." And at the end say, "God is a refuge for [me]." By doing this you can quickly realize that God is not a distant deity who merely makes sure his subjects are behaving. The reality is that God is a loving parent who wants to hold us and comfort us no matter what we're going through.

God is the ultimate musical master. He knows when the song is about someone else and when it's about the person singing the tune. Sing to him.

To God alone be glory!

Walking in the Light

If we walk in the light as He is in the light,
we have fellowship with one another,
and the blood of Jesus Christ His Son cleanses us from all sin.

1 JOHN 1:7

New York is the hub and home of the Broadway musical. One of the big-time favorites is *Hello Dolly*. One woman who's a big music buff says the opening number, "Put on Your Sunday Clothes," occasionally brings her to tears. It's not because the song is particularly emotional but because it displays in musical form what happens when we all "walk in the light." By that she means when we all walk in the same Light.

In the musical, we see all sorts of people joyfully anticipating their excursion into town. They're all dancing to the tune of the same music, the same composer. They each have their individual reasons for hopping on the train, but they're moving to the same rhythm.

Herbert Schlossberg wrote that "universals transcend particulars."[8] Whatever differences we have among us—age, race, height, culture, or others—pale in God's Light. To walk in God's universal Light helps us overcome our differences. But more than that, it helps us respond with great joy as we're all cleansed in the blood of the Lamb. It helps us put on our Sunday clothes seven days a week.

To God alone be glory!

Protections Known and Unknown

Preserve me, O God,
for in You I put my trust.
PSALM 16:1

I know a couple with several cats, and they explained to me how they're constantly picking up things around their home that could be dangerous to kittens. The little furry ones seem to enjoy chewing on, scratching on, and chasing around all sorts of items that to humans are just innocuous, inanimate objects. But for kittens, these playthings could be lethal.

If the straight pins my friend uses for sewing become lodged in the carpet, they can puncture a paw; the power cord to the phone chargers can administer an electric shock if a cat chews on it; earplugs, necessary to New York city apartment dwelling, are small enough for a cat to choke on. There are scores of examples, and the felines have no idea the dangers their pet-parents protect them from. It's exactly the same for us in God's world.

How many potential hazards does God remove from our lives without our ever being aware of the dangers? How many times has God protected us from untold harm? We'll probably never know this side of heaven. It's just good to know that there is a God who loves us enough to be our armor and shield and never ask for credit for all the things he has done to keep us from harm. But one thing he has done that we do know about is sacrifice his Son for us. Thank him for all things. Both known and unknown.

To God alone be glory!

Putting Trust Only in God

Those who know Your name will put their trust in You;
for You, Lord, have not forsaken those who seek You.
PSALM 9:10

New York City is the mecca of fine dining. It doesn't necessarily mean five-star and white-tablecloth dining, although there's plenty of that. There is a plethora of good places to eat; even a hole-in-the-wall diner can have excellent and amazing tasting food. So competition is stiff.

One Thai restaurant tried to entice would-be diners with a sign that said, "In noodles and rice we trust." It was a lighthearted play on the phrase on our legal tender, "In God we trust." But it gnawed on the conscience of more than one passerby because trust is such a crucial thing. Declaring our trust in God is appropriate for our money because it's saying that even something as valuable as the almighty dollar must come second to our need for God.

Making a joke of the phrase could create a tendency to forget the importance of trusting in God. We all have a choice of where to place our trust. Noodles and rice are wonderful but hardly something you can trust. And if you ever eat at that restaurant, it'll be a good thing to make sure to thank God for them.

To God alone be glory!

God's Plan Prevails

[Abraham] believed in the LORD,
and He accounted it to him for righteousness.
GENESIS 15:6

The story of God's great prophet Abraham and his journey to becoming the father of many nations and the patriarch of Judaism and Christianity is a great example of how, despite our sins, God is faithful. Despite our getting in the way, God is masterful at detours.

Abraham lied, cheated, and committed adultery. And yet God still worked through him to complete his plan for redemption and salvation through Jesus Christ. It's easy to look at Abraham and think his story is all about his actions, but no. It's about God's hand always being in control. As one theologian said, "It is a story about God's choice of you and how he successfully executes his will in you."⁹

We are weak vessels. But God is our strength. At crucial moments in our life, when there seems to be no path ahead, that is when God does his most spectacular work. All we need to do is be still and know that he is God (see Psalm 46:10). Have faith in that.

To God alone be glory!

A Most Satisfying Love

Know the love of Christ which passes knowledge;
that you may be filled with all the fullness of God.
EPHESIANS 3:19

None of us is perfect, and that means that none of us had perfect parents, which also means there's always going to be some sin we tend to crawl back to, as the wants of the flesh are never quite in line with God's truth. Even sins can be so embedded in our way of being that we don't notice them or we even misidentify them as virtues. Perhaps we gossip but only see ourselves as being honest. Or maybe we make snarky remarks that belittle others but only believe we're being harmlessly witty.

What the Bible understands and what God certainly knows is that we're all on a kind of salvation project. We're all trying to repair what's wrong with us, to create in our lives what we feel is missing; oddly enough, what we're missing is a love that surpasses all understanding. However, the only way to truly love someone is to truly know them. And the only Being capable of thoroughly knowing us, our thoughts, hopes, hurts, desires, past, present, and future is the Lord Almighty: Father, Son, and Holy Spirit. He is love. And he is perfection.

To God alone be glory!

Choose Wisely

*"If it seems evil to you to serve the LORD,
choose for yourselves this day whom you will serve."*

JOSHUA 24:15

Chocolate, strawberry, or vanilla? When it comes to ice cream, those three are rarely the only flavors available in today's specialty ice cream shops with their myriad of palate pleasing options. The great news is that choosing an ice cream flavor has little impact on your life's destiny. We make choices every day; some easy and some quite difficult.

When Joshua spoke to the Israelites on the eve of their going into the promised land, the choice of whether to serve God or one of a variety of pagan gods was up to them. Even though God had brought them out of slavery in Egypt and watched over them through forty years of wandering, he still gave them a choice. Why? Even though he provided food, shelter, and refuge for them, one could assume they would naturally be grateful and want to live thankful lives. But godly love never assumes.

God understands that true love doesn't coerce. It's possible the Israelites would only serve him out of obligation, not true devotion. It's the same with us. God, out of his infinite love, has provided a whole world filled with endless possibilities of goods, including ice cream! And ice cream is a good example of the irony of making choices. We may think that in choosing the ice cream flavor, we are in control, that we have the authority. But once that sweet creaminess touches the tongue, it's pretty certain that it's the ice cream that has mastered us. Choose wisely!

To God alone be glory!

Boundaries Bring Freedom

I will walk at liberty,
for I seek Your precepts.
PSALM 119:45

Years ago, a journalist covered the famous Van Cliburn International Piano Competition in Fort Worth, Texas. More than thirty pianists from all over the world competed for the gold medal that would practically guarantee them a lucrative concert career. Even though the pianists played music that had been written decades and even centuries before, they were all able to create something unique within the confines of the prescribed notes. One competitor from Russia told the journalist something never to be forgotten. She said music competitions are difficult to judge because "how do you compare one person's soul to another?"

What she expressed is the paradox of freedom. The law of staying within the boundaries of what a Bach or Bartok had written somehow allowed for a flexibility of expression. This is similar to the fence around a playground that allows children to play safely with total abandon or guard rails on a winding road that let you drive with total confidence at a higher speed because you know there's something guiding the path. C. S. Lewis wrote of this paradox, "Obedience is the road to freedom, humility the road to pleasure, unity the road to personality."[10]

We all crave to make beautiful music of our lives, to sing our heart's song. God wants that as well. The key is to learn the musical notes God provides, and the possibilities of what we can sing are endless.

To God alone be glory!

God Creates the Party

*Draw near to God
and He will draw near to you.*

James 4:8

People always say that a great place to meet a mate is at a wedding. That's certainly true for one couple who often regale their friends with the story of how they met at a high-profile wedding in New York City. Neither was supposed to be there. She wasn't on the original guest list. He was invited but didn't want to go.

After the couple married, the wife meditated over this verse in James and was reminded that all she had done was to ask a friend of the bride's father if she could attend the wedding. If she had never asked and assumed she couldn't go, her whole life would have taken a completely different turn. All it took was one simple request. A humorous thought also popped into her mind: God is certainly no party crasher. He won't show up where he's not invited. God doesn't draw near to us on an equal footing with our step. Instead, we draw near just a wee bit, and he's ready to sweep us off our feet. What a party!

To God alone be glory!

Sacrament of Baptism

I am the bread of life.
JOHN 6:48

Baptism is a sacrament in every Christian denomination. But there are different approaches. The Orthodox and Baptists practice full immersion. Many Protestants and Catholics sprinkle the water over the head. Some baptize infants and others only those old enough to make their own profession of faith. Each can seem strange to someone not raised in the tradition. For example, a woman raised mainline Protestant attended a Greek Orthodox baptism of twin baby girls. Instead of the infants wearing the long, flowing dresses, they were clothed only in onesies. To the woman it was like showing up at a wedding in your underwear.

As the service began, she kept wondering, *Will no one put some clothes on these babies?* Then she realized why. The Greek Orthodox church baptizes children by full immersion, dressing them afterward. But something amazing took place she'd never seen before. The priest cut a lock of hair from each of the newly baptized children. The priest said it was a physical symbol of them growing in Christ as new creations. From that moment on, whatever they ingested would feed not only their newly formed physical bodies but also their souls and spirits.

It's a reminder of how vitally important it is to seek the best nutrients for healthy growth, both physical and spiritual. No matter what stage we are in life when baptized, growing in Christ is a daily process, and we feed on the Bread of Life.

To God alone be glory!

Healing the Brokenness

Now as they came out, they found a man of Cyrene, Simon by name.
Him they compelled to bear His cross.

MATTHEW 27:32

Wounds from major surgery like hip or knee replacement sometimes take a very long time to heal and often leave a scar. But the joy of being rid of arthritic pain far outweighs the ugliness of the scars. Although the body is healing, the mark of the wound that allowed for the brokenness to be fixed remains.

That is what the cross of Jesus is like. It is a wound in the collective consciousness of human existence. To bear it means to always have a visual reminder of the heavenly surgeon's scalpel that removed the scourge of sin so the healing could begin.

The cross we wear around our necks or on our hearts reminds us that we need not fear the pain of brokenness, for we have been redeemed. Let the healing begin.

To God alone be glory!

ⅅISCERNING GOOD FROM EVIL

Woe to those who call evil good, and good evil;
who put darkness for light, and light for darkness;
who put bitter for sweet, and sweet for bitter!

ISAIAH 5:20

These days, it's sometimes hard to discern what is evil and what is good, what is darkness and what is light. The entertainment world has especially played a major role in blurring the lines between the two, presenting adultery, profanity, and all sorts of sexual immorality in a positive light. The industry has tremendous influence over generations of young people who grow up learning their morality only from television or social media.

What God wants us to know and be wary of is that evil has power—and it is a power that can only destroy what is good. The Bible warns against evil's allure. It's usually quite attractive. If evil showed its true face of ugliness, of unsightly disease and death, we could always avoid it. But evil is usually disguised as something or someone we find enticing or pleasant.

Rest assured, as the old saying goes, that "evil carries within it the seeds of its own destruction." Jesus on the cross defeated Satan and his lies; Satan's power is limited. Look to Jesus, and you will have no trouble discerning the difference between darkness and Light.

To God alone be glory!

Death Is Not Natural

"God will wipe away every tear from their eyes;
there shall be no more death, nor sorrow, nor crying.
There shall be no more pain, for the former things have passed away."

REVELATION 21:4

Within one week, a certain woman attended two funerals. One was for an elderly woman who'd lived a full and rich life. She had been devoted to her church, her children, grandchildren, and great grandchildren, who were all present as the priests offered final prayers. The other was for a man in his late forties who died suddenly of a heart attack. He had no children or wife, just grieving parents and friends who didn't understand why someone so talented and in his prime should suddenly be taken from this world.

The "whys" of death are never easy to answer. No one on earth can really make sense of it. But all of us, whether we believe in God or not, feel at some deep level that death is wrong, that it's some kind of mistake.

And it is. We were never meant to suffer and die. God made us for joyful communion with him in a beautiful garden. But our ancient ancestors, Adam and Eve, ruined that. Jesus destroyed death on the cross and put humanity back on the path to returning things to the way they should be. Death will not have the final say! Be assured of that because Jesus said, "It is finished" (John 19:30).

To God alone be glory!

QUESTIONING GOD'S LOVE

My son, do not despise the chastening of the LORD,
nor detest His correction;
for whom the LORD loves He corrects,
just as a father the son in whom he delights.

PROVERBS 3:11–12

Rosaries are a symbol often associated with Catholicism. However, a woman who is Protestant talked with reverence about the privilege of having acquired several rosaries from travels to Rome. Most were blessed by the pope himself. She displays them in her home, and when people ask about them, it's an opening to talking about faith in Jesus Christ.

However, her kittens have no such reverence, and only see the dangling beads as wonderful jingly-jangly things to play with. For that reason, she tries to keep the rosaries out of their reach. She caught one kitten on hind legs with his body stretched upward, his mouth firmly clamped on one of the rosaries and in the process of pulling it down. She shouted, "No! No! No!" And gave the kitten a firm pat on the rump. He released the beads ran.

She thought of the God lesson: How many "jingly-jangly things" had God removed from her life because she didn't appreciate their value and treated them with little to no reverence? All those times she said, *Why can't I have this?* Or *What harm could it be?* Like those kittens, we all want what is attractive and alluring, no matter the conditions or obstacles, not realizing that sometimes God's response is "No!" without explanation. The hard part is understanding that sometimes when God's love speaks the loudest, it can hurt the most.

To God alone be glory!

The God Who Is

God said to Moses, "I AM WHO I AM." And He said,
"Thus you shall say to the children of Israel, 'I AM has sent me to you.'"
Exodus 3:14

Learning any new language can be a struggle. But one of the very first things we learn is conjugating the verb "to be." It's essential for anyone to be able to tell their story, to tell people about themselves, to say who they are and where they come from and where they're going. In English, it's "I am." In German, *Ich bin*; in French, *Je suis*.

But nowhere in any form of language is this phrase a proper name except in the Bible. When God reveals who he is to Moses, God calls himself I AM. In the exchange, Moses doesn't correct God's grammar. What God is saying is something so off-the-charts mindboggling. He's saying that he is existence itself.

It also means that the Bible is not just *a* story but *the* story. It is the grand narrative above all narratives: who God is and who we are. All of us have a defining story that gives meaning to life. But all those stories are tethered in some way to the story of the great I AM. No matter what language you speak, there's always I AM!

To God alone be glory!

Preventing Flabby Faith

Whenever I am afraid, I will trust in You. In God (I will praise His word),
in God I have put my trust; I will not fear. What can flesh do to me?
PSALM 56:3–4

Working out is a great way to stay in shape. Exercising those muscles routinely is good for mental as well as physical health. But if you stop working out for any reason, it doesn't take long for muscles to fall prey to the power of gravity. It can turn a six pack into a bowl of Jell-O in no time.

Faith muscles are just like physical muscles. They both need an opposing force to build them up and constant attention to keep them strong. When we neglect our faith muscles, they get flabby too. When our first response if things don't go our way is to fear the future, that's how we know our faith is flabby.

But thankfully, we have the best trainer in Jesus Christ. He can help us build up faith muscles wherever we need it. For he has given us a spirit of strength, not of fear (see 2 Timothy 1:7). Neglecting your physique can add a few pounds, but ignoring your faith muscles can bring you to despair. The latter is far more dangerous.

To God alone be glory!

Bearing Our Burdens

The children of Israel said to the Lord, "We have sinned!
Do to us whatever seems best to You; only deliver us this day, we pray."
So they put away the foreign gods from among them and served the Lord.
And His soul could no longer endure the misery of Israel.

JUDGES 10:15–16

There was a six-year-old boy whose father was the consummate handyman around the house. He was carpenter, electrician, and plumber rolled into one. One day, the boy's father was fixing the plumbing in the only bathroom in the house. There was a long, metal tube lying on the floor, so the little boy picked it up. He was amazed that it was so lightweight that even he could hold it. And he could bend it with his own little hands. So he did, shouting to his father, "Look, Daddy, what I can do!"

The look on his father's face was a mixture of shear pain and agony. He cried, "Oh son, no!" Apparently, that metal tube was the crucial piece he needed for the repair job, and here the little boy had contorted its shape just to show off. Realizing that what he'd done was horribly wrong and caused his father so much grief, the little boy began to cry. His father's anger lasted only a split second, replaced by concern for his son's pain. Soon the father was comforting the little boy, reassuring him of his love, that all was well, despite the boy's actions costing him more time and money.

Not all children have such earthly fathers whose anger lasts only for a moment. But thankfully, we all have a heavenly Father, who hurts when his children are hurting and would bear the burden of their mistakes rather than see them suffer.

To God alone be glory!

LEARNING FROM THE LORD

They continued steadfastly in the apostles' doctrine and fellowship, in the breaking of bread, and in prayers. Then fear came upon every soul, and many wonders and signs were done through the apostles.

ACTS 2:42–43

By the time we're in our forties, we will have watched hundreds of hours of commercials and even more before we start collecting Social Security. That's a lot of TV time. Whatever the stats show, it's likely we don't spend as much time praying, reading God's Word, or attending Bible study or church.

The early Christians understood the importance of community. Whatever and whoever we spend time with shapes who we are, how we see ourselves in the world. That's why this gathering in the book of Acts is inspiring: "They continued steadfastly." These days, it's not practical to stop watching television cold turkey, but the point is, if we are a reflection of our community, getting our values from that community, and if the main source of community is TV, then how can God's Word have authority over us?

In his book *Amusing Ourselves to Death*, Neil Postman writes, "The mind [is] a garden that yearns to be cultivated."[11] There's no doubt prayer is a powerful tool for tilling our mind's garden. It lets us commune with God. It changes us. It tells God we're inviting him into our world to be the authority. It is a great antidote to the power of what should be lesser influences.

To God alone be glory!

Our Gifts Are from God

*There are diversities of gifts,
but the same Spirit.*

1 CORINTHIANS 12:4

New York City is brimming with talented and smart people. It is a place filled with the best and brightest in every field, be it the arts, fashion, finance, or food. In the Big Apple, there is no shortage of beauty and brains. But most of those with these talents, unfortunately, use their gift to glorify themselves. They develop their talents and grow them with the goal of being a star in their respective fields.

When we recognize our talents as gifts from God, they take on a whole new purpose, for "Whatever gifts we receive, whether tangible or intangible in character, are not only a blessing but a trust to be used responsibly in His service."[12]

Imagine a place where all people use their talents in service to the living God, to glorify the Son, Jesus, to be a vessel in the kingdom of the Lord of Lords. This can begin with you. It only takes saying the words of St. Francis of Assisi, "Lord, make me an instrument of your peace."

To God alone be glory!

THE MIND OF THE HEART

*Out of the abundance of the heart
the mouth speaks.*
MATTHEW 12:34

None of us says everything that's on our minds. If we did, we would be diagnosed with some kind of mental illness. Constant jabbering in a stream of consciousness is not normal. So we hold back most of our thoughts. And thankfully, only God knows them.

But even though we don't speak everything that's on our minds, like unkind remarks, biting criticisms, or insulting words, they still are part of our psyches, burrowing into our hearts. And that's dangerous. It's like a filthiness that builds up and eventually dirties the whole of us. As one minister wrote, "Defilement is what sin does to us; damnation is what sin introduces as our eternal end. Except for God's intervention."[13]

Being careful of what we think, blessing instead of cursing, builds up beauty in our hearts. And when we are filled with the "fruit of the Spirit" (Galatians 5:22–23), it overflows into what we say. Jesus knows there is a deeper self that we keep hidden from the world. But he also wants us to understand that we can never hide it from him. But he loves us still.

To God alone be glory!

THE VALUE OF WISDOM

Whoever has, to him more will be given, and he will have abundance;
but whoever does not have, even what he has will be taken away from him.
MATTHEW 13:12

When he was ten years old, a concert pianist was very nervous about his first piano recital. He shook like a leaf. Nothing prepared him for the terror of performing in front of all those people. *What if I forget my music?* he thought. Fear gripped him. But since that fateful evening, he has gone on to give many solo piano recitals, and the fear of a memory slip has dissipated. He said that over the years, the more he performed, the more music he memorized. And the more he memorized, the easier it got. Eventually, preparing a two-hour program of very complicated music seemed almost like child's play.

For so long, he thought this parable of the talents was only about money, but there's something else in the works here. As always, Jesus is much more concerned about our spiritual health than our monetary condition. He used a parable about money to give us an understanding of the value of wisdom in God's kingdom. "The more wisdom you have, the more wisdom you will gain in every turn in the road of life."[14]

Like memorization, we attain wisdom by actively seeking it. It is not a passive quest. But Scripture says there's something else that's crucial about wisdom, something so imperative that it makes this claim: it is the only path to truly knowing God. And that's worth memorizing!

To God alone be glory!

The Bible: The Owner's Manual

The entrance of Your words gives light;
it gives understanding to the simple.
PSALM 119:130

Car shows attract thousands, if not millions, of people each year. The new cars shine and gleam in perfect lighting in convention centers across the country. For some folks, it's the look of the car that's appealing while other aficionados prefer to pour over the brochures the car company's hand out detailing what makes the car unique and attractive, its engine, torque ratio, V6 or V8. But the manual is also a guide that tells potential owners what the car was created to do. For example, sports cars are short on interior space but have an abundance of speed. On the other hand, SUVs tout their cargo capacity, not how fast they can go from zero to sixty.

Wouldn't it be great if humanity had an owner's manual? Wait! We do. It's called the Bible. And as one learned theologian wrote of our manual, "The things it commands are the very things we were created to do."[15]

The difference between us and any car is that we are far more complex than even the most intricate of automobiles, and our manual is incredibly more nuanced. It is simple yet multifaceted. It is intelligible but multilayered. What's great about our manual is that it applies to all models for all years. And the same expert mechanic can fix whatever is broken.

To God alone be glory!

Bitter or Better?

God so loved the world that He gave His only begotten Son,
that whoever believes in Him should not perish but have everlasting life.
JOHN 3:16

The bells of Valentine's Day are pealing loudly today. So many of us look forward to some special something from a special person. There's no better verse for Valentine's Day than the apostle John's words about God's love for the world, giving love not because we are lovable but because God *is* love.

Valentine's Day is always close to, give or take a few days or weeks, the start of Lent, Ash Wednesday. Lent is the forty days leading up to Easter when we ponder God's love through Jesus' sacrifice on the cross. How suffering ties into love is something that is hard to grasp. In a theological sense, suffering is a discipline. We choose how we respond to it.

Take, for instance, the woman in a Midwestern town who responded to God's love by building a shelter to feed and house homeless women and their children. A reporter asked why, even though she had children and a home of her own, the woman would build the facility. She replied, "You can either become bitter or better from the things that happen to you." She was showing women whose lives hit rock bottom that God still loved them and was caring for them. Jesus was her example. We can share in his suffering by the way we endure the bad things that come our way. But then, because of his great love, we can also rejoice and share in the resurrection as we let God make us better for it.

To God alone be glory!

Hidden Deceptions

The serpent was more cunning than any beast of the field which the Lord God had made. And he said to the woman, "Has God indeed said, 'You shall not eat of every tree of the garden'?"

GENESIS 3:1

And so it began. From this one inquiry is born the Eddie Haskell's of the world, the Wicked Witches of the West or wherever they're from, and all other malcontents bent on all sorts of deceptions and great evils, both fictional and real. The real issue here for Eve, and for us, is the supplanting of God's authority with her own.

Here's a more modern take. As you raise children and watch them grow from infancy, there is inevitably a stage in their early years when they use a paraphrase of the devil's words to Eve in order to get something they want: "Why not?" or "You didn't tell me I couldn't." A child may decide to change the rules of checkers to help him win the game. It is a lie as easy to see through as plastic wrap.

As we get older, if we are not properly guided, we improve on delivery of said deceptions. In adulthood, those same indiscretions can blossom into something far worse. These are the sins that become news stories: fraud, identity theft, political intrigue. It's all part and parcel of the devil's agenda. As the great preacher Jonathan Edwards wrote, "In the midst of this confusion, the devil has great opportunity to advance his own interest."[16] The antidote? Ask yourself, *Under whose authority do I live? God's or my own?*

To God alone be glory!

Mercy in Healing

Have mercy on me, O Lord, for I am weak;
O Lord, heal me, for my bones are troubled.

Psalm 6:2

If you've ever rescued an animal from a shelter, it's likely you saved it from certain death. One cat owner said his feline was found on the side of a road after getting hit by a car. Its hip was broken. Thankfully, a good Samaritan brought the cat to an animal hospital where a vet healed his brokenness.

As the cat knew it had been saved from the brink of death, it was incredibly affectionate and loving, purring at the slightest touch. The owner realized that in giving the animal love, he himself felt loved. He said he thinks often of what that kitten endured, alone on the side of a highway, crying for help, maybe for its mother or just for someone to take the pain away. And then the man realized that he was often just like that kitten, feeling alone, hurting on the side of a road, crying for someone to hold him.

As one pastor says, "It's good to have love with some skin on it sometimes."[17] And that's where each of us can be the substitute for God's loving arms. Sometimes we all feel like that kitten on the side of the road, battered and broken, unable to help ourselves let alone heal the wounds that cripple us. We need a loving touch, a hand to hold, a shoulder to cry on. All of us can be aid to the Great Physician, helping to bind up the wounds of those who are too hurt to help themselves.

To God alone be glory!

THE GREATEST OF THESE

Now abide faith, hope, love, these three;
but the greatest of these is love.
1 CORINTHIANS 13:13

This verse is a staple at weddings, showing what great importance we place on giving our hearts to one person for the rest of our lives. But the Bible tells us that few of us truly know our own hearts and that our hearts are deceitful (see Jeremiah 17:9).

The great theologian Augustine of Hippo wrote in his famous book, *The Confessions*, "My weight is my love."[18] He meant that whatever controls him, whatever he is seeking after, reaching for, his greatest fundamental trust, that is what he really loves and that is what he really worships.

"Love determines all of our human existence and is the greatest of the gifts of the Spirit."[19] The love we've been seeking our whole lives is available to us now, this very moment. It's the love of Jesus. What we're all looking for is an eternal love, and only that love will satisfy us. That is what propelled Augustine's famous words, "You have made us and drawn us to yourself, and our heart is unquiet until it rests in you."[20]

To God alone be glory!

Honoring God with Our Words

*With the tongue we praise our Lord and Father,
and with it we curse human beings,
who have been made in God's likeness.*

JAMES 3:9 NIV

Have you ever heard the phrase, "A saint on Sunday and a devil the rest of the week"? Divided lives of honoring God with our singing and prayers on Sunday but swearing and being an unkind neighbor Monday through Saturday is unfortunately a plague of humanity.

In reality, church on Sunday is where we get our spiritual batteries recharged. But it's the rest of the week where we live out the gospel. Therefore, we are called upon to "Let your faith not just be external, but let the internal match."[21]

In other words, we are to honor God with our heart and deeds not just our words.

If our first impulse is to speak sharply, criticize, or gossip, it's not enough to just bite our tongues and keep the words in our mouths. We must change our hearts so those thoughts and words are no longer part of us. Think about Jesus on the cross saying, "Father, forgive them" (Luke 23:34). Imagine what incredible conviction of faith-matching deeds that is. Thank God for his guiding Light!

To God alone be glory!

Being Right with God

The LORD is near to all who call upon Him,
to all who call upon Him in truth.

PSALM 145:18

Finding the right person to be your husband or wife can be so difficult. The dating scene in today's world is even more treacherous because of what's called the "hookup" culture: the pressure to have an intimate encounter with someone you barely know.

The irony about this way of forming relationships is that it actually makes you less able to draw near to someone emotionally. It makes you less able to bond for fear of being hurt. But bonding is always required in healthy relationships. God knows that the best way to find a healthy earthly relationship is to pursue a passionate relationship with him. It's what he longs for because it is what's best for us.

At the end of the day, God is not an academic pursuit. He is not a theology class, although we can learn much about him by studying his Word. He is the ultimate relationship partner. While other religions give you a set of dos and don'ts, Christianity gives you a person, Jesus. It is Jesus with whom we can expose all our weaknesses and wants, our hopes and our fears, our never-ending quest to be wholly and fully loved. It is with Jesus that we have a love that will never die.

To God alone be glory!

FREEDOM IN TRUTH

"You will know the truth,
and the truth will set you free."
JOHN 8:32 NIV

A few weeks after a rather invasive surgery on his legs, a middle-aged man said he began to heal well enough to get by without a cane while walking inside his home. He actually felt like he walked almost normally. That is, until he got a glimpse of himself in a mirror.

He saw his wonky side-to-side walk that looked more like an imitation of Frankenstein rather than a sophisticated man-about-town. It was visual proof that he was not as healed as he thought. That realization made him humbler during physical therapy and more determined to do all the exercises the therapist prescribed. He said it was funny how what he felt was so different from reality. It was only by facing the truth that he could really begin his road to recovery.

This man's experience is a good reminder that, in God's eyes, we will always be spiritually on the road to recovery. We will always need the picture of the perfect image of Jesus Christ. He is the most loving and gentle therapist, wanting only for us to see the truth of his gospel that will set us on the road to true healing.

To God alone be glory!

All a Part of Christ

If one part suffers, every part suffers with it;
if one part is honored, every part rejoices with it.
Now you are the body of Christ, and each one of you is a part of it.

1 CORINTHIANS 12:26–27 NIV

A few years back, a well-known musician developed a neurological problem in her right hand that painfully restricted the movement of the thumb and index finger. The condition is called focal dystonia, and it has plagued many a musician, perhaps because of the repetitive motion of practicing. She went to see a specialist who said that although the tendency is to work only with the affected fingers, the real solution is for all the fingers to be a part of the healing. In all instruments, playing with all fingers brings a particular strength to a musician's ability to play.

When playing the piano, the thumb provides the pivoting motion so scales are smooth and seemingly effortless. The index finger must follow the thumb's lead. Somehow this musician's index finger started acting like the thumb and made intricate finger work sound clumsy. Only by bringing all the fingers into the recovery process could the affected ones improve. As the two fingers improved, all the fingers improved.

This is another God lesson. The musician said she believed God allowed her to suffer this malady related to something that she loves so dearly, music, to help her understand the value of community in Christ. We are not alone but part of a body with many members.

To God alone be glory!

Obeying out of Love

"As the Father has loved me, so have I loved you. Now remain in my love.
If you keep my commands, you will remain in my love,
just as I have kept my Father's commands and remain in his love."
JOHN 15:9–10 NIV

There's a difference between being good out of fear of punishment and being good out of love for the one who makes the rules. One older gentleman looking back at his childhood said, "Honest to goodness, I can't remember having a lot of rules in our home growing up. Maybe it's my age-related memory loss. But I still remember when some of my friends would talk about being grounded because of some curfew or other rule they violated, and I couldn't relate. I'd ask, 'What does "being grounded" mean?'"

He said his parents disciplined him and his siblings. But it was as if the motivation for being good had nothing to do with punishment. It had everything to do with loving their mom and dad and not wanting ever to disappoint them. We can learn a lot of rules and their penalties in a classroom. But grace is something we have to experience. The man said he was good not to get something from his parents but because of what he already had: their unconditional love.

No one takes a class to learn how to love their parents. It's an organic relationship that nurtures children's love for their mom and dad. It is the same with our heavenly Father. We are so loved and so accepted that nothing can separate us from his love. It's a gift that keeps on giving. That's a rule worth remembering.

To God alone be glory!

God's Communications

He said, "The knowledge of the secrets of the kingdom of God has been given to you, but to others I speak in parables, so that, 'though seeing, they may not see; though hearing, they may not understand.'"

LUKE 8:10 NIV

Our pets don't speak words, but they find ways to communicate. If they're hungry, a good tip of the food bowl will send a message. Pet owners learn to read the signs. The two, owner and pet, know what's going on. The godlike being in a pet's life responds not only to the animal's wants but also to its needs.

The back and forth can be described as a sort of earthly version of what theologians call *divine accommodation*. Divine accommodation is God's way of simplifying concepts that might be too difficult for our finite minds to comprehend. For example, using simple words that we can understand, Scripture explains the incomprehensible act of creation when it says, "God said, 'Let there be a dome in the midst of the waters, and let it separate the waters from the waters'" (1:6 NRSVA).

As historian Rodney Stark wrote, "God's revelations are always limited to the current capacity of humans to comprehend—that in order to communicate with humans God is forced to accommodate their incomprehension by resorting to the equivalent of 'baby talk.'"[22] Well, it seems plausible that our "pet talk" is sort of the same. However, we're *not* God's pets; we're his beloved sons and daughters. Jesus' parables are another example of God allowing us to reach the unreachable. They help us dig deeper into God's relationship with us so we can see that he is responding not just to our wants but also to our deepest needs.

To God alone be glory!

THE GIFT OF SALVATION

God spoke all these words: "I am the LORD your God,
who brought you out of Egypt, out of the land of slavery.
You shall have no other gods before me."

EXODUS 20:1–3 NIV

God set the Israelites free, and then he gave them the law. He didn't give them the law first and tell them that only if they could live up to it, God would free them from slavery in Egypt. No. Their freedom was God's gift.

The narrative of the Israelites journey from slavery tells us that salvation is not something we can earn. Our good behavior, while a nice way to live, does not pave our way into God's good graces.

We have been freed from slavery to sin through the sacrifice of Jesus Christ on the cross. "Christian obedience does not earn our salvation any more than Israelite obedience earned deliverance from Egypt. Salvation is a gift."[23] Now we are called to obey God as grateful recipients of his mercy and grace.

To God alone be glory!

His Peace

"Peace I leave with you; my peace I give you.
I do not give to you as the world gives.
Do not let your hearts be troubled and do not be afraid."
JOHN 14:27 NIV

Jesus' final parting words to his apostles and to us give comfort and strength. Many times we forget that he really is our refuge in life's daily challenges.

We worry needlessly and become the source of our own anxieties, often making ourselves feel far worse than necessary in a given situation—sometimes it's fretting over a few minced words and blowing things out of proportion, and sometimes it's losing sleep over a doctor's appointment or a job interview. On the other hand, when things are going well, we like to take credit for the success. But to ignore Jesus and the peace he offers in the process of our lives is a little like forgetting to put on shoes to go to work. It's just not going to turn out well.

One theologian famously said, "I forget your wisdom and so I worry. I forget your grace and so I get complacent."[24] Many of us have faced this same dilemma. We must strive to trust in him instead. Look to Jesus, and he will give you a rest and a peace that passes all understanding.

To God alone be glory!

Strength in Weakness

"So do not fear, for I am with you;
do not be dismayed, for I am your God.
I will strengthen you and help you;
I will uphold you with my righteous right hand."

Isaiah 41:10 NIV

There is hardly a more vulnerable moment after invasive surgery than the first two days of physical therapy in the hospital. The medications sometimes cause nausea, and the muscles around the area of surgery are weak.

A man who'd just gone through surgery said he used to think of the above passage in Isaiah as his physical therapy nurse followed close behind while he made his way around the halls of the hospital with a walker. The nurse had a wheelchair just in case the patient got weak and couldn't stand. They were not going to let him fall. At one point, the nausea overtook him, and he collapsed in the wheelchair to rest. He thought of these words of Isaiah. "Do not be afraid. I am with you." This must be how God is with us. Following us around with a divine wheelchair just in case we suddenly tire and collapse. Only instead, his wheelchair is his loving arms.

The man keeps a mental picture of the hospital experience and the wheelchair episode as a reminder of how God is taking care of him and holding him up. He is constantly reminded that God is in control and that, if we fall, we can trust that he is there to catch us.

To God alone be glory!

No Fear of Hell

Because of the Lord's great love we are not consumed,
for his compassions never fail.
They are new every morning; great is your faithfulness.

LAMENTATIONS 3:22–23 NIV

Years ago, before the advent of clean air laws, residents in many cities used to burn their own trash in big metal cans in the alley, backyard, or by the garage. For little kids who watched their dads and older siblings light the fires, it was a visual lesson that fire needs fuel to burn.

It was also before the creation of a lot of synthetic materials, which proved to be toxic when set on fire. So most things burned were paper products. It was fascinating to watch how fire consumed the different items like egg and milk cartons, cardboard, and wrappers. The heat of the flames was so intense that you had to stand several feet back. For people in that era, the imagery of fire as a metaphor for hell and damnation was quite real. Young people saw how fire consumed and destroyed, how getting close to flames could burn you. Because of this up-close exposure to fire, that generation was astounded to read that God would appear to Moses in a burning bush that was *not* consumed by the flames. How could a fire not consume all in its path?

Lamentations understands it perfectly. Hell is fire without God. It's the separation from the Almighty we experience when passions overrule God's law. It's a fire that consumes. Heaven is the "burning bush" where God's love and his law are one, providing the safe place for the fires of our passions, the fuel of his faithfulness to us.

To God alone be glory!

To Be Known and Loved

Where can I go from your Spirit?
Where can I flee from your presence?
PSALM 139:7 NIV

Every year, millions of women compete in beauty pageants. These pageants can be quite challenging events in a young woman's life, physically, emotionally, and spiritually. Those who choose to enter them often undergo interviews that include a lot of interesting questions.

One judge asked a contestant, "If you were at a party and God walked in, what would you do?" The contestant's answer showed not only how much she understood Psalm 139 but also that she lived by its knowledge. She answered, "I would do nothing different, for God is always present. He is in the room. He already knows I am there and what I am doing."

That mindset can truly change your thinking about God. This reality of God always being present is at once comforting and scary. Comforting because we need not worry about ever being alone or having to face anything life brings without the power of God's presence. But scary because there's no time when we can hide what we're doing from the all-knowing, omnipresent Being. But here's the great part—we serve a loving and forgiving God, who, through Jesus Christ, offers us mercy and grace. How precious to be truly known *and* thoroughly loved.

To God alone be glory!

The Perfect Beauty

Never be lacking in zeal,
but keep your spiritual fervor,
serving the Lord.
ROMANS 12:11 NIV

Sometimes a spiritual battle wages within us as to whether to serve the Lord or ourselves.

Here's a visual that can help us understand whom we are meant to serve. Let's say you're a man of average looks, and the most beautiful woman you have ever seen in your life starts working in your office. You can't help but stare at her. Her smile, her figure, her walk all have you mesmerized. Just being within a few yards of her gives you joy.

And then one day she speaks to you. She asks you, "Can you help me with this?" You don't even know what "this" is. But you spring into action ready to serve. Without realizing it, you have been conquered. You serve not because you've lost a war but because you were attracted to a being of incredible beauty.

That is how we are to see Jesus. That is how we are to serve him. We offer ourselves in service not because we have been conquered but rather because we have been attracted like a moth to a flame, a honeybee to a flower, by the perfect beauty, the "justice and compassion of this king."[25]

To God alone be glory!

MILE MARKER POINTING TO JESUS

"I am the LORD your God;
consecrate yourselves and be holy, because I am holy."
LEVITICUS 11:44 NIV

The One Year Bible is a great way to read the Holy Scriptures all the way through in twelve months, fulfilling many a New Year's resolution to read the Bible in its entirety. This time of year, readers would be tackling the book of Leviticus. You might also call Leviticus "the graveyard of good intentions to reading the Bible all the way through."

This third book in the Bible is like quicksand to modern readers. Whereas Genesis and Exodus have so many of the Bible's great Sunday school stories of God's triumph and miraculous works—like creation itself, Noah and the flood, and the parting of the Red Sea—Leviticus slows to a snail's pace as it carefully and methodically explains to the Israelites what it takes to be a covenant community. Every aspect of their lives was governed by whether they were clean or unclean, righteous or unrighteous. Leviticus slows down the biblical narrative because this Holy God was giving his chosen race something so important: the guidelines for how they were to separate themselves from a pagan world around them and draw near to that same Holy God.

Leviticus is a mile marker, a landmark pointing to what Jesus has done. Why don't we sacrifice bulls or goats today? It's because Jesus' death and resurrection have wiped our sins clean, made us white as snow. "That we should receive the love of a holy God—is a miracle of grace."[26] Amen.

To God alone be glory!

The Most Loving Father

*With praise and thanksgiving
they sang to the Lord.*
EZRA 3:11 NIV

We don't choose our parents. So it is all the more joyous if we are blessed with a mother and father who love us more than life itself and who worry about us more than we could ever imagine. Some people have not been so lucky to have had godly parents. Some parents leave. Some die prematurely. Others may be close physically but emotionally distant. In those cases, it's a little harder to "rejoice always, pray without ceasing, [and] in everything give thanks" (1 Thessalonians 5:16–18). However, we should take comfort that God knows our hearts and knows that we need the kind of love no earthly parent can offer.

God would not tell us to rejoice, pray, and give thanks if there weren't something to be joyful about. This trifecta of your will becomes a self-fulfilling prophecy. The more we rejoice, the more joyful we become. The more we give thanks, the more thankful we become. And the more we pray, the closer we draw to the Lord, who is our eternal Father, the parent who will never leave us or forsake us.

To God alone be glory!

Light in Darkness

Even in darkness light dawns for the upright,
for those who are gracious and compassionate and righteous.
PSALM 112:4 NIV

A darkness has settled over this country, over this world. It's a deep darkness that has taken the place of light. And because it's happened slowly, many in the world do not recognize the darkness.

That all life is precious and a gift of God Almighty is written in the Scriptures. That we have disregarded God's plan for humanity, of male and female filling the earth and glorifying God with their lives, has become a dangerous and subversive way of thinking in this darkened habitat. The prophet Isaiah sent his warning centuries ago: "Woe to those who call evil good and good evil" (5:20 NIV). But as Thomas Jefferson wrote, "I tremble for my country when I reflect that God is just; that his justice cannot sleep forever."

Jesus died on the cross, enduring the existential separation from his Father, so that we would not have to suffer such agony. Now in gratitude, we must actively shine his light, being beacons of his goodness. Let no one look upon us and see anything but his grace, mercy, and righteousness. Dispel the darkness. Make his light shine.

To God alone be glory!

Staying Close to God

"Return to me, and I will return to you,"
says the Lord Almighty.
MALACHI 3:7 NIV

In big cities like New York, there is much less personal space in public areas than in smaller, less populated towns, and because of that, people are sometimes willing to risk danger to protect their comfort zones. For example, on the subway platform, there's a yellow line that warns people to stay back from the tracks. Getting too close to the edge of the platform is dangerous. Trains come in hard and fast. But because the platforms can get very congested, many people ignore the warnings and step over the line in hopes of grabbing a seat before others in the crowd claim them all. It illustrates how, on some level, we all do a cost-benefit analysis of which rules we must obey and which ones we can ignore.

God has established safety zones too. He gave us the Ten Commandments to provide limits that keep us safe. And he warns us continually to stay close to him. In the Gospels, the woman knew that if she could just touch the hem of Jesus' garment, she would be safe and healed. We can be like this woman, not allowing anything to separate us from our Lord. In actions, words, and deeds, stay close to God's life-giving truths. Anywhere else is a precarious place to be.

To God alone be glory!

GROWING IN WISDOM

I have set the LORD always before me:
because he is at my right hand, I shall not be moved.
PSALM 16:8 KJV

Youth is a wonderful thing. We've all experienced it. Even when we get old, we still remember some of our early years with fondness. Ideally, as we age, we gain wisdom. But that's not always the case. Some people just get old. They have all the physical signs of aging—gray hair, bulging waistlines, and some wrinkles—but they have not matured in understanding life's varied events any more than they did as a young adult or teen, still acting as if life owes them something. In other words, everyone ages but not everyone grows up.

What makes the difference? Years ago a woman in her early sixties had accomplished many things as a performer. She was still youthful in energy as well as quite wise in understanding the meaning of life. She talked about places she had been and people she had met. She even sang for a pope. She said the difference for her was not just believing in God. That's just the first step. Most children believe in God. The real difference, she said, is trusting God and being grateful for whatever he brings into your life. The important thing is being able to stand your ground and trust God even when things are bleak.

To God alone be glory!

GOD SEES OUR NEEDS

Let us therefore cast off the works of darkness,
and let us put on the armour of light.
ROMANS 13:12 KJV

It's normal for married couples to be challenged by their different likes and dislikes. One of the ways their clashing tastes are exposed is when they are looking for a home. One may be more concerned about the views and ambiance, while the other is focused on the budget. One would go over the budget for a wonderful view and grandeur, but the other would be satisfied with looking at a brick wall if it doesn't break the bank. Praying to the God who loves them both equally is the best solution to finding common ground. It doesn't mean praying for God to change your spouse's desires.

Our wants tend to darken even prayer. Instead of praying truly for God's light to guide, we try to dictate to God what we think our spouse needs. We forget who's ultimately in control.

As C. S. Lewis wrote, "Whether we like it or not, God intends to give us what we need, not what we now think we want. Once more, we are embarrassed by the intolerable compliment, by too much love, not too little."[27] God in his love always has the best plan even if we can't see it or understand it. Therefore, any house will make the perfect home, as long as its inhabitants serve the Lord.

To God alone be glory!

Blood Transfusions

Therefore, brothers and sisters...we have confidence
to enter the Most Holy Place by the blood of Jesus.
HEBREWS 10:19 NIV

Children seem to understand things that adults often misinterpret. A concerned mother of a small girl consulted with a doctor because the child was fascinated with the sight of blood. Whenever a car crash occurred in their inner-city neighborhood, the child would want to run to it, telling her mother excitedly, "I want to see the blood!" Luckily the child grew out of the fascination and has no memory of the obsession. An explanation from one expert was simply that blood meant something different to a curious child than to an adult, who only could see tragedy in its loss.

The Bible and modern science both say that blood is the source of life. God says in Leviticus, "For the life of a creature is in the blood" (17:11 NIV). When people suffer a great loss of blood in accidents or due to illnesses, doctors give them transfusions. But there's another reason for blood transfusions that both the Bible and modern science agree on, and that is to rid the body of disease.

Whereas science can tackle things like anemia, cancer, or kidney disease, God has taken on the very insidious disease we all suffer from: sin. Healthy people's blood can help with medical transfusions, but only the blood of Jesus shed on the cross can cleanse us of our ubiquitous malady. The good news is that we don't have to wait to be rushed to a hospital for this transfusion. It's available any place and any time.

To God alone be glory!

Miraculous Miracles

There some people brought to him a man who was deaf and could hardly talk, and they begged Jesus to place his hand on him...At this, the man's ears were opened, his tongue was loosened and he began to speak plainly.

MARK 7:32, 35 NIV

We sometimes get so used to the accounts of Jesus healing the lame, the blind, and the deaf that we may lose true insight of just how great those miracles are.

In the case of the deaf man who began to speak plainly, this is an off-the-charts medical miracle because of what we know about how people learn to speak. Neurologists have discovered that unless someone begins to hear language at an early age, their brains cannot process the spoken word. If they suddenly hear decades later, as an adult, someone speaking would sound like gibberish. It might as well be the sound of dogs barking. Their brains can't make sense of what they hear, and their mouths can't reproduce it.[28]

For the deaf man to suddenly start speaking plainly means Jesus did a lot more than open his ears. Jesus made it as if the infirmity never existed in the first place. This is the physical embodiment of the promised new heavens and new earth, where the mind represents the heavens and the body represents the new earth. When God brings the promised new heavens and new earth for us all, he brings us more than joy. He makes it as though our sorrows and pain never happened in the first place. That is indeed a miracle.

To God alone be glory!

Helping Our Unbelief

Immediately the boy's father exclaimed,
"I do believe; help me overcome my unbelief!"
MARK 9:24 NIV

People sometimes think that if they don't have unflinching faith, it's a sign of weakness, that their walk with Christ is defective. If some prayer isn't answered the way we want or things don't turn out the way we expect, we may blame our lack of faith.

But in Mark's Gospel, we see a man desperate for Jesus to heal his son. Jesus tells him to have faith. The man answers with one of the most honest outbursts of faith in the history of mankind. It's the reality of the commingling of faith and doubt. He's saying, "I have faith, but I've lived a life of doubting and unbelief that's hard to overcome. Please, Jesus, overcome my unbelief. Please, be my strength."

Doubt and unbelief are real aspects of our lives. Sometimes we're embarrassed to admit we have doubts, but Jesus understands. There's hardly more motivation to have super-powered faith than to witness the miraculous healing of a desperately ill loved one, especially when a parent is seeking a cure for their child. Jesus knows that the world's sounds and visions, what we see and hear, are so strong that they often have greater influence on us. It's the "seeing is believing" philosophy. But Jesus operates on the "believing is seeing" track. He has compassion for our unbelief especially when we boldly admit it and ask for his help to overcome it.

To God alone be glory!

Being Rooted in Christ

A shoot will come up from the stump of Jesse;
from his roots a Branch will bear fruit.
ISAIAH 11:1 NIV

All of us came into this world through the wills of other people, primarily our father's and mother's. Even if you're adopted and have never known your biological parents, you are still connected to them through DNA. In other words, we all have roots.

We had no choice about whether we were born or when. A person of faith knows it's by grace that we are even alive. It's a good reminder to not only value life but to also acknowledge the wisdom and experiences of the generations before who have provided centuries of roots. As the ancient proverb says, "Young people walk fast, but older people know the way."

If we understand the value of our roots, we are also wise to understand the importance of the past, learning how to live (and how not to live) in order to help us protect our futures. Jesus' earthly ancestry is through King David of the tribe of Judah. Before that, it goes all the way to Adam. His divinity, though, has no beginning. He is the great I AM, the Creator and cause of all roots, all beginnings. The deeper we put our faith in Christ, the stronger we will stand against the inclement elements of the present and future.

To God alone be glory!

Spiritual Diagnostics

*Furthermore, just as they did not think it worthwhile to retain the knowledge
of God, so God gave them over to a depraved mind,
so that they do what ought not to be done.*

ROMANS 1:28 NIV

One thing we should never do is believe our spiritual situation is fixed
and permanent. That's the good and bad news about this verse. We've all
seen good people do bad things and bad people do good things. The only
person who ever did and does right all the time is Jesus Christ. Verses like
this in Romans are for us all, for all have sinned.

It also helps us to do a self-examination, a sort of spiritual
diagnostics test, to see where we've fallen short. Maybe we have been
jealous of our neighbor. Maybe we have been prideful or unkind. Maybe
we are lying to our loved ones. Maybe we are struggling with a secret
addiction. Whatever the sin, it can be overcome through God. Without
him, it will only fester.

As one pastor says, "Every sin is a kind of practical atheism—it is
acting as if God were not there."[29] Our goal is to turn that around, to believe
in the Lord Jesus Christ. He will help us overcome the sin that is within.

To God alone be glory!

Accessing the Tree of Life

On each side of the river stood the tree of life,
bearing twelve crops of fruit, yielding its fruit every month.
And the leaves of the tree are for the healing of the nations.

REVELATION 22:2 NIV

Having a green thumb is a gift from God. Those who don't possess this attribute have other gifts, to be sure. But there's something to be envied about the ability to make green things grow and prosper. Indoor potted plants are particularly challenging to maintain. But one such "brown thumber" was amazed at how a gift of a potted plant thrived despite his lack of talent. Every spring, a new set of leaves replaced the previous ones. And beautiful new flowers bloomed. He called it his personal Tree of Life, reminding him of what God has promised all of us.

Only one other place in the Bible is there a mention of a Tree of Life, and that's in the garden of Eden. But because our ancient ancestors chose to eat of another tree, the forbidden tree, we have been blocked access to this Tree of Life, with all its promise of a pain free life with no disease and no death. Thankfully, God had a plan. It is because "Jesus was hung on a tree of death" that we now have access to the Tree of Life.[30]

As C. H. Spurgeon said, "We believe our Lord Jesus Christ to be none other than that tree of life, whose leaves are for the healing of the nations."[31]

To God alone be glory!

God Is Our Strength

"The spirit is willing,
but the flesh is weak."
MATTHEW 26:41 NIV

During the Lenten season, Christians are called to fast. Some people fast from certain foods the entire forty days, others only on certain days, like abstaining from meat on Fridays. One newly baptized Christian decided he would eat no meat or dairy for the entire Lenten period. It didn't take more than three days for him to realize how dependent he was on burgers, chicken, cheese, yogurt, and his favorite—pizza!

Food is necessary to keep us alive. Not until we make the sacrifice of fasting do we realize how much power food has over us. Prayer is an essential partner to fasting because "without prayer, fasting is just a diet."[32] During a fast, our bodies, conditioned to eating whatever they want, suddenly taste the fruit of being denied. We discover we are far weaker than we ever imagined or care to admit.

But the joy this Lenten season brings is that we ourselves are more in dialogue with God, even when we try to renegotiate the terms of the fast (*God, how about this? Can't I have that?*). That conversation illustrates why we fast in the first place: to learn to be more dependent on God's strength rather than our own. God knows we are weak. We are the ones in denial.

To God alone be glory!

Painful to Forgive

"When you stand praying, if you hold anything against anyone, forgive them, so that your Father in heaven may forgive you your sins."
MARK 11:25 NIV

Major repairs on an expressway can stymie many a traveler, whether locals or visitors. The roadblocks and detours cause traffic to slow down and tempers to heat up.

It was in one of those traffic challenges that a Christian asked herself, *What could God be trying to teach me here? Besides patience, that is.* She realized that perhaps she needed forgiveness for her impatience. She began to recite the Lord's Prayer. The part about forgiving our trespasses as God forgives us struck a chord. God is saying that when we don't forgive others, it's like putting up a roadblock to God forgiving us. How can we accept God's forgiveness if we have not opened the portals of its power by forgiving others?

Forgiveness is a two-lane street. When we are unforgiving, we've blocked all the benefits of forgiveness from entering our lives. And unlike the expressway, there are no detours. Forgiving people who've wronged us is certainly not easy. It's downright difficult, sometimes excruciatingly difficult. In fact, the word *excruciating* is rooted in the horrors of the word *crucifixion*. Yes, forgiveness is painful.

To God alone be glory!

Quenching Our Thirst

"The LORD will guide you always;
he will satisfy your needs in a sun-scorched land
and will strengthen your frame.
You will be like a well-watered garden,
like a spring whose waters never fail."
ISAIAH 58:11 NIV

In cold climates, the spring rains usually bring high waters and sometimes flooding, as the ground is still too hard and frozen to absorb the melting snow and the water coming from the clouds. In the heat of summer, the ground is more than willing to take what water it can find.

But waters coming from springs underground don't rely on seasonal weather conditions. They are always available. The water table from the aquifer is deep enough that it provides a continual supply. It's this water that provides promise that the spring rains will eventually have a place to go and, when the rains stop, will supply moisture to a parched land. The underground spring water is a continual reminder that God's wisdom is not like the seasonal rains but is a continual source of refreshing liquid.

When we're in a dry season, we only need remember that there is always available Living Water, the refreshing knowledge that God can and will quench any thirst.

To God alone be glory!

He Is with You

"The Lord, He is the One who goes before you.
He will be with you, He will not leave you nor forsake you;
do not fear nor be dismayed."

DEUTERONOMY 31:8

Facing an uncertain future can be so difficult, especially when everything is out of your control. Extreme anxiety and stress can make us distrust the advice of even our closest friends.

God never promised us smooth sailing or a perfectly paved road on our journey through this life. In fact, in numerous places, the Bible promises the life of the Christian will be filled with suffering, persecution, and death, perhaps even martyrdom. But he has promised to either calm the storms or walk through them with us.

The future is indeed uncertain. But we know who holds the future. And there's no place where his arm can't reach in order to calm our fears and ease our pain. As writer Thomas Moore said, "Earth has no sorrow that heaven cannot heal."

To God alone be glory!

Tell God Your Pain

From the end of the earth I will cry to You, when my heart is overwhelmed;
lead me to the rock that is higher than I.

PSALM 61:2

While God knows all things, even the deepest recesses of our hearts and minds, we still need to be honest with him about our feelings. Why? It's not for God's benefit but for ours. God already loves us and wants to comfort us. The only thing preventing us from receiving that comfort is our thinking that we have it all taken care of. We put up barricades to our own comfort.

When children get upset, they often throw open the floodgates of tears, wailing their discontent, which their parents already fully understand. As children of the living God, we should do the same, truthfully telling our heavenly Father what he already knows, that we hurt, that we're in pain. It opens a pathway for us to receive God's help.

On the cross, Jesus cried out to God his anguish at being separated from his Father and suffering the tortures of death. We can be assured that no pain is too heavy for God to handle and no situation too tangled for him to unravel.

To God alone be glory!

GROWING IN GOD'S LOVE

"Whoever receives one little child like this in My name receives Me."
MATTHEW 18:5

There's a natural way to grow and accumulate knowledge and wisdom. From the time we are conceived in our mother's womb this natural order of growth is always at work. Cells divide, synapses form in the brain, bones strengthen.

The Lord Jesus, when he talked about how we should receive him like a little child, was inviting us to let his love, his wisdom, his Word penetrate and guide that natural process. When we are babies, toddlers, and children, our parents are charged with this task. But as we get older, it is our own responsibility.

God is all about love. He loves us not because we have earned his love, but because he is love. It is his nature. He has watched us grow our entire lives, and nothing pleases him more than when we follow the path he has set out for us, claiming the purpose he has designed for us. "God's ultimate purpose is that His Son might be manifested in [your] mortal flesh."[33]

To God alone be glory!

GOD'S NATURAL HEALING

Heal me, LORD, and I will be healed;
save me and I will be saved, for you are the one I praise.
JEREMIAH 17:14 NIV

It can take several weeks or longer for a body to heal after an accident. During this slow process, we might not notice the progress we are making. Just ask anyone who has broken an arm or leg or even suffered a traumatic injury. God in his wisdom has equipped the human body with the miracle of self-healing, the ability to reknit the sinews, restore the muscle, and remap the synaptic connections in order for us to have the possibility of being renewed.

Depending on the severity and location of the injury, some repair work takes a few short days, some a few weeks, and some require months. But God's wisdom is always behind the process. What can work for our bodies can also work for our hearts and emotions. Although we cannot see the scar tissue from the pain of a broken heart, the wound is just as devastating, if not more so, than any damage we might suffer to our bodies.

God's words from the prophet Isaiah still ring true: "I will strengthen you, I will help you" (41:10 ESV). Whatever you may be going through, God not only knows but also is slowly guiding the healing process. And soon, what you thought was impossible to endure you will overcome.

To God alone be glory!

Fearing the Future

All the children of Israel complained against Moses and Aaron, and the whole congregation said to them, "If only we had died in the land of Egypt! Or if only we had died in this wilderness!"

NUMBERS 14:2

The future sometimes can be scary. Although we try to make plans, we have no reliable maps to chart a definitive course. When difficulties come, the knee jerk reaction is to retreat, to believe that God doesn't hold our best interest and is not to be trusted.

That's certainly the case here with the Israelites. Even though God had shown them miracle after miracle, when they were on the verge of taking the promised land, they feared a scary report. They put more faith in their fears than in God. Their self-talk reinforced their fears: "We will be destroyed. We will never survive this." Then they immediately jumped to blaming God, questioning his authority and this guy Moses. To top it off, they voiced a preference for returning to slavery under Pharaoh in Egypt rather than freedom with God.

The story of Israel's distrust of God in the Old Testament is our New Testament story on a larger scale. Each one of us is Israel. We, however, have one huge advantage. We are bound to God by the resurrection of Jesus Christ. We have a new relationship with God based on his law of grace. God has shown us his amazing power and love by raising Jesus from the dead. If he can do that, then he can do anything, including help us face whatever challenges lay ahead in our lives.

To God alone be glory!

The Riches of God

Oh, the depth of the riches both of the wisdom and knowledge of God!
ROMANS 11:33

In the musical *Fiddler on the Roof*, the main character Tevye, describes his idea of a perfect life. It would be spending his days exploring Scripture because God's Word held so much value to him.

That kind of devotion is a foreign concept today. We can understand imagining a life of leisure activities, even pursuing passions like art and music. But reading God's Word? What Tevye discovered, like many people of faith, is that the more we read Scripture, the more we *want* to read God's Word. Wisdom and knowledge are to knowing God what winning the lottery is to your bank account. Only knowing God is infinitely more valuable.

Scripture is not just about tradition, as the song says, it's about a treasure trove of riches with no ending. It's a mindset of being content with the fullness of God's presence so that we can enjoy all other passions of life so much more fully. Scripture is not merely something we read and see; it's the glass through which we see everything else more clearly.

To God alone be glory!

Jesus Is Our Lifeline

He said to them, "Go into all the world and preach the gospel to every creature. He who believes and is baptized will be saved; but he who does not believe will be condemned."

MARK 16:15–16

Swimming in a backyard pool is fairly easy with few risks. But swimming in the ocean or the open sea has many more challenges. A man I once spoke to recounted how he almost drowned in the waters off a Greek island. He was on vacation, enjoying a swim off the back of a boat, when the boat began to pull away. He realized he didn't have the swimming skills to catch up to it. Thinking this could be it for him, he began to panic in the deep waters. Suddenly a friend spotted him and came to his rescue. Suffice it to say he was incredibly grateful. It occurred to him, while safely back on the boat, that in a way, we are all swimming in the sea of life and in danger of drowning.

The Gospel of Mark's words here may seem harsh to many modern folks bathed in the politics of tolerance. The idea of a loving God condemning people for their "wrong beliefs" rankles us. But if the Gospel is true, meaning objectively true, then it is true for all people, whether they choose to believe or not. So, this warning is not meant to harm people but to save them from drowning in that sea of life. Can you imagine the person who rescued that man saying, "I respected his wish to swim alone, even if it meant drowning"? No, Jesus is and always will be the lifeline to keep us from drowning.

To God alone be glory!

God Tools in Marriage

A quarrelsome wife is like the dripping of a leaky roof in a rainstorm.
PROVERBS 27:15 NIV

While on vacation, a couple rented a house for a week where they could bring the family pets. When they arrived, the leasing agent apologized for a leak in the bathtub faucet and hoped it would be okay. Fixing it required a part that was on back order and probably wouldn't be in before their vacation ended. They thought, "No problem. We can handle a leaky faucet."

But then they saw that it was not a small drip but a full running flow of water that never ceased. Twenty-four-seven it gushed. They jerry-rigged a solution that muted the sound a bit, but it never fully quieted for an entire week. It was just irritating background noise with no discernible purpose. The couple now look back on that week and only laugh about it, and credit that faucet with a tool to ending their arguments quickly. Neither wanted to be like that broken faucet, gushing with no purpose. They also know that the tool to fixing what's broken in the marriage is always in stock. It's prayer and leaning on God's Word. God created marriage. He knows how to repair even the most damaged relationships.

To God alone be glory!

The Power of Patience

If we hope for what we do not yet have,
we wait for it patiently.
ROMANS 8:25 NIV

In the Old Testament, the diviner Balaam had a vision of light and power of how God would accomplish his salvation work through his son Jesus Christ (see Numbers 22). But from the time of that vision to Jesus' appearance on earth took a thousand years. Yet Balaam believed because he saw it as clear as day. He didn't know the time, didn't know the year. Yet it was so sure a vision that he placed total trust in it, even though this resulted in death threats from an angry king.

There's power in waiting patiently. Patience is one of those spiritual muscles that only becomes stronger through challenges and practice. There's strength in waiting on God's time. "Be still, and know" that he is God (Psalm 46:10). He will accomplish his work in you. It may not be what you expect, but it will be to his glory. Open your heart and let Jesus in. Let him lead you in all that you do.

To God alone be glory!

LOVE'S DIVINE ORDER

"If anyone causes one of these little ones—those who believe in me—
to stumble, it would be better for them to have a large millstone hung around
their neck and to be drowned in the depths of the sea."

MATTHEW 18:6 NIV

This verse could be one way God is saying there's a special place in hell for those who would abuse a child. One of the most vulnerable times in our life is when we are children. We all come into the world needing to be loved and to give love. Childhood is when we learn the parameters: What are love's boundaries? How do we order love in our lives and prioritize people and things?

Whatever we learn in childhood we take into adolescence and adulthood. As we become adults, we express that early training of what love is and should be in the relationships we create outside our immediate family.

Jesus warns of what will happen to people who violate a child's innocence, who cause them to learn to love in sinful ways. Such people distort what is good and make it something God has called evil. But if we teach a child to love Jesus purely, to come to him first with their expressions of heartfelt emotions, he will give them the gracious hearts required to love others properly and more joyously.

To God alone be glory!

MASTERING THE SIN WITHIN

"If you [Cain] do what is right, will you not be accepted?
But if you do not do what is right, sin is crouching at your door;
it desires to have you, but you must rule over it."

GENESIS 4:7 NIV

Even with this warning and teaching directly from God, Cain still killed his brother Abel, the first recorded murder in human history. And when confronted by God, Cain showed no remorse or admission of guilt.

The Lenten season is about the healing of the Cain in us all. Where Abel's blood crying out from the ground was the first of much shed blood of brother against brother, it is Jesus' blood shed on the cross that will repair the breach between God and humanity.

Just like Cain, we are all both "a potential prey and a potential master of a predator called 'sin'; Cain murdered, because he fell prey to what he refused to master."[34] This season reminds us to embrace Jesus, marking each day as he draws nearer to his crucifixion, death, and resurrection. His sacrifice can only heal us if we learn to love him, the one who has embraced us.[35]

To God alone be glory!

GETTING OUT OF OUR RUTS

He makes my feet like the feet of a deer;
he causes me to stand on the heights.
PSALM 18:33 NIV

Getting us out of our ruts is God's specialty. The problem with ruts is that they promise only deeper ruts, constantly burrowing downward. When you're in a rut, it's hard to escape from it. When you're in an emotional rut, your comfort comes from the rut itself, and you have no desire to escape from it. You may think, *It's cradling me, propping me up. If I get out of the rut, what will hold me up?*

There's an evil attitude lurking in our ruts; it's the fear that God's Word won't be as comforting as our complaints, won't be as self-justifying as our snarky opinions. And won't be nearly as fun either. Ruts are dangerous places precisely because they are familiar territory. But when we make God's Word our familiar landscape, it forms an off-ramp for the rut. Complaints? God is my refuge (see Psalm 46:1). Sorrow? He turns my mourning into dancing (see Psalm 30:11–12). Anxiety? The battle belongs to the Lord (see 2 Chronicles 20:15).

Satan thought Jesus was in a rut when he confronted him in the wilderness. But for every twisted use of Scripture Satan threw at him, Jesus answered with its truth. And the truth will make us free from the ruts in our lives.

To God alone be glory!

TRULY KNOWN, TRULY LOVED

Then one of the Twelve—the one called Judas Iscariot—went to the chief priests and asked, "What are you willing to give me if I deliver him over to you?" So they counted out for him thirty pieces of silver. From then on Judas watched for an opportunity to hand him over.

MATTHEW 26:14–16 NIV

In a conversation with me, Hank Hanegraaff, the "Bible Answer Man," remarked that Judas mistook the "menu for the meal" and, in doing so, missed the experience it pointed to.

There are some scholars who argue that Judas was a willing foil to Jesus' plan to be arrested and turned over to the authorities. But this theory is shortsighted, as all the apostles showed human weakness at a certain point. One of the most shortsighted was Peter, who vowed to stand by Jesus but ended up denying him three times.

The truth is, Judas was no different from any of us. It's so easy to say, "I would never do that!" But most of us don't know our own hearts well enough to know what we would or would not do. What we think we will do and what we actually do are often on two different paths. And God knows this. He knows our frailty. Jesus could see into Judas' heart, and he understood the conflict. But Jesus died for all our sins, Judas', Peter's, yours, and your neighbors. We are truly loved because we are truly known.

To God alone be glory!

God Watching Over

Shout for joy to God, all the earth! Sing the glory of his name; make his praise glorious. Say to God, "How awesome are your deeds!"

PSALM 66:1–3 NIV

While on vacation in a rental house, a couple once had a terrible scare with one of their children. No one could find her. They searched the house and realized the front door was not only unlocked but also wide open. They feared she'd gotten lost in the woods. Their anxiety mounted and their imaginations went wild believing something horrible had happened. They frantically shouted her name, searching through the woods around the property.

They came back to the house and were about to call the police from the master bedroom when the wife spotted something lumpy under the covers. She pulled back the blanket and found the child sleeping soundly. The unfamiliar house made her seek refuge in her parents' room for naptime.

The emotions of that moment went beyond ecstasy. The relief the parents experienced felt like heaven itself, where God has promised us that heaven will be, as Tolkien's Samwise Gamgee expressed, where "Everything sad [is] going to come untrue."[36] God had watched over this child as his Word promised. How incredibly awesome are your deeds!

To God alone be glory!

ᏴEARING ᎤUR ᏚINS

They brought Jesus to the place called Golgotha (which means "the place of the skull"). Then they offered him wine mixed with myrrh, but he did not take it. And they crucified him. Dividing up his clothes, they cast lots to see what each would get.

MARK 15:22–24 NIV

How quickly fortunes change. Just a few days before this scene on Golgotha, the crowds had heralded Jesus as a king, waving palm branches during his triumphant entry to Jerusalem. But this day, this solemn day, the forces of jealousy, of political intrigue, of power plays, and the whole gamut of human sin culminated in Jesus' crucifixion.

We call it Good Friday. And we can only call it that in a post resurrection world. We know what good came from this tragedy. But it doesn't lessen the severity of what Jesus endured. On Good Friday, we remember how Jesus took upon himself the weight of human sin in its totality. Whatever sins had been or would ever be committed, he bore on the cross. He took the wrath of God's judgment so that we wouldn't have to.

There's a great feeling of freedom in knowing how much we are loved, that the God who created the universe would bend so low as to save a people who are so sinful. And yet, he did. Praise God from whom all blessings flow!

To God alone be glory!

Two Choices

Jesus looked directly at them and asked,
"Then what is the meaning of that which is written:
'The stone the builders rejected has become the cornerstone'?"

LUKE 20:17 NIV

Holy Week was the climax of Jesus' three-year ministry. He had gained a lot of followers through his reputation for miraculously healing the sick and teaching a new way of relating to God. It is now during this week we see Jesus confronting his most ardent detractors, the Jewish hierarchy of priest and Pharisee.

After Jesus' triumphant entrance into Jerusalem (Palm Sunday), the priests realized Jesus was a threat to their power. They began a series of theological challenges. It was during one of those challenges that the Jewish religious leaders realized what Jesus was saying to them: "Follow me or be crushed by me."[37] That choice left them no wiggle room. Whenever human sin is challenged, it plots to take out the challenger. And so, the people plotted to have Jesus killed. The priests were under greater obligation than most to see God, to see Jesus as their Savior, the Messiah. But their religiosity and status in the community became their god, their false idol.

In the Holy Week saga, we are also called to see not only Jesus' ultimate victorious resurrection but also our own sinful part in his arrest, trial, and death sentence. Just like the Pharisee and priests, "With our greater spiritual resources God holds us more responsible for living as he prescribes."[38]

To God alone be glory!

OPENING OUR SOULS TO GOD

Search me, God, and know my heart;
test me and know my anxious thoughts.
See if there is any offensive way in me,
and lead me in the way everlasting.

PSALM 139:23–24 NIV

Your life matters tremendously. Each of our lives is a unique drama. Ultimately God is the author of all our life stories as we become characters in his grand narrative of redemption and salvation. To a certain extent, he lets us participate in our own salvation. We have agency, the ability to choose whether to open our hearts to his redemptive work.

In order for us to see his providence in our lives, we must be honest about how we're feeling. The psalmist cries out, asking God to search the psalmist's inner self. It's the soul opening up, inviting God in to complete his work. Crying out to God is what our heavenly Father wants us to do. Anger and disappointment are honest antidotes to pride, an acknowledgment of God's authority.

Jesus on the cross cried out to God, "Why have you forsaken me?" (Psalm 22:1 NIV). Our challenge now is seeing "The story of God's interventions in our lives as a significant subplot to the bigger story of his bringing salvation to the world. Take some time to review the chapters of his story of salvation in your life."[39]

To God alone be glory!

FORGIVE

In him we have redemption through his blood,
the forgiveness of sins, in accordance with the riches of God's grace.
EPHESIANS 1:7 NIV

Many of us had a pen pal when we were children. When one Black woman was young, she had a pen pal who lived in an all-white neighborhood. One day, the pen pal invited her to the school carnival. The woman recounts how she was very excited to go and that her mother dressed her in a freshly washed and ironed sundress with her hair neatly combed. The experience started out fun as the two young girls from different racial backgrounds met for the first time and attended the carnival. But it quickly turned sour as two boys dogged their every move. Whatever fun games the girls tried to play, the two boys followed them for the sole purpose of calling the young Black girl every racial slur they could think of.

The two girls tried to ignore the boys, but the boys wouldn't stop. And no adult stepped in to help. The woman said she never told her parents about it. She just wanted to forget the whole evening. But she never wrote back to the pen pal.

Years later, she realized what an emotional scar that event left on her entire childhood. But then she learned how Jesus on the cross forgave the people who mocked him, abandoned him, and killed him. That gave her the strength decades later to forgive those boys, realizing that they, too, probably didn't understand what they were doing. The woman understood that Jesus died for all sinners, those two little boys, her pen pal, her, and all the adults at the carnival who stood by and did nothing to help. And if Jesus can forgive them, so could she.

To God alone be glory!

Perfect Advocate

Create in me a pure heart, O God, and renew a steadfast spirit within me. Do not cast me from your presence or take your Holy Spirit from me. Restore to me the joy of your salvation and grant me a willing spirit, to sustain me.
PSALM 51:10–12 NIV

If we are strong enough to face the truth, we must admit that we are never quite as good at something as we think we are. Anyone who has learned a musical instrument can testify to that. Just when you think you've mastered a difficult piece, you hear someone else play it infinitely better. And certainly, athletes know the struggle to achieve physical perfection, the hours of preparation and practice they sacrifice, only to be outdone by a faster athlete.

It can be terribly disheartening when imperfection is confronted with what seems like perfection. If we can experience it on an earthly level between fellow image bearers, think what a great chasm exists between us and the Almighty.

But the good news is that Jesus, through his sacrifice on the cross, has filled the chasm between imperfect humans and a holy and perfect God. Where once no one could stand before God as a perfect human, we are now assured that it is Jesus' record that allows us to lay bare every sin, and we know that even though we may never attain perfection, we have an advocate standing in our place who has.

To God alone be glory!

EVIL IS DEFEATED

*We know that all things work together for good to those who love God,
to those who are the called according to His purpose.*

ROMANS 8:28

Evil cannot win. It simply cannot. God has declared it. He will always have the upper hand. Oh yes, evil seems the victor in many situations; that temptation in the garden is certainly a good example. But evil will never have the last word. Satan thought he'd won in his tormenting of Job. But Job learned a deeper faith through those trials and said at the end, "I know that my Redeemer lives" (Job 19:25).

Job knew and now we know, too, that our souls belong to the living God. Whatever this world and its evil can do to our bodies either through the natural decay of aging, traumatic disease, or tragic injury is inconsequential to the great joy the Ancient of Days can make of it.

The challenge, of course, is to stand strong in that knowledge when pain and anguish enter our lives. But here's a thought that can be very helpful, "Evil [always] serves the larger good."[40] No matter what evil wills, God's higher purpose always reigns. Evil has already been defeated.

To God alone be glory!

Author of Our Faith

[Look] unto Jesus, the author and finisher of our faith, who for the joy that was set before Him endured the cross, despising the shame, and has sat down at the right hand of the throne of God.

HEBREWS 12:2

Teen years bring self-discovery and a longed-for self-awareness. When a woman was in her late teens, she remembers thinking, *What is the one question that answers every other question?* In other words, "What is the one thing that all life is drawn from, from which all existence gets its marching orders?"

She believed in God and grew up going to Sunday school, celebrating Christmas, and observing the Easter season. As a child she said her bedtime prayers. But in all those encounters, she did not relate her inquiry to the question of who God is. However, God, in his wisdom and his incredible loving-kindness and mercy, set her on a journey to discovering the answers she sought.

Faith is a journey for which there is no final destination here on earth. Every age and stage of life holds new challenges to understanding and growing in faith and knowing God. What we can be assured of is that God the Father, God the Son, and God the Holy Spirit is the author of our faith. God was always the answer to the question and still is.

To God alone be glory!

Humbled by Holy Love

God, who is rich in mercy, because of His great love with which He loved us, even when we were dead in trespasses, made us alive together with Christ (by grace you have been saved).

EPHESIANS 2:4–5

Being humble is one of those attributes that can never boast about itself. Humility is a label others must bestow on us and not we on ourselves. The moment we utter the words, "I am humble," we negate the sentiment.

But there's another kind of humbleness that we can use when speaking of ourselves as we learn to understand that we don't deserve the love God has given us—yet we are still receiving it. There's a threshold we pass when we realize that despite growing in our faith, it is God's love and gentle guidance that has steered us toward him.

As C. S. Lewis said, "[The Christian] does not think God will love us because we are good, but that God will make us good because He loves us."[41] To be loved so much is almost overwhelming. It is indeed humbling.

To God alone be glory!

The Lord Hears All

*"You are not grumbling against us,
but against the Lord."*
EXODUS 16:8 NIV

To say God has perfect hearing is an understatement. He is omniscient, all knowing, and omnipresent, everywhere. Nothing happens without the Lord's knowledge. Even our grumbling underneath our breaths or in our minds is not out of God's earshot. That should give us both comfort and a cold dose of reality. Ultimately, like sin, all grumbling is first against God. At the moment we do it, we forget who God is and that he is in control.

Let's say you complain with coworkers about the boss; it's like savory morsels. It tastes so good to vent about someone who frustrates you. But if your boss overheard that conversation, it would be the same as speaking those words directly to him or her. Instead of a tasty treat, it would be as bitter as gall. Same words, different taste. We should then remember to take all our dissatisfactions first to God. Then let Jesus help us speak the truth in love.

To God alone be glory!

CHOOSE EACH DAY

"If serving the LORD seems undesirable to you,
then choose for yourselves this day whom you will serve,…
But as for me and my household, we will serve the LORD."

JOSHUA 24:15 NIV

In our world today, distractions abound, tugging and pulling us away from God's Word and faith in Jesus Christ. That's why Joshua's words spoken centuries before the resurrection are a daily guide.

Every moment of every day we are called to make a conscious or even subconscious choice of whom or what we will serve, worship, or bow down to. What should concern us most is that it is easy to make tacit decisions, ones we make through omission, simply by forgetting God in the process.

Some people say, "I don't want to bother God with this. He has more to worry about than this." But it's in those little steps, not the gigantic leaps, where it's easier to move further and further away from God, our refuge. Joshua is saying, "Accept the rule of God or rebel against it."[42] But choose you must.

To God alone be glory!

True Lies Distort

*They exchanged the truth about God for a lie, and worshiped and served
created things rather than the Creator—who is forever praised. Amen.*
ROMANS 1:25 NIV

A young woman distraught over a breakup tearfully cried out to God,
believing with all her heart that life would be perfect if only that man
would again adore her. Young people today put a lot of faith in their
feelings, which then get elevated to the position of being arbiter of what's
truly right or wrong. They might think, *If I feel strongly about it, it must be
true. It must be right for me.*

Generations of young people have grown up believing they are the
center of their world, and by default, their feelings are the only tangible
standard for truth. God warns us constantly that this is a form of idol
worship. It's really self-worship, but it's a kind of sin whose immense
destructiveness is hidden from us because its effects happen over a longer
period of time. It's like the small boy who tells little white lies and never
gets caught. As an adult, he tells even bigger lies that eventually ruin lives
and distort relationships. When God's truth is the standard, we are blessed.
God's wisdom is true wisdom.

To God alone be glory!

Brothers and Sisters All

A friend loves at all times,
and a brother is born for a time of adversity.

PROVERBS 17:17 NIV

Siblings can sometimes be our closest companions. Even though they sometimes fight like cats and dogs, love is always present. You can be archenemies one day and best buddies the next. Friends, however, are different. Throughout our time on earth, we traverse life's many paths and byways, encountering people whom we are called to love in various ways, as friends, family, coworkers, or acquaintances.

Sometimes the closer people are to us, the more difficult they are to love as they should be loved, because we are more emotionally vulnerable to them. Others with whom we are less intimate are sometimes easier to reach out to. We need both in our lives in order to truly test our faith.

Relationships are one mechanism through which faith grows in us. These are trenches on the battlefield of life. Whenever you have a conflict with someone, ask God to help you see that person the way he sees them, their hurts and pains, struggles, and fears. If we are all made in God's image, then all our fellow image bearers are our siblings.

To God alone be glory!

Never Alone

You will keep in perfect peace those whose minds are steadfast,
because they trust in you.

ISAIAH 26:3 NIV

A young nun from Belarus was traveling in the United States to raise money for her convent's new women's health center. She stopped in a large church in a major metropolitan city. Despite being diminutive in stature, she was a powerhouse of energy, with a joyful demeanor, a quick smile, and an eager handshake and hug for everyone.

She'd been gone for more than a month from her home and familiar surroundings. In the church social hall, someone asked her if she was at all lonely because she was on this journey by herself. She said that she was not alone, that God was with her and that traveling by herself gave her an opportunity to become even closer to God, relying on him and trusting in his ability to help her in her quest.

Sometimes big cities can make for the loneliest places because of the anonymity. But if we can learn anything from that nun, it's that because of God's great love, even if we feel lonely, we are never forsaken. And we will never, ever be alone.

To God alone be glory!

Putting God First

"The Lord bless you and keep you;
the Lord make his face shine on you and be gracious to you;
the Lord turn his face toward you and give you peace."

NUMBERS 6:24–26 NIV

All the good things in life we are seeking come from the Lord. All our hopes, goals, pursuits, and happiness come from God. Sometimes, though, we pursue the things of this world like designer clothes or a prestigious job and put them on a pedestal of "must haves." We then end up quite stressed and anxious if we don't get them. But there's a sure way to be happy in this world. And that is to put the Lord Almighty at the apex of the hierarchy of all your wants and dreams. You're guaranteed to enjoy things, and life, more.[43]

Wise people of faith counsel that most of us need a constant gut check of how we're ordering the loves of our lives. It is a daily process of reordering our loves based on the knowledge of truth. For instance, "The problem with the workaholic…is not that we love work too much, but that we love God too little, relative to our career."[44] God has created a world in which we are happiest when we put him first.

To God alone be glory!

DELIGHT IN GOD'S LAW

Blessed is the one who does not walk in step with the wicked
or stand in the way that sinners take or sit in the company of mockers,
but whose delight is in the law of the LORD,
and who meditates on his law day and night.

PSALM 1:1–2 NIV

Accents can sometimes tell a listener where someone is from. A Texan's drawl or a Briton's clipped speech give geographic clues. Some accents aren't quite as distinctive, like in the Midwest for instance. But regardless, social scientists tell us that the community in which we were raised gives us our language as well as our accents. Our community is also a big influence on our understanding of right and wrong. That's why parents are concerned about the people with whom their children socialize.

The influencing doesn't stop as we move into adulthood. That is why the Bible warns us to be aware of who counsels us. Like Tim Keller wrote, "When we shed the constraints of traditional values and morality… in reality we are simply allowing a new community to tell us who we are… Communities create the paths we walk."[45]

Understanding that not all family upbringings are the greatest, God tells us to align our values with his law. He is our ultimate parent and our supporting community.

To God alone be glory!

GIFTS ABOUND

Every good and perfect gift is from above,
coming down from the Father of the heavenly lights,
who does not change like shifting shadows.

JAMES 1:17 NIV

God showers his gifts on us 24/7. They may not always be the kind of gifts we can see with our eyes or touch with our hands. And sometimes they may not even seem like blessings at all, but hardships. However, if we accept everything that comes into our lives as part of God's redemptive plan to bless us, we can "count it all joy" (James 1:2).

Instead of continually wishing for future prosperity, we should be thankful for what God has already given us. From the simplest things, like a child's smile or a neighbor's hello, to the grandest, like a comforting home, the miraculous conversion of a loved one, or physical healing, God's gifts are set right before our eyes daily. Imagine what would happen in our hearts if we acknowledged and received each one, saying, "God, I don't always understand how you are moving in my life, but I know you love me, and I trust in that truth."

Life is so much more enjoyable when we stop and see all the blessings from God. And to think, we also have the greatest gift of all: Jesus! It's simply amazing.

To God alone be glory!

Preparing for Planting

"He who received seed on the good ground is he who hears the word and understands it, who indeed bears fruit and produces: some a hundredfold, some sixty, some thirty."

MATTHEW 13:23

What does it take to make good soil for planting? Preparing soil to receive seed is a process. Farmers begin to ready the soil for their crops well before planting time. God, of course, helps by keeping the seasons, sending the rain and freezing cold to preserve the moisture so the thawing earth is moist and ready to receive the seed in the spring.

How do we prepare the ground of our souls to receive God's Word to the point of understanding it and living it out? One way is to read God's Word in a certain way, letting it test you, allowing it to land on the soil of your life.

Reading God's Word over and over is the start of the process. Choose a verse and memorize it. Let it seep into your life. You'll find that one verse can find many paths to more growing roots. Jesus is God's Word made flesh. Let his love take root and grow in you daily.

To God alone be glory!

Fashionably Praiseworthy

Do not let your adorning be external—the braiding of hair and the putting on of gold jewelry, or the clothing you wear— but let your adorning be the hidden person of the heart with the imperishable beauty of a gentle and quiet spirit, which in God's sight is very precious.

1 Peter 3:3–4 esv

Fashion is such a personal thing. And yet all our apparel decisions are swayed by an industry that comes out with new styles every season. We believe we are making independent decisions, but in reality, we have only a limited number of choices. And who among us would return to the big hair and broad shoulders of the eighties or the wide bell-bottoms and short-hemline skirts of the seventies?

The greatest fashion advice is found in Scripture. It's a warning that we become what we praise. We mold ourselves into the likeness of what we find attractive. And we continually seek opportunities to express it.

God wants to clothe us with garments that will never go out of style and never wear out: his righteousness and his love. And the cost is simply to praise him and worship him. His beauty is eternally attractive. Sing praises to it!

To God alone be glory!

The Mind and the Spirit

For to be carnally minded is death,
but to be spiritually minded is life and peace.
Because the carnal mind is enmity against God;
for it is not subject to the law of God, nor indeed can be.

ROMANS 8:6–7

We all have a favorite food or type of food. Pizza, ice cream, Mexican, or Italian. Whatever it is for you, it can be especially hard to resist when dieting. That's usually when the temptation to eat our favorites grows stronger.

Food is just one example of how the flesh seems to operate independently from the mind. But notice in this passage from Romans that the mind is in control. The flesh isn't operating independently. The mind is in control in both scenarios, whether it's focused on the flesh or on the Spirit. The flesh doesn't suddenly become weak. There's a tipping point. It starts with the mind innocently giving reasons why you deserve that little piece of this or a slight indulgence in that. *After all*, the mind says, *it's not going to harm you. You can control it.*

This is the process of addiction. We strengthen the mind in whatever we set it on, whether for good or for sin. God wants us to train our minds on his Spirit. He will do the rest.

To God alone be glory!

God's Everlasting Arms

The eternal God is your dwelling place,
and underneath are the everlasting arms.
DEUTERONOMY 33:27 ESV

Our childhood memories are so powerful, setting the stage for what we will value as adults. And parents play a huge role in the many ups and downs of our younger years. A woman I know talks of having fond memories of her father coming home at precisely the same time every day. And every time, she would hide behind the door and surprise him. He would always play along, acting amazed just to see the joy on her face.

Today she still thinks of that and imagines doing the same with her eternal Father. He smiles, pretending he's surprised. He lets her walk alongside him and sit on his lap with his arms around her, where nothing can harm her.

The world's version of this verse from Deuteronomy could be translated as, "Don't worry. Be happy." God's interpretation is, "Don't worry. Be joyful!" There is no greater joy than to know that you're resting in the protective arms of a Father who loves you and will never leave you.

To God alone be glory!

Growing Better Each Day

We do not lose heart. Though our outer self is wasting away, our inner self is being renewed day by day. For this light momentary affliction is preparing for us an eternal weight of glory beyond all comparison.

2 CORINTHIANS 4:16–17 ESV

It's not easy getting older. The body breaks down; there's creaking and cracking. Eyes that once had a solid 20/20 vision now need readers to see the small print. In our youth, all the possibilities lie ahead. We are healthy and strong with a quick mind and jubilant heart. But as we age, the body breaks down while the mind grows in knowledge. Our energy decreases, but our desires expand.

God gives us encouraging words about what we're really doing in life. We are gaining wisdom. It's not just any old kind of wisdom but the kind that comes from him. We are called to constantly renew our minds and souls to center on Jesus.

When trouble comes, God's wisdom tells us he has overcome the world, so we need not worry. When the body falters, we can be confident that one day we will have a new one, and when we are sad, God assures as that, through Jesus, he transformed the saddest event into the greatest joy. God's wisdom is the source of all wisdom. Getting older in Jesus just means getting better and better.

To God alone be glory!

Your Words Are Your Testimony

Do not let any unwholesome talk come out of your mouths,
but only what is helpful for building others up according to their needs,
that it may benefit those who listen.

EPHESIANS 4:29 NIV

Today it's become quite common to use rather salty language. Most of the words cannot be repeated here. If you ever pass a group of young people conversing, it seems every other word they use is one that, a generation or two ago, would get a child's mouth washed out with soap. Today, young people seem oblivious to the impression they make on others around them. But it's not just the youth. Even adults now, walking along the streets or in stores, talk the same way, their conversations peppered with words that offend or shock.

We must all remember that we are children of the living God. His light is in all of us. God's Word instructs, "Do not let any unwholesome talk come out of your mouths, but only what is helpful for building others up" (NIV).

As Austrian Philosopher Ludwig Wittgenstein wrote, "The limits of my language mean the limits of my world." Or as Rev. Casey Baggott said, "Your life is your sermon!"[46] How we live preaches to others of what we glorify, what we love, and what we worship.

To God alone be glory!

SUDDEN DEATH

"Therefore keep watch,
because you do not know the day or the hour."
MATTHEW 25:13 NIV

At the Metropolitan Museum of Art in New York City, there's a marble wall sculpture called "Angel of Death." It portrays an artist's final moment on earth. Death is pictured as a beautiful angel, holding her hand in front of the sculptor's tool, stopping him in mid-stroke before he can wield the hammer again. It doesn't matter that the artist is in the midst of a job or a big project he needs to complete or that he thinks he has more work to do, more success to achieve. God has called him home according to God's timing, not according to the man's schedule.

It's a sad reminder. But it can also encourage us to always stay close to God. As one pastor said, we tend to live our lives acting as if God is not there, but we die praying he is. Death is the reality none of us can escape. But because Jesus defeated death on the cross, all that believers experience now is its shadow. Stay close to the living God. Know him and love him because Jesus is our refuge for all eternity.

To God alone be glory!

He Will Help You

*"I am the Lord your God who takes hold of your right hand
and says to you, Do not fear; I will help you."*

ISAIAH 41:13 NIV

There are times in life when you just run out of the bravery you need to tackle what's ahead. Life can be scary sometimes, and even the strongest believers may find themselves trembling at the thought of facing the trial or challenge that's looming before them. Sometimes, you may feel as though you don't have enough bravery, or enough gumption, left to persevere.

That is when you must trust God to be your strength—not just an invisible man in the sky or words in a Bible but a means of survival. It's a time when faith becomes all you have. As the apostle Paul wrote to the Hebrews, your faith becomes evidence (see Hebrews 11:1). You see what you believe. Believing is seeing God's Word as truth, betting all your life on God saying to you, "Do not fear. I will help you."

To God alone be glory!

Divine Superhero

Jesus looked at them and said,
"With man this is impossible,
but with God all things are possible."
MATTHEW 19:26 NIV

Superhero action movies are wonderful ways to be plunged into a world where the good guys always win. We all know that in real life, if there were beings who could, like Superman, leap tall buildings in a single bound or fly faster than a speeding bullet, we would all be quite afraid of them unless, of course, they were also loving and kind and protected the innocent.

We want heroes, people who can save us from the evil of this world. We want an all-powerful, all loving hero, who will be at our beck and call. In actuality, we have a superhero that all other movie versions point to: Jesus. There's a big difference though. Jesus never performed "naked displays of power."[47] His power resides in healing the sick, comforting the lost, and saving us from our own sins.

After his resurrection, Jesus appeared to the disciples and ate with them. The Bible says he walked through a closed door and sat down beside them. As one priest said to his congregation, "He who entered the room when the doors were closed can certainly enter your life and give you hope."[48] That is super!

To God alone be glory!

GIVING OF GIFTS

Do not forget to do good and to share with others,
for with such sacrifices God is pleased.

HEBREWS 13:16 NIV

Some people love to give gifts. Others love to receive them. Giving doesn't necessarily have to cost us anything in order to bring joy. For instance, a woman working in the media said a company had given her a case of promotional coffee mugs with a big logo on them. The woman had no use for them. But her father eyed them and asked if he could take them to his office. She asked, "What could you possibly want with so many cups from a company no one has heard of?" Her dad, in his wisdom, replied, "You'd be surprised how something like a coffee cup can brighten someone's day."

It wasn't about the cup; it was about caring for people and showing them that they were appreciated. It was about the care and love of the gift-giver. The woman's father never rose above middle management, but she considered him a career success because he made the working environment a joyous place. His greatest accomplishment was his impact on others. From the janitor to the company's CEO, they all knew his name, and they were all his friends.

God always calls us to give to others without hesitating. God gave us the gift of his Son, Jesus. It doesn't take a lot of money to be generous. It only takes a loving heart and a willing spirit.

To God alone be glory!

Plans to Succeed

Commit to the LORD whatever you do,
and he will establish your plans.
PROVERBS 16:3 NIV

Many times, we become excited about our plans and projects.
Young people especially like to talk about how they envision their
future. Committing our plans to the Lord is noble and certainly what God
asks of us. And on the surface, we may think that means our plans will
succeed. But it doesn't always mean that.

Committing whatever we do to the Lord means surrendering it to
the omniscient God so that his plans will succeed through us. Our plans
may be well and good, but God's plans will help them turn out in ways we
might never imagine.

It means our plans will succeed exactly as we would want them to
if we knew what God knows. We would have never understood the need
for Jesus' death on the cross. We would never have required it because our
vision is limited. But God sees eternity. His ways are higher than our ways.
His plans are higher than ours. That is something we can rely on.

To God alone be glory!

Loving to Please Him

Through love and faithfulness sin is atoned for;
through the fear of the Lord evil is avoided.
PROVERBS 16:6 NIV

There are several stages in every child's life when they become a bit surly with their parents. The terrible twos come to mind. Children will talk back and test the limits of parents' rules. For some children the stage starts early. And for others it never seems to end.

One woman says her surly stage was but a fleeting moment, thanks to parents who'd had four before her and knew how to nip it in the bud. But she remembered being saucy once with her mother. And her mother's look of disappointment and hurt cut through her like a knife. The mother said nothing; she didn't have to.

For the next week, the little girl voluntarily cleaned the house, did laundry, and was meekly respectful. She didn't do it because she was afraid of her mother but because she loved her mother. The woman recalls how she hated that part of her that had broken her mother's heart. Years later, she had grown to understand that that is why we obey God. Loving God as an eternal parent, changes us into children whose desire is to please the one who loves us most.

To God alone be glory!

Rising to Serve

You, my brothers and sisters, were called to be free.
But do not use your freedom to indulge the flesh;
rather, serve one another humbly in love.

Galatians 5:13 niv

The best bosses are those who care about their employees and make the work environment pleasant. They are essentially serving their employees. On the other hand, the worst bosses are those who treat employees like personal servants who must bow to them and do their bidding. We hope those bosses won't last long in their leadership roles.

Even if we are the boss at work, having a servant's attitude of humility is how we can all be like Jesus, who put aside his kingship to walk beside us and see to our needs. It doesn't matter who we are or what we do; we should strive to be like Jesus, who rose only to serve.

To God alone be glory!

Heeding God's Wisdom

"Those who find me [wisdom] find life and receive favor from the Lord.
But those who fail to find me harm themselves; all who hate me love death."

PROVERBS 8:35–36 NIV

If this verse is correct and true, then there is no gray area for what we should be pursuing: wisdom. Finding wisdom, seeking her out continuously brings life and health. But sometimes we don't consciously turn away from wisdom. It's a sin of omission rather than commission. Even then, Scripture tells us, failing to find wisdom will have severe consequences.

Not seeking wisdom is like traveling to an unfamiliar town and instead of asking the locals for directions or consulting a map or GPS, you just wing it.

There's harm in turning away from wisdom by either ignorance or arrogance. But the deliberate shunning of God's wisdom is essentially a love of death. Jesus' death on the cross and his resurrection changed the world forever and put us on a path of redemption and salvation. That's either universally and objectively true, or it is not. There's no gray area. But believing it makes an eternal difference in our lives.

To God alone be glory!

He Gave Us Himself

Jesus spoke to them again, saying, "I am the light of the world.
He who follows Me shall not walk in darkness, but have the light of life."
JOHN 8:12

Christianity is about putting our faith in Jesus. While there is much ritual involved in worship services through the sacraments of communion and baptism, this faith is primarily about the relationship we have with our Lord and Savior.

There are plenty of religions that give instructions for how to be saved. Do this to get blessed, say this to be right with your God, or eat this and you will find favor with the object of your worship.

But Christianity is different from them all. Jesus doesn't say "do this or that and God will bless you." He says to believe in him. He doesn't point to the way of salvation. He says, "I am the way." God didn't give us a rule book to save us. He gave us himself. He gave us Jesus.

To God alone be glory!

HE CARES

[Cast] all your care upon Him,
for He cares for you.
1 PETER 5:7

Life's tests and trials seem to put verses like this in better focus. If you've ever experienced the trifecta of anxiousness when your career, family, and friendships are all challenging and stressful at the same time, it's a recipe for personal disaster. We cry out to God wondering if he really knows what we're going through or if he cares. Scripture assures us that God hears us and cares for us. But God also tells us that we can prepare for those difficult times by daily prayer and the reading of his Word.

An athlete preparing for a competition doesn't wait for the day of the event to begin training. A musician preparing for a recital doesn't wait till the week before to memorize the music. It takes weeks and sometimes months and years to adequately train in order to respond properly to the challenge.

When we trust that God cares and loves us more than anyone, including ourselves, we must believe in that daily. Then we can be confident that the God who moves mountains can make a way out of no way and help us through whatever difficulties we face.

To God alone be glory!

Whom Do You Serve?

This day I call the heavens and the earth as witnesses against you that I have set before you life and death, blessings and curses. Now choose life, so that you and your children may live.

DEUTERONOMY 30:19 NIV

A young mother explained to a pastor that she would not impose a religion on her child and that as the child grew up, she would let him decide where to place his faith. The pastor asked the mother if she thought it was important to teach the child the meanings of red lights, yellow lights, and green lights when crossing the street.

No doubt the answer would be, "Of course." And the reason we would teach a child to obey stop lights when crossing a street is to keep the child safe from harm—maybe even saving his life. The same is true for teaching a child about faith in the living God, about Jesus, about God's plan for the redemption of all mankind. This, too, can save a child's life.

In his famous commencement speech, American writer David Foster Wallace made the same observation, "If you worship money and things—if they are where you tap real meaning in life—then you will never have enough. Never feel you have enough…Worship your own body and beauty and sexual allure and you will always feel ugly, and when time and age start showing, you will die a million deaths before they finally plant you."[49] Teaching a child to worship a transcendent God will nurture his soul and his spirit. All life long, it's the red, yellow, and green lights of God's kingdom.

To God alone be glory!

SPIRITUAL AMNESIA

*By this gospel you are saved, if you hold firmly to the word
I preached to you. Otherwise, you have believed in vain.*

1 CORINTHIANS 15:2 NIV

Do you ever walk back into a room because you forgot something only to forget what you forgot when you get to the room? Those of a certain age will have some experience with that. For those who don't yet know, wait a few years. We call it forgetfulness, but it's also like short term amnesia. Without the constant reminder of something, you're apt to forget it.

Faith can have the same problem. We're all sin-based creatures, tending to "forget that God is God and that we are not," if we're not constantly thinking about what God has done and is doing for us.[50] The Israelites were always forgetting how God saved them, brought them out of slavery in Egypt, and led them to the promised land. But they couldn't keep their devotion longer than a generation or two and had to be brought back to the fold by prophets and judges.

However, we have the saving grace of Jesus Christ, through whom our redemption is secured. It is important that we do whatever it takes to remember and have faith in the God who loves and saves.

To God alone be glory!

Strength Even in the Storm

You will seek Me and find Me,
when you search for Me with all your heart.
JEREMIAH 29:13

Faith is hardest to hold on to during the storms of life, even the small ones that pop up quickly. The perfect conditions create the proverbial little tempests in teapots. For example, after a long day at work, it began to rain, and one woman left the office believing she had an umbrella in her tote bag. Once in the lobby, she searched the bag but found no umbrella. She was so tired that she considered it was almost worth braving the pouring rain rather than going back to the office to get the umbrella. But she knew she'd be soaked in seconds if she didn't. So she returned to her desk to find her umbrella.

The next morning, she discovered two umbrellas in the tote bag. She simply hadn't looked hard enough for what was already with her. Why? The storm inside her and the one outside had weakened her faith and shortened the search for what would shield her.

It's tempting to fall apart when life gets rough. Even the little things like fatigue can alter faith's course. But God's Word is true, and we can rely on it even in the storms.

To God alone be glory!

Sabbath Rest in God

By the seventh day God had finished the work he had been doing;
so on the seventh day he rested from all his work.

GENESIS 2:2 NIV

In musical notation, the rests are as important as the musical notes. Rests are the spaces in the music when no notes are played; it's just waiting. A rest either helps emphasize a rhythmic beat or enhance a melody. That's why in written music, rests are actually notated. Musicians learn how to recognize the value or length of rests. Without rests, music would have no boundaries, no proper phrasing, no emotional highs or lows. It would be chaotic, especially when more than one musician plays together.

God knows the value of rest, especially rest from work. It is so important for us, so much so that God has commanded us to rest. We rest from our work to rejuvenate and reflect, to once again "re-enter the creation story" and understand who we are as created in the image of the Almighty.[51]

God rested, too, from his work. But unlike us, he didn't rest because he was tired. He rested because he was "satisfied with His work."[52] The only way we can achieve satisfaction in our lives and our work is to rest in God. He knows how we are made and knows what we need. Our Sabbath rest is resting in him.

To God alone be glory!

LIVING IN GOD'S TIME

My times are in your hands;
deliver me from the hands of my enemies,
from those who pursue me.
PSALM 31:15 NIV

Deo Volente is a Latin phrase that was commonly used at the end of letters or messages in the 1900s and simply abbreviated *DV*. It means "God willing" or "If God is willing." It is an acknowledgement that whatever plans we may have, whatever future we foresee, God is ultimately in charge and will order our steps as he sees fit.[53]

Time is one of those valuable things we cannot buy in a store. It is not on the New York Stock Exchange. It cannot be bargained with. It is totally in the possession of an almighty God, who has ordered this world in his image and to suit his purposes. Even Jesus, seeing his approaching death and tasting the suffering that lay ahead on the cross, pleaded to God to "remove this cup" from him but then said, "not my will, but thine, be done" (Luke 22:42).

The Lenten season is just a brief time. But we should carry its lessons throughout the year. We are to understand the meaning of the cross and how everything—every precious moment, no matter how brief—is part of God's plan. Our time is always in God's hands.

To God alone be glory!

Love Songs to Jesus

Come, let us sing for joy to the LORD;
let us shout aloud to the Rock of our salvation.

PSALM 95:1 NIV

Songs are often how we express our love for someone or something. That is why countries have national anthems. They unify people in praising their native land. We also express our love for God through music, using hymns, praise music, and, yes, love songs. Many popular love songs, if you examine their words, are really songs you could only sing to an eternal God. Songs that promise a love that will never fail can only describe God's love for us. People leave us through death or their own will, but God's love is for eternity.

Think about the song from the late 1960s called "Never My Love." Its lyrics profess a love that will always be strong and never waver. The only human in history to keep such a promise is Jesus. Yes, we are a community of Christians, but there is also an intimacy with God we gain through expressing our love for him. Songs are our heart's pathway to praising what we love.

How do we obey Jesus and make submission to him more desirable than the lure of sin? By singing love songs to him. Because, as the love songs say, being loved (by Jesus) is the sweetest thing.

To God alone be glory!

God as Our Ultimate Parent

Train up a child in the way he should go,
and when he is old he will not depart from it.

PROVERBS 22:6

You never know who you may sit next to on a flight. Some of us prefer not to engage in conversation with our seat mates while others like to get to know the person with whom they'll be spending an hour or two. A woman I spoke to recalled a flight when she stepped out of her normal "no talking rule" and chatted with a woman who turned out to be an efficiency and organization expert. She made her living showing others how to keep their offices and homes neat and perfectly organized. She said what drove her to be so proficient at it was that she had vowed never to be like her parents, who were the exact opposite.

Today's verse from Proverbs tells us that parents have an indelible influence over how their children grow. By default, we are like our parents in many ways. For example, how we learn to love or not love can depend a lot on how they loved us. Or like this woman on the plane who, by design and effort, became *unlike* her parents.

Parents are the authority in children's lives. How good or not good they are at raising their children depends on who the authority is in their lives. Is it a transcendent God or something else? God is our ultimate parent. None of us has perfect earthly parents. But we will always have a loving holy Father wanting to guide us in the way that we should go.

To God alone be glory!

Landing on Your Feet

All things are lawful for me, but all things are not helpful.
All things are lawful for me,
but I will not be brought under the power of any.

1 CORINTHIANS 6:12

One of the favorite toys for one woman's young kitten is a small stuffed tiger with a bell attached by a ribbon. The kitten will carry it around and throw it in the air and jump up and catch it then pounce on it again, repeating the action over and over.

The woman once found the beloved toy on the top of the stairway and decided to throw it down the stairs. Suddenly a flash of fur jumped through the second-floor railing and onto the steps below to capture the toy. The kitten had no fear, even seemed caught off guard, landing with her four paws on three different steps. The woman wondered, "Wow! Is this what God sees when we voraciously go after something? When we leap for our favorite things without knowing where we'll land?"

Freedom is a wonderful thing. But ironically, we can only be truly free when we live according to God's design for us. Cats are designed to land on their feet no matter what. Humans are not. As author and speaker Abdu Murray said, "God, knowing us, has established the boundaries of freedom that keep us from running blindly into traffic, childishly chasing after the bouncing ball of our liberty."[54] That's a good warning to us all.

To God alone be glory!

God's Loving Vengeance

Beloved, do not avenge yourselves, but rather give place to wrath;
for it is written, "Vengeance is Mine, I will repay," says the Lord.
ROMANS 12:19

Anger is an emotion that is often misunderstood. Many times it's linked to hate or disapproval. But it's actually quite complex. Anger is also an expression of love. If we love someone or something, we get angry at what may be hurting them, whether it is a terrible situation like war or abuse or their own self-destructive behavior. We also get angry because we want to protect what we love, whether it's another person or our own choices we make for our lives. However, because we're sin-based creatures, our loves—and hence our anger—are never perfect.

Only God's anger is justified because only God has all the facts. "God knows all that was in the person's heart and what they deserve."[55] Our endgame tends to be revenge, to see the other person suffer, to exact a heavy price for their misdeeds. But God's endgame is repentance and redemption. Our anger leans toward retaliation. God's anger is based on love for the saving of souls. That's why it is a blessing to serve this living God whose Word promises his anger lasts only for a moment but that his love endures forever (see Psalm 30:5).

To God alone be glory!

Perfect Law, Perfect Peace

Open my eyes that I may see wonderful things in your law.
PSALM 119:18 NIV

We are all imperfect human beings, struggling daily with what our sin-based instincts drive us to do, things which often run counter to what God requires of us.

We'd like to think, *Hey, I'm not so bad, at least not as bad as some other folks.* But the reality is that we are often out of sync with God's expectations, sometimes just a little and sometimes quite a lot. When a vengeful and angry spirit rises up in us, the mind seems like a weakened vessel precariously perched on a precipice, helpless to hold on.

But the mind is a muscle. And like all muscles it must be trained in order to be strengthened. And the perfect workout is lifting up the perfect law of God and bowing down to it. Over time, the mind trains the body and the spirit to know their proper place. Thanks be to God that when we fall short even after striving for perfection, he gives us the grace and mercy to try again. Meditating on his law will keep us in his perfect peace.

To God alone be glory!

GOD'S CURRENCY

*Now in Christ Jesus you who once were far away
have been brought near by the blood of Christ.*
EPHESIANS 2:13 NIV

Every country or group of countries has a currency used to buy and sell goods. When you travel to a different country, one of the first practical things to do is exchange currency. The exchange rate varies from day to day, so sometimes you get more or less money for your American dollars.

God has a currency too. But it has no equivalent value among man's dollars, Euros, or rubles. God's currency is the blood of Jesus. His blood is for the purchasing of souls. And although our souls cost him a cosmic sum, his saving blood is free for those who ask and put their trust in it. Maybe God's not a very good accountant. But he has all the purchasing power that's necessary and the only currency that has eternal and ultimate value.

To God alone be glory!

God's Simple Light

God said, "Let there be light,"
and there was light.
GENESIS 1:3 NIV

Is it that simple? Is God that close? Look out the window at a tree and realize the God of the universe is holding it up. And he's not grunting and sweating but carrying it by the tip of his pinky, by the laws he created.

In world speak, it's the tree's roots, gravity, the intricate balance of branches, the angle of the trunk, that's holding it all together. You can even call it a scientific model. But the forces that keep a tree standing are the same powers that keep our hearts beating, our lungs breathing. The same God created it all.

For God, who made light out of darkness, order out of chaos, and love to bind it all, it is simple. And yet, its complexity is a wonder and sometimes even a mystery for us to uncover through scientific discovery. Science alone cannot save us; believing in the one who designed the created order is the only pathway to salvation. It is Jesus who saves. Nothing and no one else. Let there be Light.

To God alone be glory!

Transformed by Trials

Joseph said to them, "Don't be afraid. Am I in the place of God?
You intended to harm me, but God intended it for good to accomplish what
is now being done, the saving of many lives."

GENESIS 50:19–20 NIV

While staying in a hotel, a woman put a hot curling iron on an unstable surface. As a result, it slid off the counter, hitting the hard bathroom floor, and she thought for sure it had broken. But it didn't. Relieved, the woman immediately found a safer place to rest the curling iron and learned to secure it better in the future.

This is a simplistic example, but it makes the point. Why does God let painful things happen to us? Because sometimes, unfortunately, it's the best way for us to learn.

Think of all the things that upset our lives, things that make us anxious, angry, or sad, things that bring difficulty into our lives. These could be God's teaching moments. Think of Joseph, who was wrongly imprisoned for years. Was it an injustice? Yes. But in the process, the arrogant young Joseph learned humility and patience, something no textbook, no lecture could have changed in him. His faith in God, his only refuge, increased. Instead of Joseph living in a prison of his own making, he was in a physical prison that, in turn, freed him from what was really his jailer: ego, pride, and ignorance.

Jesus is the only human to live a perfect life. The rest of us can only strive for it. But if we put our faith in Jesus' perfection, his redeeming work on the cross, our striving won't be in vain.

To God alone be glory!

ONLY ONE WAY

I pray that you, being rooted and established in love, may have power, together with all the Lord's holy people, to grasp how wide and long and high and deep is the love of Christ.

EPHESIANS 3:17–18 NIV

The only limits to God's love are those we put on it. Love, however, is complicated. The touchy-feely, emotionally satisfying love we crave from another imperfect human is not the kind of love we're talking about. It's a love that is greater than our wants and desires and sees right to our needs. That's God's love for us.

God sees eternity and knows our every thought and feeling. He is molding us for salvation. We want to pay the rent on our studio apartment, but he wants to give us a mansion; we want to fit into a swimming suit, but he wants to fit us for eternity. These are vastly different priorities. As C. S. Lewis said, "Aim at heaven and you'll get earth thrown in. Aim at earth and you'll get neither."[56]

Jesus, God made flesh, died on a cross to bridge the cosmic chasm that existed between us and the divine. If we could be saved by any other means, don't you think a God of that kind of infinite love would have told us?

To God alone be glory!

Healthy and Healing Praise

Rejoice in the LORD, O you righteous!
For praise from the upright is beautiful.

PSALM 33:1

Have you ever noticed that when you're cheering on your favorite sports team to a glorious victory your heart feels only good things? That's what praise and gratefulness do for us. They are twin elixirs of good fortune and a talisman against a bad mood. In other words, "A grateful heart protects you from negative thinking."[57]

God commands us to praise him not because he's an egomaniac but because it is good for our souls. What we praise we worship. But only God can give us a constant flow of love and good will. Praising shapes our character.

C. S. Lewis wrote, "I had not noticed how the humblest, and at the same time most balanced and capacious, minds praised most, while the cranks, misfits, and malcontents praised least."[58] A God who would give up his glory to save even those who don't believe in him is one who deserves our constant praise.

To God alone be glory!

Never Forsaken

*"Have I not commanded you? Be strong and of good courage;
do not be afraid, nor be dismayed, for the LORD your God
is with you wherever you go."*

JOSHUA 1:9

All of us worry about something. Whether it's the future, the past, or the present. Am I going to get into that school? Will I get that scholarship? Will I get that promotion or that job? When will I find the right person to marry?

But God tells us that worrying can also be a form of rebellion against him and his Word. We sometimes tend to pride ourselves in our ability to worry, as if worrying makes us deeper or more caring. Worrying, though, can also drive us down a path that makes us "doubt God's promises."[59]

God said, "I will never leave you nor forsake you" (Hebrews 13:5). You can depend on that promise because he didn't abandoned Jesus in the grave. Jesus' resurrection is our assurance that we can always put our faith in God's promises.

To God alone be glory!

SPIRITUAL JUSTICE

*"Do not pervert justice; do not show partiality to the poor
or favoritism to the great, but judge your neighbor fairly."*
LEVITICUS 19:15 NIV

The conventional wisdom down through the ages is that poor people
did something wrong and that's why they're poor, or wealthy people are
morally righteous and that's why they have riches. But even in the Old
Testament, God shows that the amount of money you have or don't have
is not an indication of your spiritual or moral strength. In fact, showing
favoritism to either economic group is a perversion of justice.

Jesus confirmed this centuries ago. Yes, he had a special place for the
economically poor and oppressed, but in his Sermon on the Mount in the
Gospel of Matthew, he says, "Blessed are the poor in spirit" (5:3), meaning
that no matter how much money or how few possessions we have, we must
all consider ourselves spiritually poverty stricken.[60] Jesus taught us that the
only true wealth is found in God Almighty.

To God alone be glory!

Worship the Giver

*Everything in the world—the lust of the flesh, the lust of the eyes,
and the pride of life—comes not from the Father but from the world.*

1 John 2:16 niv

In an off-Broadway play called *The Mother*, written by Florian Zeller, a woman is obsessed with her son. She reminisces about when he was a child, how much she enjoyed fixing him breakfast and walking him to school. She called it the happiest time of her life. But now that the son she adores is an adult and living his own life, she is angry and confused. She lives now only to be near him and is sullen and depressed when he doesn't call. At the end of the play, she lies in a hospital bed after trying to commit suicide and wonders bitterly what all that early life was for.

You see, the character in Zeller's play, like many people, took something good and turned it into an idol. The routine of caring for her child became ritual and eventually progressed imperceptibly to worship. When her son no longer needed her care, the mother felt she had no reason to live.

We have many good things that God has given us, but they are the means through which we glorify him. We are called to worship the Giver not the gifts, the Creator not the creation. There is only one gift we should worship, and that is the gift of God himself in Jesus Christ.

To God alone be glory!

Satan's Full-Court Press

The one who does what is sinful is of the devil,
because the devil has been sinning from the beginning.
The reason the Son of God appeared was to destroy the devil's work.

1 John 3:8 niv

Have you ever thought, when watching a heated competition between two top basketball teams, that the term *full-court press* could also describe Satan's efforts to corrupt God's image bearers? Basketball is certainly not evil. But that's why the analogy works. Satan has everything good at his disposal. He takes what God means for good and makes it for evil.

Think about the wonders of music. We have beautiful symphonies and love songs. But then there's also other varieties containing some of the most offensive language and derogatory descriptions of women.

Even in the church, we describe God's love as his highest good but forget that love also involves discipline and sacrifice, which means not always getting what we want. That, too, can be Satan's tool. He turns the gift of love into an evil when he convinces us that pursuing whatever our hearts dictate is the highest form of good. Jesus defeated Satan on the cross so that Satan's evil work on us now is nothing more than a vanquished enemy in the throes of death. Love Jesus first, and all other loves will take their proper place.

To God alone be glory!

Victory over Death

"Whoever lives by believing in me will never die.
Do you believe this?"

JOHN 11:26 NIV

What does it mean to die and yet live? It seems like a paradox. We tend to think of death in purely biological or physical terms. The body dies. There is a funeral and mourning for the loved one who has passed on.

But there is another kind of death that we experience, one that occurs while our bodies are biologically alive. It's a sort of existential death that can take many forms. A disappointment, a sadness, a loss. These are ways a bit of death "invades our existence" giving us a taste of its ultimate power over us, the power to take everything we love away from us.[61]

Jesus has defeated death on the cross. It no longer has that power over us. All we need to do is put our faith in the one whose ultimate sacrifice changed the trajectory of human existence. And just as Jesus rose from the dead, he can also resurrect our lives from their disappointments and sorrows. Living for Jesus means living in total victory over death.

To God alone be glory!

Prideful Destruction

*Pride goes before destruction,
and a haughty spirit before a fall.*
PROVERBS 16:18 ESV

Oh how I love a new pair of shoes! The smell of fresh leather, the crispy tissue in the new box, the anticipation of pairing them with just the right outfit. These are all signs of retail therapy's effects on us. One woman reveled in a new pair of expensive designer heels as they glittered and sparkled on her feet. But before she had a chance to break them in, she tripped on the stairs while wearing them. Only by clinging to a banister did she avoid suffering serious injury. Literally speaking, pride came before a fall. As you already know, though, this is not the only kind of *fall* Solomon had in mind with this proverb.

Pride in a new piece of apparel may seem innocent. But pride in our psyches can be like a dark power that masquerades as a bright light shining down on all our efforts. Pride "blinds us to our flaws."[62] It's fuel for the engine powering unforgiveness, jealousy, envy, and spiteful anger. In short, pride includes a lot of the stuff that ruins lives and distorts relationships.

Jesus is our example of the perfect anti-prideful human being: always giving, always loving, and, most of all, always forgiving. Be thankful that our pride will always be overcome by his grace and mercy.

To God alone be glory!

Peace and Safety

See what great love the Father has lavished on us, that we should be called children of God! And that is what we are! The reason the world does not know us is that it did not know him.

1 JOHN 3:1 NIV

Cats aren't known for being man's best friend, but they are more loyal than most people give them credit for. Many cat owners are surprised at how their cats always stay close by. If they move into the bedroom, the cats follow. If they go into the living room, the cats again follow. Even if you go into the bathroom, your cat may follow you there. In each room, they either play or find a resting place for a cat nap. As long as they're near their humans, they are happy.

It's a great feeling for many cat owners because they know that if the cats are close by, they are out of trouble and safe from danger. And because they're near, it's easier to pet them and hold them and make them feel even more loved. This must be how God feels toward us. He wishes we would stay near him to soak up his "unlimited and unfailing love."[63]

How many of us truly take advantage of it? What does it feel like and what does it look like when we experience how precious we are to him? You might imagine it is like someone's cats, slumbering peacefully at the foot of the bed, knowing they are loved and forever safe. Thank you, Jesus, for loving us more than we could ever imagine.

To God alone be glory!

Serving God, Not Our Talents

"All this I will give you," he said, "if you will bow down and worship me."
Jesus said to him, "Away from me, Satan! For it is written:
'Worship the Lord your God, and serve him only.'"
MATTHEW 4:9–10 NIV

Journalists meet some pretty talented and famous people in their line of work: musicians, actors, athletes, politicians, you name it. One journalist said the happiest celebrities always seem to be able to let their talent serve them and not the other way around. The unhappiest people had turned their gifts into idols, little *g* gods. They were driven to succeed in order to prove their self-worth. Whether or not you believe in Satan's schemes matters not to Satan. For this is one of his greatest ways he controls humans, making them slaves to their own talents.

The fact is, God has given us all gifts but for the purpose of growing them for his glory. When those gifts become what we trust most, they cease to serve their rightful purpose and instead become slave masters.

Like Reverend Peter Nicholas said, like any drug, "you can become addicted to your search for success."[64] Gifts are God's way of telling us, "I have great plans for you." Our gift to God is how we use those gifts to further his kingdom.

To God alone be glory!

Amazing Grace

The grace of God has appeared,
bringing salvation for all people.
TITUS 2:11 ESV

Very few people, living or dead, understand or understood the concept of grace better than John Newton. Not only was he a slave trader but also among the worst of them. Brutal and ruthless, he was the one that other slave traders looked down on. But on a stormy voyage in rough seas that was certain to be his end, he cried out to God. He was saved, and his conversion began.

John Newton would eventually go on to become an Anglican priest and hymn writer and fight against the slave trade along with William Wilberforce. Newton's most famous hymn is one we sing so often today, "Amazing Grace."[65]

Believers who travel to London experience incredible joy when they visit Newton's church, St. Mary Woolnoth. On his memorial plaque on the church wall are Newton's own words, which say in part, "Once an infidel and libertine…was by the rich mercy of our Lord and Saviour Jesus Christ, preserved, restored, [and] pardoned."[66] If you're ever in London, don't miss the opportunity to sing his beloved hymn in the church. Tears will flow.

To God alone be glory!

CONDITIONED TO OBEY

Make me understand the way of your precepts,
and I will meditate on your wondrous works.
PSALM 119:27 ESV

In England, traffic stays to the left. It's a little disconcerting for American tourists who live by the rule of keeping to the right. It can also be dangerous for Americans who are crossing the street as a pedestrian. We naturally look left for oncoming traffic. But when traffic stays to the left we have to look right. And the city tries to help out by painting on the curb, "Look to the right."

But no matter what the words say, after looking right, Americans can't help but look left as well. So conditioned are we of one way of doing things that even when the rule is spelled out right in front of us, we still can't fully live by it. It's a simple case of conditioning and what we experienced growing up.

It's also an example of how even God's laws can seem counter to everything we feel and think. Just as the sign on London's curbs are meant to save us from harm, so, too, are God's laws. Only God established his laws because he loves us. God's laws come from love because "God is love" (1 John 4:8).

To God alone be glory!

Enemies Become Friends

If, while we were God's enemies, we were reconciled to him through the death of his Son, how much more, having been reconciled, shall we be saved through his life!

ROMANS 5:10 NIV

Memorial Day should be a somber day honoring the men and women who died defending America. The idea of war, of course, is that we have enemies whom we must be willing to kill or be killed by in order to secure peace.

But think of Abraham Lincoln, who led this country through the tumultuous Civil War. At the end of the war, Lincoln made a profound statement describing how best to be truly rid of enemies: "Do I not destroy my enemies when I make them my friends?"

Jesus is our example of how to truly reconcile with our enemies to make them our friends. Forgiveness is the first step, of course. But then comes the hard part: blessing them. Jesus instructs us in his Sermon on the Mount to "Bless those who curse you, and pray for those who spitefully use you" (Luke 6:28). It not only "destroys" enemies, but it also chisels away Satan's power, which is ultimately the force behind many of our conflicts. Jesus is our perfect example for turning enemies into brothers. With Jesus as our Light, we can also strive to make friends of our enemies.

To God alone be glory!

Ɗeepest Ꝇove Ꝑossible

This is how God showed his love among us:
He sent his one and only Son into the world
that we might live through him.

1 John 4:9 niv

We tend to think of our love for God like that of a love for another human being or for a treasured hobby or passion. In other words, we think of it from the perspective of *our* ability and capacity to love. But this love the apostle John is speaking of is a different kind of love altogether; it's off the charts really. First of all, it's a love that God has for us and his creation. It's a love that fulfills all our deepest longings, so much so that, in its presence, we no longer need food, water, or the right temperature.

Love repels insults like a gnat hitting a stone wall. This kind of love is transformative. This kind of love is "gift love."[67] It wants to give out of its abundance. This kind of love is the fundamental element of creation. It is the "Divine energy" that put forth the world.[68]

This love truly surpasses all understanding as it is the basis of all our scientific laws that we have yet to fully understand, and yet, it is totally comprehensible as it is also the love of a mother for her child. All this, the total spectrum of what love is, was present on the cross. It is truly amazing.

To God alone be glory!

Unique Paths, Same Destination

The LORD makes firm the steps of the one who delights in him.
PSALM 37:23 NIV

Some experience God in feelings, others do so in intellectual pursuits, like science and literature. But no one path is enough if our faith is lifelong.

The emotional person may need hard facts to quell a moment of confusion. And a person heavily into science may need a passionate moment of the heart to feel God's presence. Each area—feelings or facts—can become an idol if we do not balance one with the other.

Knowledge and faith. Mind and heart. They go together because God is both love and law. Both were captured on the cross. It is because of God's law that Christ sacrificed himself. Sin must be atoned for. But it was because of his love that Jesus did it willingly. All paths are unique but find their true direction moving toward the risen Savior.

To God alone be glory!

Nature and Nurture

In your hearts revere Christ as Lord. Always be prepared to give an answer to everyone who asks you to give the reason for the hope that you have. But do this with gentleness and respect.

1 PETER 3:15 NIV

Scientists continue to debate the relationship between nature and nurture, your genes or your environment. Most agree that both have a tremendous effect on how a person turns out as an adult, but how much each one contributes is, well, not an exact science.

One thing is for sure. There is a cause behind who we are, why we exist, and the purpose of our lives. That we even ponder these ideas is unique to the human species. Cats and dogs, as far as anyone knows, don't brood over such existential matters. But we do.

What the Bible is saying in this wonderful message from the apostle Peter is that no matter what your genes or your upbringing has caused to happen in your life, your true hope is in Christ Jesus. Every good thing comes from our Lord, but those good things can be taken away. People die, we lose jobs, and bank accounts dwindle. But Christ will never be taken away. Putting our ultimate hope in him brings us joy each day and for all eternity.

To God alone be glory!

In God's Garden

Blessed are the people who know the festal shout,
who walk, O Lord, in the light of your face.
PSALM 89:15 ESV

To have a beautiful garden is the dream of many people. But when you live in a big city apartment with no outdoor space, you may be limited to fantasizing about open landscapes of green and hues of floral beauty.

Gardens are perfect places to spend time with God, the ultimate gardener. As C. Austin Miles' old hymn "In the Garden" says, "I come to the garden alone…and He walks with me, and He talks with me, and He tells me I am His own." The beauty of a garden and the beauty of the love of God join together in one blissful, heavenly experience.

Luckily for all city dwellers, they can experience God's love everywhere, in the garden of life. Springtime is a reminder that God can make all things new. He can turn darkness into light and death into life. That is the beauty of a garden that what was once dead is again full of life. This is the hope for our lives. Disappointment and sorrows are not the end of the story. Joy and life and the beauty of God's garden is the everlasting saga.

To God alone be glory!

A New Heart

"I will give you a new heart, and a new spirit I will put within you.
And I will remove the heart of stone from your flesh
and give you a heart of flesh."
EZEKIEL 36:26 ESV

A certain little girl, like a lot of little girls, loved horses. Every summer at camp, she couldn't wait to go horseback riding. For every birthday, that's what she wanted to do as well. She even believed she could raise a horse in the middle of the inner city. City restrictions had no bearing on her desires. She would sometimes gaze out her bedroom window, imagining her horse casually chewing on grass in the backyard. You see, passion and desire kept any kind of intellectual argument from getting through to her.

A wise reverend said the same things about our ability to believe in God: "We're not shaped by our intellect, but by our desires."[69] It's the same thing with food, love, or anything we become passionate about. Our desires shape and control our actions. Intellectually we know that we shouldn't have that second piece of cake or enter a relationship with someone who's not in line with God's plan for our life. Ironically, it's the passionate heart that becomes like stone. Nothing can get through. What's the solution? A new heart, one that is soft enough to desire and allow God's hand to mold it.

To God alone be glory!

Problems Solved

God does not show favoritism.
ROMANS 2:11 NIV

An older woman coming back into the city on a train had a bit of a chuckle. She heard a couple of teenagers sitting behind her having somewhat of a philosophical discussion about life, relationships, marriage, and the state of the world and how to solve its problems. They were quite sure they had figured it all out, and one of them finally surmised, "Wait, if everyone were like us, there'd be no wars. So everyone should be like us!" Ah, youth!

At one point, perhaps we all thought like this, that there would be no problems if we would all get on the same page and work toward the same goals. But God loves variety. And we all have different strengths and different life experiences that have molded us into the people we are. However, there was still an inkling of truth nestled in what those young people said. And it's these words: "If everyone."

God gives us all a choice in how to finish that sentence. But he knows the real lesson is when we change the words from "If everyone" to "If I." We stop looking at the world as being the problem and instead look at how we've contributed to it. That's when God can truly help us solve the problems of the world.

To God alone be glory!

Spiritual Cancer

*Keep your servant also from willful sins;
may they not rule over me.*

PSALM 19:13 NIV

Sin is spiritual cancer. Like the physical disease, it has no respect for individuals. It will eat up and destroy its host until it either kills it or is killed. Take adultery for instance. A man decides to leave his wife and young children to be with another woman. The affair creates many victims. In their zeal to find true love, the two lovers fail to admit how their own sinful hearts, invaded by this cancer, contribute to the pain and suffering they create in their respective families. But God knows.

Sin begins small, even imperceptibly. If left unexamined, it simply continues to grow. Fear of God is the chemotherapy against the cancer of sin. *Fear* in this case means "in awe of." Our self-understanding grows with our increasing reverence for God.

The good news is that Jesus Christ defeated sin's ultimate power over us, which is death. But he also defeated death's little minions, the cancerous pawns prowling to invade our lives. The Bible also says, "The fear of the Lord is the beginning of wisdom" (Proverbs 9:10). The fear of the Lord is a defensive castle wall against sin's attacks.

To God alone be glory!

A Leap of Faith

Those who belong to Christ Jesus have crucified the flesh with its passions and desires. Since we live by the Spirit, let us keep in step with the Spirit.
GALATIANS 5:24–25 NIV

Living by the Spirit is a challenge. But there's a moment in our lives when faith becomes sight, when the hoping and praying become physical or emotional realities. It's then that we know we've grown spiritually.

A good visual reminder of what this time of growth might look like is a scene from the movie *Indiana Jones and the Last Crusade*. Indiana, the hardened and practical archeologist and action hero, must take a step off a ledge onto what appears to be thin air in order to find the cup of Christ, the Holy Grail. And he must take this terrifying step not only because it's a professional quest but also to save his father, who has just been shot. It's a literal leap of faith. He knows he's never had to have that kind of faith before. But he has no choice. He steps out and lands on solid ground.

Of course, it is a movie. But it's true that God communicates through such mysterious circumstances because he always meets us where we are. The bottom line is that whether our faith is bold like Paul's or barely there like the convictions of Indiana Jones, God rises to the occasion.

To God alone be glory!

God Is Never Mocked

Do not be deceived: God is not mocked,
for whatever one sows, that will he also reap.

GALATIANS 6:7 ESV

I knew a man who became quite boastful about his relationship with God. He was a Christian by tradition but rarely went to church or prayed. But he was utterly convinced that he and God had a good rapport and that God was okay with his life choices.

Scripture says this man was fooling himself (Proverbs 12:15). The only way God could be okay with every choice we make is if God didn't care about us. Only an uncaring parent never corrects a child. You see, this man is like many people, mistaking God's patience with God's affirmation. People don't live in a vacuum, and each choice we make is guided by a previous choice and another one before it and another before that, on and on down the line. It's not totally this man's fault. Background and upbringing contribute as well.

One reason there are four Gospels in the Bible—Matthew, Mark, Luke, and John—is because they each focus on different viewpoints of Jesus' life and ministry. But all end the same, with his crucifixion and resurrection. God understands we're all different, and each one of us is carving a unique path to him. But we are all the same in that Jesus will always be "the way, the truth, and the life. No one comes to the Father except through" him (John 14:6).

To God alone be glory!

Living in Beauty

Finally, brothers and sisters, whatever is true, whatever is noble, whatever is right, whatever is pure, whatever is lovely, whatever is admirable— if anything is excellent or praiseworthy—think about such things.

PHILIPPIANS 4:8 NIV

Most of us believe we act rationally. But God understands that we are often controlled by our heart's desires. For the ancient prophets and philosophers, the heart was not just a muscle that pumps the blood through the body. The heart was the source of all our wants and passions. So the Bible talks a lot about helping us create a new heart (Psalm 51:10), one that seeks to do God's will and strives to please the one who created us.

We can change our hearts by first asking God for help. Second, we must understand the complex interplay between our heart and mind. We become what we think about. If we think and see beauty in people, people will see much beauty in us. If our mind seeks truth, we will work to speak truthfully. And if we see excellence all around, it will compel us to strive for it in our own lives. Changing our hearts is a process. But the living God of this world stands at the ready to be our help and guide.

To God alone be glory!

Successful Failures

"When I fed them, they were satisfied;
when they were satisfied, they became proud;
then they forgot me."
HOSEA 13:6 NIV

A church marquis announcing the title of Sunday's sermon said, "Success has made failures of many people." That one sentence pretty much sums up our dilemma of trying to balance career, family, and our walk with God. It encompasses the Bible's warning about serving two masters. We simply cannot (see Matthew 6:24).

God knows that there's only room in our lives to live under the authority of one master. Many a marriage has been crippled, damaged, or destroyed because one spouse put career or pride ahead of family. A lot of athletes and actors have become famous and wealthy only to see their personal lives fall apart.

Success in any category can be a great thing. But when it becomes the ultimate thing and our foundational trust, then it becomes an idol and, in the end, our master. Success cannot comfort us or love us. It can only demand more and more from us. But God's love is so all satisfying that it enables us to love what we have and to be content with it. When opportunities come, we see them for what they are: a gift from God for us to use in service to him.

To God alone be glory!

Clothed in God's Love

Oh give thanks to the Lord, for he is good,
for his steadfast love endures forever!
PSALM 107:1 ESV

Every spring when it's time to put the winter clothes away and bring out the lighter weight garments, I find in my closet items of clothing I had long forgotten about. Sometimes it's an item I have barely worn, or it may still have the tags on it. It's like shopping without spending any money.

Being thankful is a great deal like that. It's a state of mind really. Expressing gratitude to God for the gifts he has given provides a whole new covering that you forgot you had. Even more, being thankful unleashes God's cosmic power that changes your world, which can also change the world of those near you.

Think about that undiscovered wardrobe. Giving thanks is like covering yourself in God's greatest garment, his love that endures forever.

To God alone be glory!

God's Precious Children

How priceless is your unfailing love, O God!
People take refuge in the shadow of your wings.
PSALM 36:7 NIV

If something is of great monetary value, we might say it is priceless. If something is of great value to us personally, we call it precious.

Priceless implies that something is objectively worth a great deal of money. But when something is personally all important to us, it can have no price tag. It is beyond the scope of being bartered for. No exchange of currency or gifts would make it worth the trade. When you recognize that something is precious, you might feel a sudden gasp of excitement in its presence, like seeing a snow-capped mountain range for the first time or receiving a beautiful heirloom quilt handmade by a beloved relative.

That is God's love. And sometimes it's hard to grasp its power. But a good example is when a mother first holds the newborn she's been carrying in her womb for months. She sees the baby's features for the first time, eyes, nose, tiny hands and feet. Babies can only demand and cry for what they need or want. But the parents still give all their love because they are overflowing with love for the infant, who is precious to them. In much the same way God loves us not because we are worthy of being loved. He loves us because he is love. And we are all precious in his sight.

To God alone be glory!

God's Victory Is Ours

He has redeemed my soul in peace from the battle that was against me, for there were many against me.

PSALM 55:18

Praying thanks during a spiritual battle or during one of life's hardships is what this brief verse teaches. And it is a good lesson.

In the verse directly before, the psalmist speaks boldly about praying to God morning, noon, and night and stating, "He shall hear my voice" (v. 17). He speaks of a future time when God will answer his prayer. But then immediately in verse 18, the tense changes. It is in the past tense, as if the redemption has already occurred. Notice also he doesn't progress to the present tense. He goes from "God shall" to "God has." There is no in-between; no "God is figuring things out." Not all translations make this distinction. It's a subtlety worth noting.

Jesus' death on the cross brought redemption to us immediately. That is why, at the moment of death, Jesus said, "It is finished" (John 19:30). The temple curtain was torn, and no longer would there be a separation between God and humanity. Prayers are our conversations with God. And the most powerful are when we listen to hear what God has already accomplished and give him our thanks!

To God alone be glory!

The Heart of the Law

*"Do not think that I came to destroy the Law or the Prophets.
I did not come to destroy but to fulfill."*

MATTHEW 5:17

The 1960s and '70s brought us many things, some good, some bad. But one legacy still apparent today is this aversion to the authority of law, preferring the supposed freedom of autonomy.

In his Sermon on the Mount, Jesus preached a deeper, fuller, and heart-level understanding of how we should interpret the Ten Commandments. He explained that "Do not kill" is not just the physical action of violently taking another life, but it is also the anger in the heart that preceded it. "Do not commit adultery" is not just about engaging in physical intimacy with someone who is not your spouse but also the lusting with the eyes that you do beforehand.

The Pharisees would narrowly interpret a law so that the sin got smaller and smaller. We all have a little Pharisee in us, never seeing the enormity of our sins, succumbing to and becoming a slave to our feelings that are breeding grounds for wrong actions. But Jesus sees into our hearts. He sees our need. And he asks for us to bow to his and only his authority and, ultimately, to the only true freedom it brings.

To God alone be glory!

Riches in God's Refuge

Do not fret because of evildoers, nor be envious of the workers of iniquity.
For they shall soon be cut down like the grass, and wither as the green herb.
Trust in the LORD, and do good; dwell in the land, and feed on His faithfulness.

PSALM 37:1–3

It's difficult to watch the rise of people who achieve their success through less-than-noble means. And we wonder, *Where is God's justice? Why would God allow "the wicked" to prosper?* The Bible is filled with passages telling us not to envy the wealthy and prosperous, but it's so easy to feel that envy, especially in a place like New York City, where being rich and famous has become the default measure of self-worth.

God is not opposed to wealth or popularity; many faithful people throughout the history of humanity have been wealthy. Abraham was quite wealthy. King Solomon's wealth rivaled anyone's in the whole of history.

But they were righteous men who valued their relationship with God above earthly wealth. "The wicked" value only what their hands have made and forget who gave them those hands. They also live fearing their fame and fortune will be taken away. But those who trust in God put virtue ahead of popularity and riches. And no one can ever take away what is ultimately most valuable.

To God alone be glory!

WALKING ALONGSIDE

To the weak I became as weak, that I might win the weak.
I have become all things to all men, that I might by all means save some.

1 CORINTHIANS 9:22

In the verse above, the apostle Paul is saying what we express today as "walking a mile in someone else's shoes." Paul does this to understand how best to open the hearts of others to the saving grace of Jesus Christ.

All of us have hidden, unfulfilled longings or pain we may keep from the world. For example, there was a man who worked in a television newsroom in a major Midwest city. He always smiled and seemed to be in a good mood. One day he committed suicide by shooting himself with one of the guns in his collection. All his colleagues were shocked. He had hidden his pain from them and the world. However, no one working alongside him daily attempted to probe beneath the surface to truly make him a friend, to become someone he could confide in and maybe even cry with.

We are built for personal relationships. We are all members of a very big club called "The Walking Wounded." Most of our wounds are below the surface where no one sees. Sometimes we even hide them from ourselves. God has called us to be his warriors in the fight against the forces that threaten our neighbors and ourselves daily. Pray without ceasing. Talk to the people in your life and go below the surface. Let them know they are loved. Be on the battlefield of God's love.

To God alone be glory!

God's Ultimate Promise

"Be strong and courageous. Do not fear or be in dread of them,
for it is the Lord your God who goes with you.
He will not leave you or forsake you."

DEUTERONOMY 31:6 ESV

Some days just don't go right. No matter how hard we try to keep matters on track, there are always things that are out of our control. We've all had those days when we discovered that something we thought had been taken care of was still not done. And what you had hoped to accomplish is nowhere near complete. Add to that the feeling that everyone and everything seems to be working against you. It's near complete frustration.

But God allows those times simply for our benefit, believe it or not, so that we will know that he is our hope, that he is who we should truly rely on. If we were totally self-reliant and had all the power we needed, we could make it rain when the flowers need watering or make the sun shine on the day we plan an outdoor affair.

If God's Word is truth, then we can trust in what it says. He does go before you. He will not leave you. He will never forsake you. No matter what you see or hear, do not fear, for the Lord is always near. So cheer up, for the Lord God Almighty has it all under control.

To God alone be glory!

Power in Every Word

God is our refuge and strength,
a very present help in trouble.
PSALM 46:1

Meditate over today's verse and you'll find that every single word in this psalm holds power and truth. Look closely at each word.

God: The omnipotent Being, all-knowing, all-present.

Is: Current, now, immediately.

Our: Every one of us, including you.

Refuge: Sanctuary, shelter, fortress, security, and shield.

And: Also, including, in conjunction with.

Strength: Power, toughness, fortitude, firmness.

A Very: At the top, intensely.

Present: Near at hand, always with you.

Help: Whatever you need, when you need it.

In Trouble: What seems unsolvable, discord, conflicts, disillusion, heartache.

What a great and quick way to tap into God's ever-abiding presence. Whatever is going on in your life, keep repeating these words. Put them on your heart and in your mind. Let your body absorb these words so that you will never be shaken by life's ups and downs.

The world would have us believe otherwise. But it's just Satan's ploy to get us to give up and give in. But God's Word shows a different plan is in place. Praise him!

To God alone be glory!

CREATION SPEAKS

The heavens declare the glory of God;
and the firmament shows His handiwork.
Day unto day utters speech, and night unto night reveals knowledge.

PSALM 19:1–2

God speaks to us every moment of every day. Are we listening? The psalmist proclaims that God's creation, the heavens and the earth, is revealing knowledge to us about him constantly.

Sometimes we take for granted that we live in a world God created. It's a little like asking a fish if he likes living in water. The fish would ask, "What's water?" So immersed in a world that sustains us, we forget to acknowledge the one who created it all.

There are many forms of communication, some verbal, some nonverbal. God has put in this world knowledge of him that comes directly to us whether we're listening or not. He's giving us the assurance that, "You can find Me in each moment, when you have eyes that see and ears that hear."[70]

God's ultimate expression of love came to us through Jesus dying on a cross, taking the wrath of his own judgment. All of creation is communicating that truth, pointing to that reality, if we have the ears to hear and the eyes to see.

To God alone be glory!

The Real Root of Evil

The love of money is a root of all kinds of evil,
for which some have strayed from the faith in their greediness,
and pierced themselves through with many sorrows.

1 TIMOTHY 6:10

We need money to pay rent and to buy food and clothing. But what is enough money? Ah yes! This is our challenge.

Today's verse is often misquoted as "money is the root of all evil." But that's not true. Money is morally neutral. It's how we value it that creates evil. It's loving money so much that it becomes your god, the thing you will sacrifice all for: your family, your virtue, God's love.

The word *strayed* is key in the verse, for it shows a gradual procession; it is not making a decisive plan, but it's unknowingly taking small steps, making decisions based upon greed, slowly drifting toward the love of money and away from God's order until one day it pierces. Then we wonder, *Why, God, did you let this happen?* Every big downfall begins with small motions. God says be careful what you love. Love God first and foremost; then you will never be conquered by the love of money.

To God alone be glory!

Mind, Body, and Soul

"'You shall love the LORD your God with all your heart,
with all your soul, with all your mind, and with all your strength.'
This is the first commandment."

MARK 12:30

What's more powerful, your mind or your body? What controls what? Scientists will say the mind controls everything, from the unconscious regulating of our heart and respiratory system to the deliberate choices we make.

But anyone who's tried to stick to a diet knows there are times when the body craves what it wants, and the mind might as well go on vacation. In this greatest commandment, Jesus tells us that we are to focus all of who we are on loving and obeying God. "We are created as whole persons by God with a body and a mind that have deep and complex effects on each other."[71]

Even scientists don't have all the answers as to how our genes and DNA react with our environments. But what the Bible tells us is that God created us in his image, male and female. And our mind/body interactions and all their complexities need to be ordered, firstly, through his love for us then, secondly, by our love for him.

To God alone be glory!

Jesus Is Truly Okay

*Blessed be God, who has not turned away my prayer,
nor His mercy from me!*
PSALM 66:20

The late sixties and seventies were a time of a lot of self-actualization and armchair psychology: "I'm okay. You're okay."[72] It was a time when people were trying to find out who they were and the grand narrative that ordered life. It was also a time of questioning all authority, especially religious doctrines.

In fact, in the seventies, many people started looking down on faith as just rigid ritual that rarely related to the ups and downs of life. It became popular to experiment with faith and seek out other forms of spirituality, like Eastern mysticism. But apart from God, there is no being "okay." There is no other real identity that lasts forever except the one we have in the eternal Being.

And by the way, Jesus does have something to say about our ups and downs. He died on a cross to make sure we can be with him for eternity, the ultimate up. Stay close to him. He's truly the only Being who is really okay.

To God alone be glory!

True Independence Declared

Jesus said to her, "I am the resurrection and the life.
He who believes in Me, though he may die, he shall live."

JOHN 11:25

These words of Jesus are on the tombstone of George Washington, the first president of the Unites States. In just a few weeks we celebrate the signing of the Declaration of Independence by the fifty-six men in the Second Continental Congress. The final draft was approved on July 4, 1776.[73] The document mentions God four times as the reason we have rights that can never be taken away, that God is higher than man's laws.

It's very comforting to know that an intellectual giant like Washington, though he was certainly not perfect, still bowed to God, still understood that Jesus Christ stands as the final arbiter of justice and mercy. America's founding document rests on a foundation infused with biblical principles.

America is imperfect and may not last forever as a country. But it is founded on the principles of one who is perfect and is eternal. Jesus has promised, "I am the resurrection and the life…Though [you] may die, [you] shall live."

To God alone be glory!

FREEDOM THROUGH RESTRICTIONS

*Live as free people, but do not use your freedom as a cover-up for evil;
live as God's slaves.*

1 PETER 2:16 NIV

Everyone submits to something or someone. In your job, you've got a boss. That boss has a boss. Even if the boss owns the company, he or she submits to clients, customers, or shareholders. Otherwise, the business will fail. Submission creates a better-run business and, hopefully, a profitable one as well.

What this means is that there's an order to freedom. A business can't be successful unless it submits to the purpose of its operation. An apparel chain that decides it wants to become a fast-food restaurant is bound to jeopardize its economic future.

In God's business plan, he has designed us for a purpose. We only have true freedom when we submit our whole being to that design. In marriage, relationships, family obligations, work, God has a design for us. And when we submit to it, only then are we truly free.

To God alone be glory!

Beliefs Have Power

*These are written that you may believe that Jesus is the Messiah,
the Son of God, and that by believing you may have life in his name.*
JOHN 20:31 NIV

One little girl thought the wars she heard about on the news were happening in her own neighborhood. She couldn't fathom the distance between her town and a war-torn country thousands of miles away. It frightened her so much that one year she thought Fourth of July fireworks were bombs and that she would soon die.

Beliefs are powerful things, and even a child's outlandish understandings can cause fear and confusion. Growing up doesn't change the fact that "beliefs shape your behavior."[74] In fact, what you believe has even more power over you as an adult.

If you're swimming in the ocean and someone tells you there could be sharks close by, chances are you will get out of the water or be much more cautious. But let's say it turns out there were no sharks. It wouldn't have changed your state of anxiety because you believed they were there. God's counsel is for us to believe in his mighty power, to believe that he is in control, and, most of all, to believe in his love that endures forever and will never leave you or forsake you. This is the only belief that should have ultimate power over us.

To God alone be glory!

FAITH IN GOD'S POWER

This is how we know that we belong to the truth and how we set our hearts at rest in his presence: If our hearts condemn us, we know that God is greater than our hearts, and he knows everything.

1 JOHN 3:19–20 NIV

Sometimes a problem can seem overwhelming. When that happens, there's a tendency to obsess over it. In every conversation, the problem just seems to get bigger and bigger. But as several preachers have said, "Stop talking about how big your problem is and start talking about how big our God is."

Instead of dwelling on the problem, we should be resting in the knowledge that God is bigger than any problem and can make a way out of no way. The Bible doesn't promise that we will never have problems or pain. It promises us that if we put our trust in the Sovereign God, we will get through it. The God who raised Jesus from the dead is a God who can solve whatever problems we may have. Let us put our faith not on the problem of pain but in the power of God.

To God alone be glory!

Surely Goodness and Mercy

The LORD is my shepherd;
I shall not want.

PSALM 23:1 KJV

Some Bible verses are so powerful that many composers through the ages have felt the need to set them to music. Psalm 23 is one of them.

There are many versions, but a famous one is from composer Franz Schubert. Even in German, the words are still powerful. But here's the English translation of Psalm 23 in the King James Version of the Bible:

> The Lord is my shepherd; I shall not want. He maketh me to lie down in green pastures: he leadeth me beside the still waters. He restoreth my soul: he leadeth me in the paths of righteousness for his name's sake. Yea, though I walk through the valley of the shadow of death, I will fear no evil: for thou art with me; thy rod and thy staff they comfort me. Thou preparest a table before me in the presence of mine enemies: thou anointest my head with oil; my cup runneth over. Surely goodness and mercy shall follow me all the days of my life: and I will dwell in the house of the Lord for ever.

The Word of God speaks to us through the psalm's six verses in a way that defines our whole being, comforting us, assuring us of God's care for us, his love for us, and his protection for us throughout eternity. God sees to our every need through the Good Shepherd, Jesus Christ. When you have time, listen and give God the glory.

To God alone be glory!

Making All Things New

*"For behold, I create new heavens and a new earth;
and the former shall not be remembered or come to mind."*
ISAIAH 65:17

Today's verse is about God's grand narrative of redeeming a fallen world.
It also defines the narratives of our individual lives and how God can
recreate in us new things, new thoughts, new visions, and, of course, new
revelations about who we are and what our purpose in life is.

In short, this Scripture verse is the description of a conversion,
heartfelt and definitive. The heavens represent the mind, which will have
a new way of understanding the world. The earth is the body that will be
transformed to carry out the mind's directives.

Even though he is sometimes called "the Ancient of Days," "God is
always young, and so are those who truly love him. He makes all things
new."[75] Jesus died to give us eternal life. Because he rose from the dead,
he is able to create in us that spirit that keeps us forever young and ever
seeking to glorify him.

To God alone be glory!

Listening for God's Voice

He said to them, "Take heed what you hear.
With the same measure you use, it will be measured to you;
and to you who hear, more will be given."

MARK 4:24

People often lament that God does not speak to them like he spoke to the Israelites or the prophets of old—plainly and simply.

But this reminds me of the story of a farmer who came to the big city to see a friend. When the two went out for a walk in the hustle and bustle, the farmer suddenly stopped because he heard a familiar sound…birds singing. His friend said, "How did you hear the tweeting of birds in all this traffic noise?" The farmer answered, "You hear what's important to you."

In the same way, we can train our ears to hear God's voice. It's just a matter of what to listen for. God's Word is "living and powerful" (Hebrews 4:12). It is by his Word the world was created: "God said, 'Let there be light'" (Genesis 1:3). Reading his Word teaches our ears to listen for God's voice.

To God alone be glory!

CELEBRATE VICTORY OVER EVIL

Whoever gloats over disaster
will not go unpunished.
PROVERBS 17:5 NIV

All eyes in the office were trained on TV monitors and computer screens watching the World Cup soccer tournament. They all rooted for their favorite team. A win by one team brought raucous cheers throughout the office. A loss, heartbreaking moans. A win for one meant a loss for someone else. It's the way of sports.

It's hard not to celebrate a win and smile at your "enemy's" downfall. But good sportsmanship is based on this verse from Proverbs. Gloating takes the honor away from doing well. By thanking your opponent when you achieve a victory, you're acknowledging his or her talents and showing respect that they fought the good fight. Good sportsmanship is also based on the reality that the only real Enemy we have is Satan. In life, to smile and take pride in our enemies' downfall essentially praises and participates in evil. And evil, God says, will never go unpunished.

Jesus died on the cross and, in so doing, defeated the devil. By his resurrection, he made it possible for us to participate in the greatest victory of all time.

To God alone be glory!

Using Words to Heal

*The words of the reckless pierce like swords,
but the tongue of the wise brings healing.*
PROVERBS 12:18 NIV

When we were children and some bully called us names, we would chant back, "Sticks and stones can break my bones, but names will never hurt me!" Maybe in a schoolyard, this little jingle can deflect a bully's taunts, but words in general do have power over us. They have the power to shape and mold us as well as cause great harm. Words can hurt. They can also heal.

There are stories about young people committing suicide after being constantly bullied online. The verbal venom they endured daily crushed their souls. Words did far more damage than sticks and stones. By the same token, if a parent constantly tells a child, "You'll never amount to much," the child will grow up either to fulfill the prediction or work to overcome it by becoming an obsessed overachiever trying to prove them wrong.

But if a child is carefully nurtured and encouraged with words of affirmation, the child will not only grow in confidence and strength but also be able to balance accomplishments with contentment. Jesus always spoke to people with words that would heal. Even in exposing their sin, his goal was to strengthen them and love them. We are called to do likewise.

To God alone be glory!

God Alone Is Our Refuge

The angel of the LORD said to Elijah the Tishbite, "Go up and meet the messengers of the king of Samaria and ask them, 'Is it because there is no God in Israel that you are going off to consult Baal-Zebub, the god of Ekron?'"

2 KINGS 1:3 NIV

Have you noticed there's been an increase in the number of shows and movies focused on evil and evil spirits and a fascination with the power of demonic forces? The programs unmask our tendency to believe in the power of spiritual evil but fail to recognize the power of God, the maker of heaven and earth.

The Philistines worshiped the god of Ekron in the Old Testament. In 2 Kings 1, Israel's King Ahaziah sent messengers to ask this false god if his body would recover from injuries following a catastrophic fall. God's prophet Elijah rebuked him for denying the true God and pronounced that Ahaziah would die. But the question remains, why didn't King Ahaziah run to the Lord Almighty first instead of consulting an evil spirit. It's the same reason for us today. We put too much faith in what evil has done and too little faith in what God can do. The Psalms remind us that God alone is our refuge. Jesus knew that. On the cross, in his greatest torment, he called out to his Father.

King Ahaziah's situation is a cautionary tale for those of us living in a post-resurrection era. We not only have proof of God's limitless power, but because of Jesus' sacrifice, we also have proof of his vast and boundless love.

To God alone be glory!

THE GIFT OF LIFE

My frame was not hidden from you when I was made in the secret place, when I was woven together in the depths of the earth. Your eyes saw my unformed body.

PSALM 139:15–16 NIV

Birthdays are wonderful. When we're young, we're excited to get older. But as we age, the number of years may not be as important as the quality of those years. It's good to celebrate being alive and to be thankful to God, the author of life.

Today's psalm is a wonderful reminder that God knows us better than any person possibly can. Even before all our physical parts were formed, the genetic blueprint existed, and God knew it intimately. God knows us so much better than even our closest friends, siblings, and even the mother who carried us in her womb. God knew you before your mother even knew she was pregnant.

Our lives have always been in the maker's hands. And we are to be grateful that God through Jesus Christ has given us tremendous and amazing grace to bring us this far. Though we fail him many times, he has never failed us. Our prayer should be that he will continually lead us through this life and one day call us home to be with him.

To God alone be glory!

A Firm Foundation

Since we are receiving a kingdom that cannot be shaken, let us be thankful, and so worship God acceptably with reverence and awe, for our "God is a consuming fire."

HEBREWS 12:28–29 NIV

It's always nice when science discovers what God always knew. In this case, it's gratefulness. God directs us to cultivate a grateful heart. It's for our own benefit. And now researchers pretty much say the same thing: "Indeed, many studies over the past decade have found that people who consciously count their blessings tend to be happier and less depressed."[76]

What secular researchers won't say is that cultivating a thankful heart is an act of faith and that more positive changes come from believing in the power of an omniscient and omnipotent Being who orders your life and all of creation.

God's plan for us is not just to be less depressed but also to be sanctified and made holy. Yes, gratitude as a discipline will change your brain. But being grateful to a God who died on a cross to save us and heal our foundational wound will transform our very existence.

To God alone be glory!

Relationships Shape Us

The Lord God said, "It is not good for the man to be alone.
I will make a helper suitable for him."
GENESIS 2:18 NIV

In this story of creation, it is the first time God says something is not good. Up until this point, everything God has created he blesses: "It is good." But not here. What this tells us is that from the very beginning of time, we were made for relationships and that being alone and isolated is not good.

There's an interconnectedness of humanity. Relationships formed us, created us, built us, molded us. From the moment of conception, we are nurtured in our mother's womb. After we are born, it's that relationship—with our fathers, too, hopefully—that continues to nurture and protect us. If we didn't have that seminal connection, we would die, not just physically but also emotionally and spiritually.

There is no part of human life that flourishes in solitude for extended periods of time, for "we can't live without meaningful personal relationships."[77] God knows this. He provided for us the ability to have a personal relationship with him. Jesus is real. He is God in the flesh, providing us with a personal relationship that orders all our other relationships.

To God alone be glory!

Speaking Truth in Love

Speaking the truth in love, may grow up in all things into Him who is the head—Christ—from whom the whole body, joined and knit together by what every joint supplies, according to the effective working by which every part does its share, causes growth of the body for the edifying of itself in love.

EPHESIANS 4:15–16

Theologically speaking, this is where the rubber meets the road. In order to get anywhere in a vehicle, how could one function without the other? It's nearly impossible. And what an apt analogy if *truth* is the road and the rubber is the *love*. Truth is the only pathway through which love can express itself properly.

Without truth, love is self-serving. Without love, truth is a hard taskmaster. Truth and love are a powerful pair that should never be parted. Depending on our temperaments, we usually lean one way or the other, toward truth or toward love. We tout truth and wield our Bible as a cudgel. Or we preach love but let people remain in their destructive sins. While truth often creates conflict among people, especially on issues of morality—who's right and who's wrong—love demands that we protect the relationship.

Jesus never told someone just what they wanted to hear. He told them what they needed to hear: truth. But he did it so lovingly that it changed their hearts and transformed their lives. The key is that he first loved them. And that's what Jesus offers us. He loves us enough to speak the truth. We should do likewise.

To God alone be glory!

TRANSFORMING LOVE

When they continued asking Him, He raised Himself up and said to them,
"He who is without sin among you, let him throw a stone at her first."
JOHN 8:7

The woman caught in adultery is a famous scene in the Bible where we learn so much about the awesome love and mercy of Jesus. The village fathers, a.k.a. the morality police, captured a woman who was guilty of a most heinous sin. They brought her to Jesus, in part to trap him as well, because the law of Moses demanded that she be stoned to death. (They obviously forgot to capture the man too!) But they wanted to see how this new rabbi with all his lofty talk of love and God's truth would handle this one.

Jesus never said anything to them about what the woman did wrong. He waited and doodled something on the ground—what he wrote the Bible never says. When they demanded that he speak, he said that whoever was perfect among them could be her judge and jury. Realizing they had no authority, they left one by one. After the accusers were gone, Jesus talked to the woman, telling her that he did not condemn her. His parting words were, "Go and sin no more."

Does she sin again? We're never told. The point for many is that Jesus never endorsed her sin. "He never celebrated something contrary to God's design."[78] Instead, Jesus showed her a compassion that perhaps she'd never received all her life. This man who saved her from certain death asked her to do one thing. Chances are her life was forever changed. Encountering the real Jesus is always transforming.

To God alone be glory!

LIFE AND LIBERTY

*The Lord is the Spirit;
and where the Spirit of the Lord is,
there is liberty.*
2 CORINTHIANS 3:17

Today we celebrate our nation's independence, the day the colonists threw off the yoke of an oppressive government and became a free country.

The irony of freedom is that it is entrenched in order and boundaries. We often call ourselves a nation of laws. But these should be laws that free us, not enslave us. Only by bowing down to an authority can there be peace and true freedom. The Founding Fathers understood this.

In fact, it was George Washington, the first president of the United States, who said, "It is the duty of all nations to acknowledge the providence of Almighty God, to obey His will, to be grateful for His benefits, and humbly to implore His protection and favor." Freedom gives us the ability to obey God's will. And God's will brings true freedom, for it is based on his designed purpose and meaning for our lives.

To God alone be glory!

Building Walls

The wealth of the rich is their fortified city;
they imagine it a wall too high to scale.

PROVERBS 18:11 NIV

There are many kinds of walls: brick walls, wooden, stone, or even walls made of straw like in the child's story of the three little piggies.

But there are walls we build that have no physical presence. They are the walls we construct throughout life to hide the hurt of our emotional scrapes and bruises. It's the soul's version of brick and mortar. Sometimes we build these walls to hide the hurt from others, but over the course of time, those same walls hide the hurt even from ourselves.

Despite the walls we build, God sees all our wounds. He will help us break down the walls. But sometimes the walls are built so strongly and fortified with so many layers that taking them down is painful too. It feels as if we will crumble into pieces as the defenses we've built up over time are torn away. Be assured that God is a safety net, just like the ones firefighters use to catch people jumping from burning buildings. Trust God first to know your pain intimately and then trust him enough to let him break down your walls in order to free you from them. Let God alone be your high tower.

To God alone be glory!

Praising What We Become

Rejoice in the Lord always.
I will say it again: Rejoice!
PHILIPPIANS 4:4 NIV

Praise is how we express our joy in something or someone we truly love or admire. That is why the Scriptures talk so much about giving praise to God. It frees us from focusing on ourselves and, instead, turns our attention toward God. What we praise we long to be close to, to model ourselves after.

Sometimes we praise what doesn't deserve our accolades, like certain kinds of bad behavior. Friends, too, can become bad influences. The movie *A Bronx Tale* is all about that dilemma. A young man is torn between striving to be like the slick gangster in the neighborhood—whom he deeply admires for his suits, cars, and money—and his allegiance to his father—a hard-working bus driver with a meager income. The young man's heart praises the gangster more than it lauds his father. A sudden tragedy makes him realize that his father is the one who really deserved all his praise. And by the end of the story, it's clear the boy will work to be more like his father.

God, our loving Father, instructs us to praise him not because he needs our praise but because out of that praise, we will strive to be more like him.

To God alone be glory!

Reflecting the True Light

Just as we have borne the image of the earthly man,
so shall we bear the image of the heavenly man.

1 CORINTHIANS 15:49 NIV

What does it mean to be made in the image of God? It means that we were created to be a reflection of his glory. What brought the world down were our ancient ancestors, Adam and Eve (the earthly man and woman). In one act of disobedience, the couple showed they were not content to be a reflection and wanted instead to be God.

Thankfully, creation is still telling us the true story. "The beauty of the world is a pointer toward the greater beauty of God, which it reflects as the moon reflects the greater light of the sun, or as a beautiful diamond scintillates as it catches the beams of the sun."[79]

We are all like mirrors, made to reflect not generate an image. And there's something crucial to being able to reflect. It requires having the proper light; otherwise, the image is distorted or darkened. God's Word tells us Jesus is "the light of the world" (John 8:12). This is the true Light through which we can reflect the image of our Creator, being the image bearers we are meant to be.

To God alone be glory!

No Gossiping Here

The words of a gossip are like choice morsels;
they go down to the inmost parts.
PROVERBS 18:8 NIV

The Bible tells us that words are like food. We take them in and digest them. Good words can heal and nurture us, bringing love and joy. That is what God calls us to do when we open our mouths to communicate.

Unlike food, though, what we speak is digested not only by us but by the people who hear us. Gossip is the junk food of the verbal world. It's hard to resist, and once you have it, you want more and more of it. Gossip comes from something sinful in our hearts. Its origins lie deep within. We may disguise it as something someone needs to know, but it comes from our need to feel superior and powerful, to belittle another person in order to feel better about ourselves.

What can change us? Knowing that our self-worth comes from the love of God the Father, Jesus the Son, and the breath of the Holy Spirit. No earthly accomplishment, whether our own or someone else's, can take that away. Gossip originates in the seed of sin. It was covered over and snuffed out at the foot of the cross, where grace, mercy, and love had the final word.

To God alone be glory!

SERVING AS WORSHIP

They would not listen, however, but persisted in their former practices. Even while these people were worshiping the Lord, they were serving their idols. To this day their children and grandchildren continue to do as their ancestors did.

2 KINGS 17:40–41 NIV

At first read, this passage in 2 Kings makes it seem like there's a difference between worshiping and serving. But because of what's known as *parallelism* in Hebrew writing, it's essentially saying they are the same thing.

Worshiping means serving. God knows it's possible to go through the motions of religious rituals but, in our heart of hearts, to be bowing down to the idols of the age like popularity, wealth, career, beauty. These are all good things that, when we serve them more than we serve God, blind us to our worshiping of false gods. In other words, it is quite possible to call yourself a Christian, a follower of Jesus, but live in the service of something else.

God wants us to bow down to him first and only. It may turn out we become popular or wealthy or anything else the world sees as wonderful. But because we serve and worship only God, if life's ups and downs take those things away, it won't destroy us because God alone is our hope.

To God alone be glory!

Be Careful What You Kill

God blessed them and said to them, "Be fruitful and increase in number; fill the earth and subdue it. Rule over the fish in the sea and the birds in the sky and over every living creature that moves on the ground."
GENESIS 1:28 NIV

It's an awesome responsibility to have "dominion" over the earth. There's a lot of controversy about what that dominion entails. But a recent radio documentary on mosquitoes encouraged listeners to find some good in those tiny insects, carriers of pestilence, disease, and general annoyance. The mosquito is so prevalent in places like Minnesota, the Land of Ten Thousand Lakes, that it's called the unofficial state bird. Mankind has been working mostly to rid the world of them. But one of the commentators said something quite powerful; he said that we should be careful about what we kill, even if it is just a pesky mosquito.

Just because you can't see the benefit of something doesn't mean there isn't one. In fact, one of the experts said that for centuries, the mosquitos' ravenous appetite for human blood protected certain parts of the world, like the rain forests, by preventing humans from colonizing them and consequently destroying their pristine nature. If you can care about harming something as tiny as a mosquito—a known carrier of malaria, Zika, West Nile virus, and other dangerous viruses—you could pretty much say that about all of God's creation, from the tiniest and youngest, to the largest and oldest.

Jesus dying on the cross was a voluntary execution, and God in his wisdom knew exactly what would come of it: our redemption. Taking care of God's creation requires us to seek his wisdom first. "Dominion" is an awesome responsibility.

To God alone be glory!

Jesus Took the Hit

*Sin will have no dominion over you,
since you are not under law but under grace.*

ROMANS 6:14 ESV

A young couple was in a very bad car accident. However, the accident that caused them pain and maybe permanent, debilitating physical injuries actually saved the life of a nine-year-old boy. They stopped so the boy could cross the road safely, and when they did, a young driver plowed into them at fifty miles per hour.

If the couple hadn't stopped, the boy may have crossed into the path of the other car. In other words, they took the hit instead of the boy. And the boy's mother, realizing their sacrifice, is forever grateful.

That is how we are to look at Jesus on the cross. He took the hit of death so that we are only touched by its shadow. When we grasp the full weight of that sacrifice, we, too, will be forever grateful.

To God alone be glory!

RELEASED FROM SHACKLES

The Spirit of the Lord GOD is upon me, because the LORD has anointed me to bring good news to the poor; he has sent me to bind up the brokenhearted, to proclaim liberty to the captives, and the opening of the prison to those who are bound.

ISAIAH 61:1 ESV

The great Old Testament prophet Isaiah may have been speaking to the Israelites here, but he is talking to us today as well. These are the words Jesus quoted in the New Testament as he began his ministry (see Luke 4:18).

Captivity has many forms. It can be physical if we are in a place where our movements are restrained. Or it can be spiritual, being captive to sin, a slave to our own desires. Take, for instance, a man who committed a crime in his youth and wound up in prison for several years. While still in jail, he met Jesus, and that encounter released him from spiritual bondage, which made him free even though he was still behind bars.

Seeking God with all our hearts removes us from bondage to sin, a much more debilitating restraint than bars or handcuffs. The power of sin follows us wherever we go as our personal jail cell. Jesus has the key to unlocking any cell anytime, anywhere, no matter how well guarded it is. And when the Son sets you free, you will be free indeed! Trust him.

To God alone be glory!

WE ARE HIS MASTERPIECE

Speak to the earth, and it will teach you, or let the fish in the sea inform you. Which of all these does not know that the hand of the LORD has done this?

JOB 12:8–9 NIV

The Great Lakes are majestic and awesome. Lake Superior is in northern Minnesota and parts of Michigan. The Ojibwe Indians called it *gichigami*, which means "great sea." And it is indeed the greatest of the Great Lakes. It is the largest fresh body of water in the world with over seventeen hundred miles of shoreline, and at its deepest, it is taller than the Empire State Building.

Over its shores, one can see the most spectacular sunrises, framed on one side by rocks and tall pines. And yet sometimes Superior's minuscule parts are just as alluring as its grand schemes. During spring, the melting ice on the rocky shores creates a beautiful picture. I saw a photo of one such image hanging on a hotel wall. The photo captured perhaps less than a square yard of white pastel ice, nestled in the nooks and crannies of the stones, the ice hugging the stones, the stones embracing the ice like a crown of glory.

Oh, the beauty of God's great artistry! If he can do that with water, ice, and rock, think of what he can do with bone, blood, sinew, and a mind that powers it all. The Bible assures us that we are God's workmanship; we are his greatest masterpiece, created in his image. We are called to embrace our majesty as a child of the living God. Be the masterpiece that God has created you to be.

To God alone be glory!

Hopeful Even in Death

Behold, I tell you a mystery:
We shall not all sleep,
but we shall all be changed.

1 CORINTHIANS 15:51

The death of a loved one brings sadness and pain, even when believers have faith in the resurrection. God understands our trepidations and mournful spirit when death comes. He often sends a ray of light at such dark times.

When one man's mother lay sleeping and close to death, a call came in the middle of the night. The exact time was 3:45 a.m. The man got up to answer the phone, but no one was on the other end. He then checked on his mother and found that her body was still warm, but she was not breathing. The home health care nurse confirmed that his mother had just died. The next day, the man checked the caller ID to see who had called in the night. It said only "Unavailable. Out of area." Maybe it was a telemarketer or a wrong number; who knows for sure. But the man firmly believes that call came at nearly the exact time of death and that it was his mother saying goodbye to her beloved son and only child.

God will never abandon us, even in the grave. And Jesus, by defeating death through death, has given us hope that we and our loved ones will live on.

To God alone be glory!

Thankful Sacrifice

I will offer to You the sacrifice of thanksgiving,
and will call upon the name of the LORD.

PSALM 116:17

God calls us to be thankful. Being thankful brightens our hearts. But thankfulness can also be an act of sacrifice. It means giving up griping or feeling sorry for yourself for the things you don't have. And let's face it, sometimes it suits our mood just to complain. It's exactly those times that being thankful can be at odds with what we feel like doing. Complaining has a negative impact on us. "When you focus on what you don't have or on situations that displease you, your mind also becomes darkened."[80]

The story of Pollyanna, written in 1913 by Eleanor H. Porter, is a wonderful tale of a young girl who, no matter the situation, could find something to be glad about. She remained cheerful even though she had recently lost both her parents and had come to live with her mother's older sister in a small town filled with unhappy people. Pollyanna was able to change an entire town's outlook on life because of her optimistic and thankful spirit.

The crucifixion and resurrection of Jesus Christ is our sign that even the seemingly most awful thing can become God's greatest victory. Be thankful and simply let God be God.

To God alone be glory!

The Nature of Sin

Everything that does not come from faith is sin.

ROMANS 14:23 NIV

Today, we have a hard time understanding the true nature of sin. When people of all ages talk about sin and what it is, they pretty much agree it's something that should be avoided. That's the good part. But who rightly can define sin is not so clear. That's the bad part.

The apostle Paul is making the case here that sin is a very broad and nuanced condition of the human soul. While we tend to think of sin as doing bad things like stealing, killing, and cursing, sin can also be doing good things for the wrong reasons. While that seems pretty harsh, it shows how self-absorbed humans are and how far we've strayed from reliance on God. As John Piper says, "This is a radical indictment of all natural 'virtue' that does not flow from a heart humbly relying on God's grace."[81]

He goes on to explain why, saying, "Not relying on God in any action or thought takes power and glory to ourselves. That is sin, even if the external deed accords with God's will."[82]

It just shows how utterly in need of salvation we are. Luckily, we have a Savior, Jesus Christ. He is our hope in being able to give glory to God in all things. Glorifying God is what we were made for. It's how we flourish. It's how we should live.

To God alone be glory!

CONCEIVING EVIL

*Whoever is pregnant with evil conceives trouble
and gives birth to disillusionment.*
PSALM 7:14 NIV

It's relatively easy to chart when a child was conceived. Start from the birth date and go back about nine months; most couples can figure it out. But how do you know when you're "pregnant with evil?" How do we know when trouble is conceived?

I heard about a successful man who was involved in a hit-and-run accident. He fled the scene rather than face the authorities. Why would someone who had never committed a crime or gotten in trouble with the law do such a thing? Perhaps, it's because somewhere back in his early life, he'd gotten away with not obeying the rules, and he profited from it. That same way of thinking followed him to the accident. Actions and ideas are conceived and gestate just like a physical birth. They don't suddenly appear out of nowhere but are cultivated and nurtured.

The Bible warns us to be aware of how we conduct our daily lives. Each encounter is a chance to do God's will or walk by the dim light of our own will. Since the resurrection, we know that if we do make mistakes, God is forgiving. Because of Jesus' sacrifice, if we confess our sins, he will lift the burden of them. We can have hope that we are not just forgiven but also loved and cherished.

To God alone be glory!

Seeking to Believe

Look to the Lord and his strength;
seek his face always.

1 Chronicles 16:11 niv

In 2018, the then president of the Philippines, Rodrigo Duterte, stirred controversy by saying that if anyone could prove to him that God exists, he'd resign as president. He later wisely walked back his comment and apologized not to the clergy with whom he had been feuding, but to God.[83] Poor soul. He should be pitied because while, as some have said, you can't prove God exists like he's a mathematical theorem, a preponderance of evidence shows he does indeed exist.

All who see that evidence must make a leap of faith to either believe or not believe. God has made the world in such a way that we can choose. We must choose to have faith in God. The evidence is always there. It's not that there isn't enough proof; it's that the heart refuses to be swayed. The Filipino president's problem wasn't a lack of information but a lack of faith.

Pray that God will open this man's eyes and the eyes of others who need only to seek God and his strength for his presence to become a reality.

To God alone be glory!

Living under the Manufacturer's Guidelines

We are his workmanship, created in Christ Jesus for good works,
which God prepared beforehand, that we should walk in them.
EPHESIANS 2:10 ESV

Someone once asked a friend of mine, "Can man live without God?"
My friend answered, "Yes, but only because God allows us to." There are
consequences to living outside of the "manufacturer's recommended
guidelines," just like with any created thing.

Take for instance the DC-10 airplane. When it came on the scene
years ago, it was touted as a marvel of transportation. Its wide body
held more passengers and traveled farther than most other planes. But
then there were a series of crashes and other problems that made many
travelers feel unsafe, and they avoided flying on the plane. Finally, after
a devastating crash in which an engine just fell off the plane, the FAA
grounded all DC-10s. What investigators discovered was that airline
crews had been ignoring the manufacturer guidelines for certain types of
maintenance because it took too long and cost too much money. The error
caused small cracks to form in the part of the plane that connected the
engines to the wing. Investigators discovered similar cracks on eight of the
grounded planes.[84]

Taking an easier, cheaper shortcut instead following the manufacturer's
manual is one way in which we worship created things instead of the Creator.
Sometimes the negative effects take years to notice. But God doesn't want our
lives to crash and burn because of an error that we can avoid. He wants us to
trust him and believe that he alone is our hope.

To God alone be glory!

Stay in Your Lane

Be still before the LORD and wait patiently for him;
do not fret when people succeed in their ways,
when they carry out their wicked schemes.

PSALM 37:7 NIV

It's understandable in any profession to want to achieve higher and higher goals. Whether you're a teacher, a lawyer, a baker, or a candlestick maker, climbing the ladder of success is part of what gets us up in the morning. However, in that striving, there's also a tendency to be jealous of what others have. That's one reason the last of all the commandments warns us, "Do not covet."

When we covet, we become blind to our own blessings; our vision is darkened, only seeing what someone else has achieved. But consider this great and simple advice from a driving instructor. She said, "Stay in your lane." When you stay in your lane you see more clearly what's ahead. It's a safer way to operate, in a car and in life.

Remember that God has blessed you too. Because of Jesus' death on the cross and his resurrection, there are even greater blessings for us in all we do. Recognize those blessings. Praise him for those blessings. Thank him constantly for them. There's so much ahead that God has in store if we just learn to stay close to him. He's in the lane with you.

To God alone be glory!

A Symbol of Death Transformed

When they came to the place called the Skull, they crucified him there,
along with the criminals—one on his right, the other on his left.

LUKE 23:33 NIV

Think about those two men crucified with Jesus, that they were criminals, taking the penalty for their crimes. It is a reminder to us through the ages that crucifixion was a sentence doled out to thieves and murderers and violators of civil laws.

Although the Romans didn't invent crucifixion, they certainly perfected it. They crucified thousands. Today, the cross is a symbol of God's victory. And Christian churches display them boldly, and believers in Christ wear them humbly.

But because of the two sinners crucified with Jesus, we shall never forget God's transformative powers over human will. For Jesus, taking the penalty of God's wrath upon himself, "transformed the symbol of Roman power, terror and death and redeemed it and made it a symbol of love and service."[85] If God can do that with an entire world order, he can certainly do that with our lives.

To God alone be glory!

Transforming Truth

Sanctify them in the truth;
your word is truth.
JOHN 17:17 ESV

Where can truth be found? Is it something that is fixed and unmovable? Or is it a personalized accessory like an outfit or fashion choice? God's Word tells us that truth is something we can know (John 8:32), which means it's available to our minds, able to be grasped intellectually. But the Bible also warns that our hearts will blind us to the truth, even making us believe a lie is truth (1 John 1:8; Isaiah 5:20).

So many of us have erred and made the heart the purveyor of Truth, then wonder why relationships end or become fractured. God tells us his truth will set us free (John 8:32), not only the big truth of Christ's grace and mercy, of his death and resurrection, but also the smaller obstacles of life's dilemmas, of work habits, money issues, conflicts.

Truth carves out pathways like a snowplow after a blizzard. Truth is God's Word, and Jesus Christ is the Word made flesh (John 1:14).

To God alone be glory!

The Only Real Salvation

As for me, I watch in hope for the Lord,
I wait for God my Savior;
my God will hear me.

Micah 7:7 niv

Many people satisfy their own cravings for a quick, feel-good pick-me-up. A little chocolate ice cream here, a bit of retail therapy there, then throw in a brief pity party, and voila! Our hurts and pains are forgotten…until the next time. Then we repeat the process.

The ultimate salvation is from the living God. Our everyday slights, struggles, and mishaps are opportunities for us to train our spiritual selves to trust in him. They are ways to say, *As for me, I will have confidence in God's ability to protect me, save me, direct me, hear my pleas, love me.*

Despite how the world directs us to save ourselves, God wants us to look to him because he is the only real salvation we have. Everything else is a temporary fix.

To God alone be glory!

God Is Doing Something

You have wearied the LORD with your words. "How have we wearied him?"
you ask. By saying, "All who do evil are good in the eyes of the Lord,
and he is pleased with them" or "Where is the God of justice?"

MALACHI 2:17 NIV

A common complaint is: "If God is God, why doesn't he do something to stop the evil in the world? Why does evil continue to flourish?" In today's verse, the prophet Malachi is responding to the Israelites who made the same complaints many centuries ago. Not much has changed with human sin.

The tendency to judge others and question God makes us blind to the sins controlling us while shining a bright light on other people's misdeeds. This is not to say that evil things are not happening. But God's judgments are based on his perfect knowledge. And by those standards, we all fall short. God is doing and has done something about the evil in this world, both our own sins and the sins of others. Jesus Christ dying on the cross was more than just one man's sacrifice for a few bad folks. It was the climax of human history that began the potential transformation of every human heart.

J. I. Packer said it so well when he explained how our natural state is to rebel against God. But when we put our faith in Jesus, we exchange our "natural enmity and rebellion against God for a spirit of grateful submission to the will of Christ through the renewing of one's heart by the Holy Spirit."[86]

To God alone be glory!

A Time and Purpose

There is a time for everything,
and a season for every activity under the heavens:
a time to be born and a time to die,
a time to plant and a time to uproot.

ECCLESIASTES 3:1–2 NIV

A recent poll found that a great majority of people believe their life has purpose and meaning, that we're not just here for no reason. It's no accident that so many feel this way. God made us in his image, and he made the whole of creation, the stars, the planets, and the moon, and they all have a purpose.

Scientists have recently discovered that our earth is unique, that its position in the universe and its ability to support life is incredibly rare among the planets because "for the physical history of the Earth to be the way it is, certain kinds and quantities of life must exist in just-right locations at just-right times."[87] This scientist is talking about life in evolutionary terms, but it emphatically applies to our lives as well.

Each one of us is unique. Each one of us has a role to play in God's grand scheme of creation's progress. Because of the redemptive work of Jesus Christ on the cross, we can all rise up and live out our true purpose and meaning: to glorify God. Whatever talent or strengths we have, we are to use them to glorify the maker.

To God alone be glory!

God's Poetry in Motion

*I will sing of steadfast love and justice;
to you, O LORD, I will make music.*
PSALM 101:1 ESV

Some of the greatest poems are on the topic of love. Think of Shakespeare's "Sonnet 116": "Love is not love / Which alters when it alteration finds, / Or bends with the remover to remove. / O no! it is an ever-fixed mark / That looks on tempests and is never shaken." Or Elizabeth Barrett Browning's "Sonnet 43," which sings, "How do I love thee?…I love thee to the depth and breadth and height my soul can reach."

When the Bible says we are God's workmanship (see Ephesians 2:10), it means so much more than hammers and nails and a physical shape. According to author and speaker Abdu Murray, "Workmanship is translated from the Greek word *poiema,* which means anything brought into existence or compiled by someone. It's where we get the English word poem from. You and I—all of us—are God's poem."[88]

What's more, each of us is a unique poem, a living sonnet created by a God who not only loves unconditionally but who is love itself. To live out our poetic natures then, we are called to Christ, to be one with the risen Savior. Each unique soul is a living testament to the power of God to transform us into his poetry in motion.

To God alone be glory!

Soul Cleansing

*Get rid of all moral filth and the evil that is so prevalent
and humbly accept the word planted in you, which can save you.*

JAMES 1:21 NIV

I heard of an elderly woman who injured her leg during a mishap in the
kitchen between her shin and the stove. It left an ugly gash. Typical of
the spry, senior citizen, she chose to use her infirmity for a gospel lesson.
She said, "Look at this scar and how unsightly it is! This must be how the
entirety of our souls looked to God. If that is true, I'd better be much more
concerned about the care of my soul than the healing of a physical scar."

And this is so true because the Bible says our best efforts are "filthy
rags" (Isaiah 64:6 NIV) compared to the righteousness of God. Our natural
opposition to God causes us to run into obstacles, whether spiritual or
physical. And it creates countless scars and ugliness in us.

God has provided the means to cleanse us of our total depravity,
to heal those unsightly wounds. Jesus Christ took on our filthiness so
that we can be cleansed and made pure by the blood of the Lamb. We are
unequipped to save ourselves. But God's salvation is the greatest hope we
have for true healing.

To God alone be glory!

Weaving Our Lives' Fabric

"No one sews a patch of unshrunk cloth on an old garment,
for the patch will pull away from the garment, making the tear worse."
Matthew 9:16 niv

Not too many generations ago, sewing class was compulsory for girls in junior high school. The conventional wisdom was that skill with a sewing needle was essential for future homemakers. One of the first things the student learned was that, before cutting a garment, the seamstress had to preshrink some fabrics, such as cotton. If she didn't, the sewn garment would shrink when washed and would be too small or short.

In the verse above, Jesus is telling his followers that even though we may all seem the same, cut of the same cloth so to speak, we receive the message of the gospel differently. Some of us are old cloths unable to hear the good news of Jesus' atoning sacrifice. In fact, when we hear it, it doesn't sit well with our traditions or conventional ideas; it doesn't fit.

One thing the gospel can do for us that old fabric cannot do for itself is to make us new again. Instead of preshrinking the fabric of the gospel to make it fit our condition, the gospel, if we let it, will weave us into a new cloth, a new life, and we will be born again.

To God alone be glory!

Appearances Can Be Deceiving

*"Beware of false prophets, who come to you in sheep's clothing,
but inwardly they are ravenous wolves."*
MATTHEW 7:15

Appearances can be deceiving. From fruit that's about to go bad to smiling faces that hide evil intent, things that seem one way but are the opposite is a common deception in the devil's tool chest for the corruption of God's creation. Think of King Saul in the Old Testament. He was tall, muscular, and handsome. He fit the image of a king. But he failed because he trusted himself rather than God. "For all his physical prowess and his popular attraction, Saul was basically defective in understanding the kingship of God."[89]

Saul died a twisted and painful death because being king was more important to him than serving God. In the end, he lost both his kingship and his relationship to God. That is the evil of good things that become our fundamental trust. We want to hold on to them so badly that we will commit crimes, even murder in extreme cases, to keep from losing them.

God will deny us no good thing if we put our trust in him. And those good things will be even more enjoyable because we receive them from the only good thing that matters.

To God alone be glory!

Our Duty Becomes Our Passion

You, brethren, have been called to liberty;
only do not use liberty as an opportunity for the flesh,
but through love serve one another.

GALATIANS 5:13

God gives us incredible freedom in this world. He has designed our common home, earth, in such a way that we don't even have to worship him for that gift of freedom. We can pursue our hearts' desires. While our freedom is enshrined in the Declaration of Independence, God first established it in the universe. However, that doesn't mean there aren't consequences for the choices we freely make. And that's when we can sometimes wish God would have prevented us from going down certain paths.

Our *choices* mostly fall into two categories: doing what we want or doing what we should. Abdu Murray, commenting on the state of our individualistic culture that is turning away from truth, wrote, "We're so obsessed over the freedom to do what we want that we've neglected the freedom to do what we should."[90]

Jesus Christ, too, had a choice to not endure the suffering on the cross. But he did it for our sakes out of love. That is the gospel message. It makes it possible for our "wants" and our "should haves" to become one and the same. With God's help, our chores are transformed into our passions.

To God alone be glory!

WORKING FOR THE LORD

Whatever you do, do it heartily, as to the Lord and not to men, knowing that from the Lord you will receive the reward of the inheritance; for you serve the Lord Christ.

COLOSSIANS 3:23–24

A prominent retail chain recently went bankrupt and closed its doors for good after several decades of robust business. There are controversies regarding why it went belly up, and it should be no surprise that some serious allegations of a lack of integrity were made. Executives received tens of millions of dollars in bonuses during the bankruptcy proceedings. When asked why a company that was going bankrupt was paying out so much, a spokesperson explained that it was to ensure that the executives would perform at a high-level during the bankruptcy.

Meanwhile, the workers who had made meager wages tending the cash registers, stocking the shelves, and greeting customers never received their promised severance pay. Supposedly, there were no funds available. At the same time, the company also paid hundreds of millions of dollars in attorneys' fees. The injustice of it boggles the mind.

You see, if we are ultimately working for God, doing what's right and just is our higher calling. All our earthly work is an opportunity to serve God and his creation. The Bible says, "The love of money is a root of all kinds of evil" (1 Timothy 6: 10). Serving God first is the way to thrive in life and in business.

To God alone be glory!

Shields against Spiritual Evil

*As for God, His way is perfect;
the word of the Lord is proven;
He is a shield to all who trust in Him.*

Psalm 18:30

It's very common and understandable to think of shields as only physical: a soldier's equipment made from hammered metal, the fence around the yard, or perhaps even just the warmth from a heavy coat. Those kinds of shields bring us protection and comfort.

But God's Word can give us ample and equal protection from the assaults that come from the spiritual realm. To know God's Word, to ingest it into every cell of our being, is like armor against the ultimate form of assault we endure daily—insults, injured pride, meanness, and bullying.

While physical harm can injure or even destroy our bodies, doctors and hospitals will aid in healing our flesh and bone. But who heals the soul? Where is the hospital that has a trauma center for spiritual evil? It is heaven's hospital. And Jesus Christ is the Great Physician. He provides the ultimate in protection, comfort, and strength.

To God alone be glory!

Honoring Parents

"Honor your father and your mother, that your days may be long upon the land which the Lord your God is giving you."

Exodus 20:12

As children, many of us had strict rules about bedtime. Often, we'd hear a parent use their stern voice to make us turn off the TV or computer and go to bed. Now that we are decades older, fatigue from a long day's work and knowing we'll need rest for another day motivates us to adhere to bedtime rules. Your mother doesn't need to call and tell you, "Turn off the TV, brush your teeth, and go to bed." As children, obeying Mom and Dad's rules is one way we honored our parents. But as adults, honoring them takes many forms. No earthly parent is perfect. Sometimes their own lives are not what God would want us to follow. Honoring them properly as an adult takes wisdom and knowledge of God's Word.

When children become adults, a parent's job is through. But a child's obligation to honor them as the reason we are living never ends. In an honor-shame culture, this obligation is clear and a matter of pride. However, in the individualistic cultures of the Western world, it's almost celebrated when children throw off the yoke of their parents' expectations.

God's Word provides us with the best resources to honor our parents with the proper allegiance no matter our cultural expectations. It is when we understand that God is our ultimate parent that we can love our earthly parents as people and as children of the living God, just like we are.

To God alone be glory!

DIFFERENT PURPOSES IN GOD'S SERVICE

Does not the potter have power over the clay, from the same lump to make one vessel for honor and another for dishonor?

ROMANS 9:21

When a couple marries, they often register for gifts at a department store or favorite shop. The typical registry includes everyday dinnerware and fine china. Why would a couple need both? The difference: Dinnerware is less expensive than fine china. If a piece of dinnerware breaks, it is usually easier to replace and not too costly. Additionally, fine china is often considered a work of art or heirloom that can be passed to the next generation while dinnerware is common enough to hold no sentimental value.

They're both used for the purpose of setting a table and enjoying a meal. But the couple will use one for everyday meals and the other for special meals like holidays and birthdays and other celebrations. Both have a purpose. Both are needed.

While we are all of equal value to God, not all of us will be called upon for special tasks. Does the dinnerware complain that it is not fine china? Does the fine china sulk because it stays in storage most of its life? It sounds ridiculous, but that's how some of us act when we don't appreciate how God has made us. Whether we're dinnerware or fine china is not the issue. It's whether we praise God for creating us to serve him and him only.

To God alone be glory!

FREEDOM IN CHRIST

It is for freedom that Christ has set us free.
Stand firm, then, and do not let yourselves
be burdened again by a yoke of slavery.

GALATIANS 5:1 NIV

Freedom is wonderful, but it is also paradoxical. God has given us freedom, which is bound in his love. We can use that freedom to love him, abide by his laws, and glorify him with our lives. Or we can use that same freedom to reject him and live by our own rules. It's our free choice.

Throughout the Bible God warns us we will only be truly free through obeying God. If we worship any other false god or idols, it is essentially like becoming a slave. With freedom comes great responsibility. Every loving parent teaches their child this concept in simple ways in hopes that they will make good choices in life. Every free choice always has consequences.

Even the most powerful Being, God, has ordered this world so that even he has limitations. Author Perry Hamalis paraphrases Russian Orthodox theologian Paul Evdokimov when he writes, "God can do anything except compel us to love Him, for love is free and thus where there is no liberty of choice there is no love."[91] Jesus freely chose to die on a cross. His love is so amazing and so divine that he took the punishment we deserve.

To God alone be glory!

POWER OF PRAYER

When the cares of my heart are many,
your consolations cheer my soul.
PSALM 94:19 ESV

Sometimes children's books teach very valuable lessons. A good example is the story of Heidi, the orphan girl who goes to live with her grandfather high up in the Swiss Alps. She adores the mountains and the goat herding life. But she's suddenly taken away from this home and brought to the big city to live with a wealthy family. The people are nice, but she desperately longs to be at home in the beautiful mountains. Her heart breaks, but she can tell no one. But one day, the elderly woman who teaches Heidi to read sees the little girl's despair and tells her to pray.

"See, Heidi, I understand now why you are so unhappy. We all need somebody to help us, and just think how wonderful it is, to be able to go to the Lord, when something distresses us and causes us pain. We can tell Him everything and ask Him to comfort us, when nobody else can do it."[92] It's a simple directive that Heidi, and we, can follow. When our hearts are heavy with burdens no one can understand, God understands them, and he can unburden us when we come to him as children, wanting comfort from a devoted Father.

From this moment Heidi learns not only to pray to God but also to trust him. God's timing is always perfect. Jesus' death and resurrection show us that what seems like the worst thing that could happen, God can turn it into an ultimate victory. He did it on the cross. Have faith he can continue to do it in your life.

To God alone be glory!

Mercy and Justice

Yet the Lord longs to be gracious to you;
therefore he will rise up to show you compassion.
For the Lord is a God of justice.
Blessed are all who wait for him!
ISAIAH 30:18 NIV

Let's say you were caught speeding. A highway patrol officer pulls you over and says, "I clocked you doing 80 in a 55 mile per hour zone. The law says I must give you a ticket. But because it's my little girl's birthday, I'm going to let you go without a ticket." Now that's mercy.

How can mercy *and* grace be part of God's justice? Only through Jesus Christ. We're guilty of sin, but God is saying that because of his Son, Jesus Christ, he will not impose the penalty we are due. Instead, we are justified through Christ's sacrifice on the cross. Therefore, mercy and grace now reign supreme. Jesus has paid the penalty for sin in full, and because God is a God of justice, it would be unjust of him to require payment for a crime already paid for.

To God alone be glory!

RELATIONSHIPS THAT HURT OR HEAL

A gentle answer turns away wrath,
but a harsh word stirs up anger.
PROVERBS 15:1 NIV

Just about everyone has, at one time or another, worked with someone who never seemed to say anything nice about anyone. It wasn't that they told lies about people; most of what they said was truthful. But they expressed their thoughts about others with such venom that it exposed more about the state of their own heart than any defect in the person or situation they talked about.

With their supposed "truthfulness," they created tension within a group. And sometimes, you might have realized how much discomfort there was in the room until the person was no longer there. While they were present, strife and discontent reigned. But after they left, the entire mood changed for the better.

As Timothy Keller wrote, "If you have a propensity for insults, you will always be undermining relationships."[93] God has built us for relationships. The ultimate relationship is with him. Because of Jesus Christ, God's only Son, we have the most loving relationship secured through all eternity. Living that out in our workplaces and in our family relationships has the power to transform any place into heaven on earth.

To God alone be glory!

Love God and Be Kind

*"Who has known the mind of the Lord? Or who has been his
counselor?" "Who has ever given to God, that God should repay them?"
For from him and through him and for him are all things.
To him be the glory forever! Amen.*

ROMANS 11:34–36 NIV

Imagine growing up with limited resources, with no prospects for the
future, and having no ability to create a path for an opportunity. Then one
day an anonymous benefactor comes into your life and offers to pay for
your college tuition and tuition for graduate school and even medical or
law school if you wanted to go. Then after you graduate, the person pays
for the costs of opening your own practice. On top of that, the benefactor
gives you millions of dollars as seed money, so you never have to worry
about your financial future. Now imagine that the only requirement of
having all that wealth is that you are grateful by using your talents wisely
and showing kindness to others.

That is essentially who God is to us. Only he is not anonymous. He
can be known if we so choose to know him and be in relationship with
him. The reality is, we are paupers. Without God we are destitute. We
owe everything to God. All we have is from him. Without Jesus, his Son,
we cannot possibly understand the depths of his care for us. His only
requirements are that we are faithful to his Son, that we be grateful for his
gifts, that we seek to know him, and that we treat others with kindness.

To God alone be glory!

Unforgiveness Devours

The God of peace will soon crush Satan under your feet.
The grace of our Lord Jesus Christ be with you.
ROMANS 16:20 ESV

If you don't believe in the devil or Satan, then his work is already done. The best way for Satan to do his evil deeds is through people who are unaware they're being used as pawns in spiritual warfare. If you do believe that Satan exists, one of the best ways to thwart his schemes is through forgiveness. Yes, forgiveness. This is also unfortunately one of the greatest hurdles we have as human beings.

When we don't forgive, evil wins. Why? Because unforgiveness hurts you more than the person who hurt you. If it hurt them to malign you, they wouldn't have done it. But if you don't forgive, then you start wanting to hurt them in the same way they hurt you, just to give them "what's due." But when you do that, "The evil done to you has come into you and is shaping you."[94] Without you knowing it, the devil has devoured you.

By forgiving, you have deflected the devil's schemes to bring you down into the grave with him. The ultimate forgiveness is Jesus dying on the cross, dying for our sins, so that we don't have to. God, through Jesus Christ, defeated Satan for good. His attacks on us now are simply the devil in the throes of death, wanting to destroy God's most valued creation. Don't let evil triumph over you. Forgive and have faith.

To God alone be glory!

Amazing Creation!

The Son is the image of the invisible God, the firstborn over all creation.
For in him all things were created: things in heaven and on earth,
visible and invisible, whether thrones or powers or rulers or authorities;
all things have been created through him and for him.

COLOSSIANS 1:15–16 NIV

Scientific inquiry has discovered countless facts about the world and the universe, like the fact there are trillions of planets or that photosynthesis helps sustain the air we breathe. But also realize that God created it to be so. He assigned hydrogen its qualities, determined how nuclear fission would continually fuel the sun and warm the earth, and that there would be gravity holding the planets in their orbits.

He also determined plate tectonics that cause the quaking movement within earth's mantle that broke apart the supercontinent called Pangaea, so earth's rotation slowed to twenty-four hours a day instead of three or four hours a day. God also created the conditions for the moon's orbit, creating the tides that filter ocean waters.[95]

All things point to a God so powerful that it's nearly impossible to truly fathom him. Then imagine he holds his creation up with his little pinky! Now, also realize that he created the universe in such a way that we could claim God had nothing to do with it. Wouldn't you prefer to live fully in awe of the majesty of God, who not only created the galaxies and the starry night but also created you? And that same God wrote himself into our story as a flesh and bone human so that we could spend eternity with him.

To God alone be glory!

WE ARE TREASONOUS TRAITORS

Against you, you only, have I sinned and done what is evil in your sight;
so you are right in your verdict and justified when you judge.
PSALM 51:4 NIV

When Nathan the prophet confronted King David about adultery and murder, David's soul was in torment as he realized he violated God's holy law. But wait, you say. David had someone killed to cover up an adulterous affair. He hurt a lot of people. Why is his sin only against God?

God made the rules. He's the one the sin ultimately offends. "Every sin is cosmic treason—it is overthrowing the rule of the one to whom you owe everything."[96] Every sin can be traced back to Adam and the original sin that started it all, overthrowing God's rule and replacing it with our own. So if one man can start the "cosmic treason," one perfect man can be judged for it as well. And that man was Jesus.

Sin is a pesky reality that God has been dealing with since the beginning of our existence. It morphs and molds itself into an opportunity, no matter what situation we find ourselves in. Sin takes on forms that masquerade as even good things. There is no escape from our sinful nature. Jesus alone can save us from its consequences. He can save us from the high court of God's tribunal for treasonous traitors. Jesus will say, "I paid her debt" and "I was judged in his place." How does it change us when someone else is judged for our treasonous wrongs? That is the glory of the cross.

To God alone be glory!

Defeating Death with Death

Since the children have flesh and blood, he too shared in their humanity so that by his death he might break the power of him who holds the power of death—that is, the devil—and free those who all their lives were held in slavery by their fear of death.

HEBREWS 2:14–15 NIV

The gospel of Jesus Christ's death and resurrection is a counterintuitive claim. It makes no sense on first glance…or even on the second or third maybe. But that's precisely why we must look closely at its claims.

How can you defeat the ultimate enemy, death? The answer: by killing it; by nullifying its power, its destructive weapons. At Easter, Greek Orthodox churches around the world shout the words, *"Christos Anesti! Alithos Anesti!"* which means, "Christ is risen. He is risen indeed!" And then they sing a centuries-old, traditional Orthodox Easter hymn, saying, "Christ is risen from the dead, trampling down death by death, and to those in the tombs, granting life."[97]

If Jesus is who he claims to be, the Creator of the universe, the ultimate power of judgment and mercy, love and law, then that changes everything. It doesn't matter what time of year it is. We can shout every day, *Christos Anesti!*

To God alone be glory!

The Heavens Declare Glory

God made the earth by his power;
he founded the world by his wisdom
and stretched out the heavens by his understanding.

JEREMIAH 10:12 NIV

In a galaxy far, far away, scientists recently detected a mysterious radio signal. What baffled them was its low frequency. Because they can't identify exactly what it is, some people have speculated that it's aliens sending signals to us. Scientists have been seeing these fast radio bursts, or FRBs, for a little over a decade now. What they know is that they're coming from a galaxy over a billion light years away. They last only milliseconds, but in that short time, they produce a total energy equal to that of what our sun produces in a month! Some media outlets taunt readers by speculating that "E.T." is still trying to phone home.[98]

But while there's still no proof these FRBs are signs of an extraterrestrial trying to reach us, there is countless evidence in the universe that one divine agent has already communicated with us and continues to do so. His name is Jesus Christ, and the heavens have been declaring his glory since time began (see Psalm 19:1).

To God alone be glory!

Building Blocks of Life

You are a chosen people, a royal priesthood, a holy nation, God's special possession, that you may declare the praises of him who called you out of darkness into his wonderful light.

1 Peter 2:9 NIV

Have you ever pondered why you are here? Well, look no further than the stars and the heavens.

God has built this world in such a way that it has all contributed to making the earth the way it is for this time in history. Long ago, the research scientists undertook often motivated them to become closer to God. Their scientific findings were not to replace God but to grow nearer to him. They surmised that if there was a Supreme Lawgiver, then the natural laws should be discoverable as part of his divine work.

While many scientists later used their craft to separate themselves from their maker, many more these days are seeing God's hand in their work. Convinced of this, scientist Dr. Hugh Ross theorized at the end of his book, *Improbable Planet,* that:

> We are here to seek and find God and then to use all the resources he has so painstakingly and generously provided, within the amazingly stable and optimal climate epoch he established, to encourage people from every ethnic and cultural group in the world to receive God's redemptive offer. God's desire to bring redemption to a vast and variegated population explains why the history of the Milky Way Galaxy, the solar system, Earth, and life looks as it does.[99]

To God alone be glory!

Acting in True Love

We have known and believed the love that God has for us.
God is love, and he who abides in love abides in God, and God in him.

1 JOHN 4:16

There's a lot of talk these days about the lack of love and caring in our world. Why can't people just love each other? Right? But do we really understand what love is and what it means when the apostle says "God is love" and that our responsibility is to do likewise?

First of all, when God loves us, it's not because we're so adorable. For many of us, the opposite is true. God loves us because he is love and that's his nature. Second of all, his love for us means he's concerned not only about the evil that others do to us but also the evil that is within us. A struggling alcoholic loves his booze and will fight the removal of it. But separating him from what he craves and getting him needed help will save him from destruction. Human traffickers are evil predators of the innocent and trusting. They make money from destroying other people's lives. Love means to fight against these kinds of evil.

Jesus Christ dying on the cross is one way we know God loves us. He gave up his comfort to save us from the evil in the world, both around us and in us.

To God alone be glory!

Our Hope and Joy

*All Scripture is breathed out by God and profitable for teaching,
for reproof, for correction, and for training in righteousness.*
2 Timothy 3:16 ESV

The Christian faith, which is the gospel of Jesus Christ, is at once quite simple and quite complex. The youngest and the least educated minds can grasp its truths, yet the most gifted intellectuals also explore all its vast wonders and theological complexities.

All that's required is taking the step to say, *Jesus, come into my heart, live in my heart; show me who you are.* God will open your heart to the Apostles' Creed, the Nicene Creed, and the Lord's Prayer. It doesn't require a degree in comparative religions. As theologian Dr. Voddie Baucham Jr., said, "I am only responsible for giving a reason for the hope that is in me, not the hope that is in others."[100]

Praise God through Jesus Christ for giving us a hope that is beyond measure, beyond our ability to squelch or change. For he is our hope and our joy.

To God alone be glory!

God's Plan A

There are many plans in a man's heart,
nevertheless the Lord's counsel—that will stand.

PROVERBS 19: 21

"I coulda been a contender! I coulda been somebody!"[101] Like the goals of young boxer Terry Malloy in the Oscar winning film *On the Waterfront*, so go many dreams of wealth, prosperity, and achievement—dashed! Goals we set for ourselves might fall short. And yet, God tells us that his plan A is still in motion. How can that be when your life is not going according to your plan?

God's ultimate purpose for us is that we know him and glorify him. Everything in our lives becomes an opportunity to do just that. We accomplish his goals when we constantly speak his truth. Even Job, with all his trials and tribulations, said in the midst of it all, "The Lord gave, and the Lord has taken away; blessed be the name of the Lord" (Job 1:21 ESV). Life brings no guarantees. While we make plans for one day, one week, or one year down the road, we can never be certain whether we may have to make a sudden turn to the left or right. What we may think of as detours and missteps are really where God has brought us, where he wanted us.

The hardest thing is to embrace these changes, to learn from them, and then to grow closer to God because of them. You never know when the worst thing that happens turns out to be the best thing in the long run. Jesus' death on the cross was a trauma beyond belief for his followers. But it became the greatest thing that ever happened for the good of all humanity.

To God alone be glory!

The Heart of Warfare

Keep your heart with all diligence,
for out of it spring the issues of life.
PROVERBS 4:23

A priest recently described the care and feeding of our hearts as a tremendous battle. He called the heart "the great unconquered territory."[102] It should make us ask ourselves, *Have I truly made Christ the Captain of my heart, the Master of my mind?*

If we're honest, we'd have to admit that there always seems to be a little bit of resistance, an area we still want to guard as our own private territory. The problem is that pockets of resistance and privacy can potentially grow into prisons of passions. That is why in the Old Testament, God gives such harsh penalties for seemingly trivial offenses, telling the Israelites to root out the evil within their community.

Evil, no matter how small or innocuous, is like a cancer that could grow and destroy the health of the whole body. Our heart "is the last bastion of rebellion."[103] Having a heart for Christ means the battle is already won.

To God alone be glory!

Daydreams Directed by Christ

As in water face reflects face,
so a man's heart reveals the man.

PROVERBS 27:19

It's the cutest thing, a photo of a kitten lounging in a tiny hammock on its back, arms stretched, eyes closed. The caption reads, "Set aside some dreaming time." It's a reminder to relax and ponder the present-day blessings, the hoped-for future. It's good to take those words to heart and remember that the mind and the spirit need rest in order to have strength for daily endeavors. But daydreaming can also be dangerous if what we focus on is not in God's will.

The Bible talks about our hearts in many different ways; some good, some bad. The prophet Jeremiah called the heart "deceitful…and desperately wicked; who can know it?" (17:9). But one way to understand it better is to "look at your daydreams. They tell you what you are living for, who you really are."[104]

We are called to set our minds on Jesus, "the author and finisher of our faith" (Hebrews 12:2). And we should also add the director of wonderful daydreams.

To God alone be glory!

Love through Faith

Praise be to the God and Father of our Lord Jesus Christ! In his great mercy he has given us new birth into a living hope through the resurrection of Jesus Christ from the dead, and into an inheritance that can never perish, spoil or fade.

1 Peter 1:3–4 NIV

We should be so thankful to God for the great people of faith who have gone before us; some have blessed us personally while others throughout history have been our tall towers of reason and passion. How does one build one's faith?

How did St. Augustine and St. Nicholas, St. Joan of Arc, and millions of others stand strong in the midst of trials? They had faith. How does one have faith? Apologetics is only part of it. The word is from the Greek *apologia*, which means "in defense of," so apologetics is defending your faith when others challenge you. This part of faith building is for the mind.

But the heart needs something in addition to facts. It needs a relationship. That's what these great people of faith had, a relationship with Jesus Christ. To know him is to love him. And love is the fundamental longing of what every heart craves. Know Christ, and you will find the love of your life.

To God alone be glory!

The Character of Christ

Pray for us. We are sure that we have a clear conscience and desire to live honorably in every way.
HEBREWS 13:18 NIV

Good character is a quality we all want from our friends, family, acquaintances, coworkers, employers, and employees. It's something we like to think we possess as well. But how do we attain it? The word *character* has its root in the ancient name for tools used for inscribing. We use pens and pencils today, which don't have as much staying power. They can be easily erased or blotted out. But think of the engravings on monuments and great buildings. They are there forever because they've literally been etched in stone. That is how we should think of our character. It takes time to develop, but once there, our character cannot be erased unless something drastic happens to it.

"Through a long path and a lot of work (Proverbs 1–4), we develop integrity and righteousness, and it is through these character traits that God guides us."[105] The source of our good character can only come from the one who is all good and his wisdom. And what happens if we fall short, as so often happens?

Remember that something drastic has already occurred that will aid our carving out good character. Jesus bore our sins, our lack of good qualities, on the cross. He is our righteousness. He is our good character.

To God alone be glory!

Free Indeed

Jesus replied, "Very truly I tell you, everyone who sins is a slave to sin. Now a slave has no permanent place in the family, but a son belongs to it forever. So if the Son sets you free, you will be free indeed."

JOHN 8:34–36 NIV

The metaphor of slavery is very apt when talking about sin. It holds us captive better than any jail cell or slave master. We sometimes forget that slavery can be a spiritual condition because our cultural reference point is the race-based, chattel slavery of early America, as well as human trafficking and forms of forced servitude today.

But understanding the wide scope of slavery is very much part of God's teaching wisdom to help us understand how slavery is not only wrong but also evil. If we are mastered by anyone or anything but almighty God, our lives become forfeit.

God is unlike any other master. For there are no bars, locked doors, or meager paychecks keeping us bound to him, only the free will to serve him if we choose to. But by serving him and him only, we are truly free, free from bondage and slavery to sin.

To God alone be glory!

Belief and Judgment

You believe that there is one God. Good!
Even the demons believe that—and shudder.
JAMES 2:19 NIV

A lot of polls today ask people about whether they believe in God or believe that God exists. It's an odd question, really, because it's almost saying that if enough people don't believe in God, that must mean God doesn't exist. But God exists independent of our beliefs.

The real question is not whether you believe in God but whether you worship God and live to serve him. As theologian Alister McGrath writes, "Faith is about commitment to God, not just belief in God."[106]

The Bible makes it very clear that even Satan believes in God, probably even more than any of us do. But Satan's problem is that he would not worship or bow down to God. While God has already passed judgment on the devil, the rest of us still have a chance to plead our case. Christ alone is our advocate before God. Run to him. Whatever judgments we deserve, he has already paid the price.

To God alone be glory!

The Heart's God-Shaped Hole

"I know that you are Abraham's descendants.
Yet you are looking for a way to kill me,
because you have no room for my word."

JOHN 8:37 NIV

The phrase "a square peg in a round hole" means something or someone doesn't properly fit the specific circumstance, so it is rejected. Seventeenth century philosopher Blaise Pascal wrote that we have an "infinite abyss"[107] in our hearts, and unless it is filled with God, we are never satisfied. But the problem is we often fill it with other things, like relationships, money, a beautiful home…believing these will give us what only God can.

If we mistakenly pursue good things for the wrong reasons, they will fill the space where only God should be. When that happens, we run the risk of rejecting God because he conflicts with our self-interests. This is why the Pharisees and rulers of the temple didn't just reject Jesus but also wanted to kill him.

Filling up on God's Word lets Jesus find his proper place. It lets us enjoy the job, relationships, and our homes for what they are: great gifts. But it allows us still to worship the gift giver.

To God alone be glory!

ULTIMATE TRUTH FROM GOD

Stand therefore,
having fastened on the belt of truth.
EPHESIANS 6:14 ESV

Writing a nonfiction book involves a lot of research. The final product usually contains quotes from other authors and sources that give credibility to the information in the book. Footnotes provide the proper details for where to find the source of a quote or fact. Footnotes are also a wonderful reminder to a writer that we are not sufficient unto ourselves. We are standing on the shoulders of greater minds who have come before, and we are sitting in the room where living great minds are speaking.

Wisdom involves seeking advice. When the accolades come, if they do, you will know there are countless people to thank who contributed to your success. The ultimate thanks, however, goes to God, our maker, who is responsible for all the great minds. For all truth belongs to God and is from God.

To God alone be glory!

Delighting in the Lord

Delight yourself also in the Lord,
and He shall give you the desires of your heart.
PSALM 37:4

This psalm is God's wink and smile. He understands its simplicity yet knows the huge difference it will make in our lives. Modern folks read this and think, *Oh good, let me delight in the Lord, and I can get (fill in the blank).* But how we should really look at this is that whatever we delight in, whatever we grow an appetite for, we want more of.

If you start running, you'll eventually get a runner's high that makes you want to keep running to keep getting that feeling. And it works with not-so-great things, too, like bad foods. If we eat a steady diet of sweets in the evening, we begin to crave sweets in the evening, and the same goes for chips and other snack foods. Whatever we delight in, we will soon crave constantly. God knows this.

Therefore, delighting in the Lord means he will become the desire of our heart.

To God alone be glory!

GOD'S SELF-HELP

*As many as received Him,
to them He gave the right to become children of God,
to those who believe in His name.*

JOHN 1:12

There are questions we all ask at life's big moments: *Am I pursuing the right career, the right relationship?* It's part of the human condition to question our existence, to wonder why we're here, for what purpose we were born. There is a plethora of self-help books that try to answer those questions. But the best book that has the answer to all of them is the Bible. God's Word.

It's the book that can tell us who God is and who we are in relation to him and his creation. The world is a crazy place filled with ideas and beliefs, many of which conflict with God's Word. Instead of asking the world to give you the answers to the biggest questions, ask the living God, ask Jesus. "Separate yourself from all the noise and ask Jesus to tell you about yourself."[108]

Jesus always understands what we really need and the deeper need behind our questioning life. Who are we? We are his children.

To God alone be glory!

All One in Christ Jesus

There is neither Jew nor Greek,
there is neither slave nor free,
there is neither male nor female;
for you are all one in Christ Jesus.

GALATIANS 3:28

What defines you? Where do you get your identity? From being a Democrat or Republican? From being male or female? Is your race or political affiliation more important than being a child of the living God? When someone from another race or political bent confronts you, do you show them only disdain? If we are all one in Christ Jesus, then that identity is the overarching existence usurping any other status. In political campaign seasons, it's easier to forget that we're ultimately part of the same tribe.

It's good to remember that God sees us all as bearing his image. It is essential that we see the same in those whose political views we oppose. Speaking the truth in love may not win votes in a political ad campaign, but it will win hearts and minds and help bring people to Christ.

To God alone be glory!

The Peace of God

The Lord is near. Do not be anxious about anything, but in every situation, by prayer and petition, with thanksgiving, present your requests to God. And the peace of God, which transcends all understanding, will guard your hearts and your minds in Christ Jesus.

PHILIPPIANS 4:5–7 NIV

These are a few of the many Bible verses that strengthen faith and put the world back into perspective. It says that God is not only near, but he's also in charge. Whatever is happening in your day, the Lord will work it out.

Knowing God is in charge and that you can tap into his comfort and nearness gives a peace that is beyond description. It's telling you, *Calm down. No problem is too big for God. No situation is so daunting that the Creator cannot dismantle or crush it.* But most of all, this protection is for both your emotionally laden heart and your reason-based mind. No matter how you feel or think, God's got it covered. His truth is truth.

To God alone be glory!

Lord over the Storm

[Jesus] said to them, "Why are you afraid, O you of little faith?"
Then he rose and rebuked the winds and the sea,
and there was a great calm.
MATTHEW 8:26 ESV

Storms can be scary things. Extreme storms like hurricanes, typhoons, and tornadoes are downright terrifying. But there are also storms like a gentle summer rain with a little thunder thrown in. These can actually be comforting.

One thing is certain, the variety of storms in each different season is very much like the variety of storms in life. Some we can handle with ease, but others are frightening, like a possible job loss or breakdown in a marriage or family relationship. And some are potentially deadly, like a health threat or simply the ravages of age.

In all cases, we must be like the apostles in the boat. We must pray to God. We must cry out to him from the depths of our hearts. The Bible assures us that God will either calm the storm or take us through it. Either way he, Jesus, is Lord over the storm.[109]

To God alone be glory!

Rest and Redemption

Your steadfast love, O Lord, extends to the heavens,
your faithfulness to the clouds.

PSALM 36:5 ESV

There's nothing like a good night's sleep. Its value is nearly immeasurable. What was a problem when we laid our heads down on the pillow the night before seems less so in the morning. The night of rest has gifted us with more clarity in the dawning hours.

God's compassions for us have made this possible. It would be easy to assign a scientific or natural explanation, saying it's some physiological way we are wired. But then we must also remember that it is God who designed us in this way, to sleep and then wake up feeling victorious.

There's no better example than Jesus' ultimate sleep, death, and then his resurrection that brought us ultimate clarity: redemption. Praise be to our Lord Jesus Christ!

To God alone be glory!

Flowing from Love

The fruit of the Spirit is love, joy, peace, patience, kindness, goodness,
faithfulness, gentleness, self-control; against such things there is no law.
GALATIANS 5:22–23 ESV

There's something very interesting about this well-known verse. It's so elementary that it's often overlooked. Notice that there's only one fruit, one divine fruit with several attributes. Not several fruits you can pick and choose from as if it's a cafeteria. A little peace here or a little faithfulness there. It's just one comprehensive fruit.

And just like in the Ten Commandments, the first one listed is the most important. In the commandments all the laws hinge on keeping God first. In the fruit of the Spirit, all its parts hinge on love. Flowing from love is joy, and from love flows peace and patience. Love brings kindness and goodness, faithfulness, gentleness, and finally self-control. All these parts are part of a whole. That's why Paul's letter to the Corinthians says, "The greatest of these is love" (1 Corinthians 13:13).

To God alone be glory!

COME AND SEE

Philip found Nathanael and said to him, "We have found him of whom Moses in the Law and also the prophets wrote, Jesus of Nazareth, the son of Joseph." Nathanael said to him, "Can anything good come out of Nazareth?" Philip said to him, "Come and see."

JOHN 1:45–46 ESV

Relationships change us. That's the only way we change. Think about it. If it hadn't been for your parents or an older brother or sister, you wouldn't have learned to tie your shoes. Maybe your dad taught you how to ride a bike without training wheels. Or think about your first crush who broke your tender heart. Then who helped mend it? Relationships shape us, mold us; that is how we become who we are.

If human beings can do so much molding and shaping of other human beings, think what an encounter with the living God can do for us! Philip knew. "Philip rightly discerns that Nathanael will be transformed not by an argument, nor even an idea, but by a personal encounter with Jesus."[110]

A personal relationship with Jesus Christ is the transcendent transformation we are all in need of and deep down are desperately seeking. He will be found if we seek him with all our hearts (see Jeremiah 29:13).

To God alone be glory!

FRUITFUL SUBMISSION

God blessed them. And God said to them,
"Be fruitful and multiply and fill the earth and subdue it."
GENESIS 1:28 ESV

It's easy to interpret this directive of filling and subduing the earth as only applying to the big things, like the general idea of having lots of children, as well as progress in agriculture, road construction, and feats of architecture.

But really, we are to bring all things under the heading of God's order. Cleaning house, raking leaves, even protocols for how we answer phones. Author Emily Post made a sizable fortune instructing millions on the proper way to handle even the smallest elements of interpersonal relations.

God's order is no different. "In the end, nothing, even table manners, is indifferent to the service of God."[111] We are to do all things in decency and to glorify God.

To God alone be glory!

Honorable Work

"Do not work for the food that perishes, but for the food that endures to eternal life, which the Son of Man will give to you. For on him God the Father has set his seal."

JOHN 6:27 ESV

Many of us, when we were young, before embarking on careers, worked in hourly jobs in retail or fast-food chains. One woman said that before she became a journalist, she worked odd jobs through a temp agency. Some of the tasks were so mundane and beneath her. Or so she thought at the time. She since learned something quite valuable about work. That is, all work is honorable as long as it's ethical and moral. That applies to a lot of different kinds of activities.

The woman's grandmother cleaned the ladies' washroom at a big department store for a living. It was one of the few jobs an African American woman could find in the 1950s and '60s. But she did it with pride, and she did it so well that the vice president of the company talked about how pristine the women's lounge was. What he didn't know was that his employee, although earning a living cleaning bathrooms, was always working for her true Master.

To God alone be glory!

Think on These Things

Finally, brothers, whatever is true, whatever is honorable, whatever is just, whatever is pure, whatever is lovely, whatever is commendable, if there is any excellence, if there is anything worthy of praise, think about these things.

PHILIPPIANS 4:8 ESV

Question: How do you clean a glass filled with muddy water without pouring the mud out?
Answer: You begin filling it with clear water to displace the dirty liquid. Today's verse is a wonderful example of how to change our thought patterns and, in the process, change ourselves.

It's so easy to get bogged down by what's going wrong in our lives—hardships and difficult situations as well as dealing with difficult people. But the God of all creation has given us a path to joy, and it's the verse above from Philippians.

We are what we think, what we mull over and ruminate about. God is telling us we can find him in all that is good in this world. And when we become the living embodiment of Philippians 4:8, we also become a source of clear waters leading all those around us to Jesus, the actual Living Water for which we all thirst.

To God alone be glory!

MY REDEEMER LIVES

"If only there were someone to mediate between us, someone to bring us together, someone to remove God's rod from me, so that his terror would frighten me no more."

JOB 9:33–34 NIV

Job's plea for mercy is a call for a Savior. It is an Old Testament prophetic call for a Redeemer. Job knows such a person must exist if humans are ever able to face an omniscient, omnipotent, and omnipresent, perfect God.

On top of all that, this God must be righteous and justice. Wrongs must be atoned for. But he must also be merciful, loving, and gracious. How does that kind of God deal with sin from the least to the greatest? On this side of the cross we know there is someone to arbitrate between us and God the Father. His name is Jesus Christ.

But think how much faith Job must have had before Jesus' incarnation to be able to say in the midst of incredible trauma and pain, "I know that my redeemer lives" (Job 19:25 NIV). He was assured even then that Jesus Christ would be his advocate before God. And we can be certain as well.

To God alone be glory!

UNSHAKABLE FAITH

For God alone my soul waits in silence;
from him comes my salvation.
He alone is my rock and my salvation,
my fortress; I shall not be greatly shaken.
PSALM 62:1–2 ESV

Today's verse offers comfort and hope. But sometimes, the comfort and hope are harder to grasp when we are "shaken" by life's many surprises. One man who has a successful career in finance laughingly told a story of his college years when, at the end of the semester, he thought he did pretty well on the final in French class. Then the professor asked, "Where's all your lab work?" Horrified, the man broke out in a cold sweat. It was a bad nightmare come to life. Somehow, he had not been aware all semester that lab work was a requirement of the course. He got a D in the class.

How does believing in God alone as your fortress and rock help you deal with something like this? The answer is by putting it in perspective.

God is still God, and he will use our earthly mishaps to better us, if we learn to rest and trust in him. Remember, the man grew to be successful in finance not French. But it was that mistake that taught him to be thorough in all his later work, which helped his career. God let him fumble through a class in order to find faith in something greater than himself.

To God alone be glory!

ᴅESIRES OF THE ꜰLESH

I say, walk by the Spirit,
and you will not gratify the desires of the flesh.
GALATIANS 5:16 ESV

This is one of those verses that can turn modern people away from faith. They say, "Here's another one those Holy Roller verses meant to shame us into behaving like automaton, goody-two-shoes Christians!" Well, not exactly.

A fascinating science article explored how the mind and body are interconnected and that the neural networks in our brain are created through our experiences. The more intense the experience, the quicker the activity is hardwired into our lexicon of behaviors. The danger is that experiences that should remain separate, like sex and anger, can get fused together as one event, and this can make a person keep repeating behaviors like abusing an intimate partner. It's the Hebb's principle that says, "Neurons that fire together, wire together."[112]

This of course has far-reaching implications for a wide variety of behaviors. And scientists are just scratching the surface as they study the interplay between our DNA and our environment. But for believers, it's an assurance that God in his wisdom spoke this truth in layman's terms thousands of years ago.

To God alone be glory!

The Healing of Humanity

*The LORD said to Abram, "Go from your country and your kindred
and your father's house to the land that I will show you."*
GENESIS 12:1 ESV

When a litter of kittens was born in their backyard, a couple tried to take care of them, feed them, and, when they could, take them to the vet. The runt of the litter needed special attention because something was wrong with its eye. The vet said the kitten had conjunctivitis. He recommended applying a medicated ointment in the cat's eyes twice a day. This is a nearly impossible task with feral cats. So the couple brought the kitten and one of its siblings into the city to a friend's apartment so they could be cared for separately. The kittens were so scared and stayed pretty much cowered in a corner of the bathroom.

The couple said that when looking at those kittens, they thought of Abram being called by God to leave the safety of his home and venture into a strange land to build up a nation. While the little kitten had no idea why it was being taken from its home, Abram at least had some knowledge of God's plan. But both were taken from their native lands for the larger good of healing, Abram for the purpose of healing the entirety of humanity. God's plans are awesome!

To God alone be glory!

CLICKBAIT FOR THE KINGDOM

Do not be conformed to this world, but be transformed by the renewal of your mind, that by testing you may discern what is the will of God, what is good and acceptable and perfect.

ROMANS 12:2 ESV

Millions of people of older generations didn't grow up with smartphones, iPads, or iWhatevers. So they tend to shy away from social media because it takes time and effort remembering all those passwords. But another reason they avoid it is because the many interactions online can breed discord between image bearers who never met face-to-face. As one pastor wrote, "Internet culture privileges mockers, whose insults and broadsides are click bait."[113]

Making every thought captive to Christ can be a challenge in a culture of anonymity, where snarky salvos rule. But just think how much more pleasant tweets and postings would be if we all learned to say what Christ taught—to speak the truth in love.

Jesus died on a cross and rose from the dead to defeat the evil in this world and in our hearts. All he asks is that we believe in his Word, trust, obey, and lead others into his kingdom.

To God alone be glory!

GOOD AND FAITHFUL SERVANT

"His master said to him,
'Well done, good and faithful servant.'"
MATTHEW 25:21 ESV

It's been more than two decades since terrorists brought down the World Trade Center towers. And not a day goes by that one particular airline pilot doesn't think about the worst terror attack in US history, not because he was there but because he wasn't there. He'd been assigned to co-pilot American Airlines Flight 11 that day. But at the last moment, a more senior pilot bumped him from the flight. That plane was hijacked by terrorists and crashed into the North Tower of the World Trade Center.

He doesn't know why God spared him. But now this man lives with a sense of urgency to spread the gospel of Jesus Christ. He's been given a rare gift of knowing what it means and feels like in real time, that someone died in his place.[114]

Life is oh so different when that transcendent truth hits you down to the very core of your being. His one wish at the end of his time here is to hear God say to him, "Well done, good and faithful servant" (Matthew 25:21).

To God alone be glory!

Don't Be Led Astray

I am afraid that as the serpent deceived Eve by his cunning, your thoughts will be led astray from a sincere and pure devotion to Christ.

2 CORINTHIANS 11:3 ESV

Two recent studies about Christians are quite interesting because they appear to address separate ideas. But a closer look reveals they are part of the same issue, except that one is a cause and the other an effect.

One study says most Christians would rather worship with people of the same political beliefs.[115] The other study reveals how many people who profess to be Christians are only nominally so. They have accepted Jesus, but they may not accept the Bible as the "reliable Word of God" or believe that "every moral choice either honors or dishonors God."[116] Although one study is from the US and the other from Europe, they're both part of the same problem: not making Christ reign in our hearts.

We as image bearers are built for worship. If we don't actively worship God through Jesus Christ, something will fill the vacuum. In seeking a savior, we tend to look at temporal powers like politics. Be assured that politics can't save your soul, although many times politicians campaign as if they could. Worship the risen Lord and him only. All other things will take their proper place.

To God alone be glory!

Existentially Complete in Christ

I am like a green olive tree in the house of God.
I trust in the steadfast love of God forever and ever.
PSALM 52:8 ESV

Despite Herculean gains in areas of technology and science in the past century, existential questions still plague us most in our darkest times. We realize that only having facts cannot comfort us.

As one theologian wrote, "The really big questions…are…, Who am I? Do I really matter? Why am I here? Can I make a difference? Neither science nor human reason can answer these questions."[117] Only God has the answers to those queries. But the simple answer is always that we live to glorify God. Whatever we do, however we do it, should be in service to him.

Why? If you knew someone gave you a priceless gift simply out of love, how would you react? You'd be quite grateful and appreciative. Now imagine that Being is the reason you are breathing. What's that worth to you? I remember someone wrote on the chalk board in my high school classroom many decades ago, "God's gift to you is your life. What you make of your life is your gift to God."

To God alone be glory!

A Light Never Failing

"I have come into the world as light,
so that whoever believes in me may not remain in darkness."

JOHN 12:46 ESV

It is at this time of year when we discern the shorter days. When we rise for work in the morning, it is still dark like the middle of night. Fall is nearly here, and the dark days of winter will soon follow.

But there is still joy because the light of the living God will never be extinguished. It will never burn out even if all things physical do. If that light is in our hearts, the physical darkness is nothing to fear or be sad about. Joy reigns because Christ reigns.

As C. S. Lewis so brilliantly said, "I believe in Christianity as I believe that the Sun has risen; not only because I see it, but because by it I see everything else."[118] Jesus is the Light of the World.

To God alone be glory!

God Controls the Winds

Let me hear in the morning of your steadfast love, for in you I trust.
Make me know the way I should go, for to you I lift up my soul.
PSALM 143:8 ESV

Recalling her life as a child in grade school, one woman remembers gazing out the classroom window at the tops of the trees as their leaves moved to a gentle breeze. The second-floor view allowed her to imagine that the whole school was surrounded by a beautiful forest instead of streets of inner-city houses. She said it was so easy to let her mind wander rather than pay attention to the teacher. Sometimes that wandering cost her a few correct answers on a test. But in the long run, it wasn't a crucial error.

But when it comes to matters of the soul, the spirit, and finding solace in a world full of challenges, the correct knowledge can be crucial. God knows that a wandering mind is a potential captive to any which way the wind blows, especially when it comes to fears about the unknown future. Money woes, a marriage on the rocks, job in turmoil, or no job at all can all make our minds slaves to despair.

God has made it clear that although we may not know what the future holds, we can be assured of who holds the future. And it is a God who not only cares which way the wind blows but is directing it as well.

To God alone be glory!

OUR LINK TO GOD

The heart knows its own bitterness,
and no stranger shares its joy.
PROVERBS 14:10 ESV

Even as we become close to the people in our lives, the human experience has an element of solitude. Ultimately, we are all independent agents.

Even close spouses, siblings who grow together, good friends who know our good days and bad days, and parents who know our every mood…they still have no access to our most intimate thoughts, our deepest longings, or our greatest desires. But one thing that should give us comfort in our perpetual state of metaphysical seclusion is that there is a God who knows us and knows our thoughts.

We are forever linked to that God. He's not a remote deity but a loving Savior who entered our world to share in that same human experience. He is fully human, Jesus, and fully divine, Lord of creation. And because of his sacrifice on the cross, we are forever entwined with the one who knows us best.

To God alone be glory!

IDENTITY IN JESUS

[Jesus] said to them,
"But who do you say that I am?"
MATTHEW 16:15 ESV

What kind of person do you think you are? Are you nice? Do you see yourself as timid or bold or self-reliant? Do you anger easily, or are you patient and kind? Do you think you're fairly good looking?

Now ask yourself this: Of all the different attributes you see yourself having, how did you come to know that you have those attributes? Who told you? If you believe you told yourself, you may be fooling yourself. You see, "your natural self-image is a compilation of verdicts that have been passed on you by various people over the years."[119] You cannot shape yourself.

Jesus already knows who he is because his identity is with God the Father. It's the only identity that matters. When he asks his disciples to tell him who do they think he is, he's not asking for his benefit, but theirs. Once they see him as the Messiah, God on earth, it is the only attribute they need for which to order their lives. And it is the only one we need as well.

To God alone be glory!

Jesus, the Eyes of Your Heart

[I pray that] the God of our Lord Jesus Christ, the Father of glory, may give to you the spirit of wisdom and revelation in the knowledge of Him, the eyes of your understanding being enlightened; that you may know what is the hope of His calling.

EPHESIANS 1:17–18

Although science figures big in this technologically driven world, the fact is that we primarily see and act with our emotions, our hearts. It's a combination of feeling and fact, where we strive to find facts that confirm our feelings. So many times, our feelings get way out of proportion, and we ignore facts altogether. And that's often when mistakes happen.

God tells us to know Christ so well that it gets into the very core of our being, to our hearts, where we do most of our decision-making. The more we align ourselves with a belief, the more we will become like it. This is a fact of science. So the more we know Jesus intimately, the more he will transform our hearts. The result is that the eyes of our hearts will be enlightened and see the true hope he has given us.

To God alone be glory!

Each Day a Teachable Moment

Teach me to do Your will, for You are my God;
Your Spirit is good.
Lead me in the land of uprightness.

PSALM 143:10

This is a wonderful verse that says two very important things: First, that we are teachable. That's the good news—that we can learn to know God's will. And the second thing is the not so good news: we may not necessarily learn naturally. If we do behave honorably, righteously, and lovingly, it may be because someone else taught us without knowing the source material or why.

Think about Wall Street, where very smart people make lots of money. In the past, brokers and financiers were ethical because it made for good business. But when some found that they could make more money, and lots of it, by skirting the rules, they did so. God was not their authority. Money was.

And as we know today, the skirting of the rules, even the bending and breaking of the law, has resulted over time in massive financial failures affecting millions of people. The best thing believers can do each day, if nothing else, is to say to God "teach me" and "lead me."

To God alone be glory!

REJOICING IN TRUTH AND LOVE

*Love does not delight in evil
but rejoices with the truth.*

1 CORINTHIANS 13:6 NIV

There's a very funny commercial where Honest Abe's wife asks him, "Does this dress make me look fat?" Lincoln, the sixteenth US president, takes way too long to answer, signaling his real thoughts. The angry look on Mrs. Lincoln's face says it all. His conflicted look spoke the truth. That commercial brings up a problem scenario we've all been in: How do you tell someone you really care about that they're doing something destructive in their lives? Do you pull up a study that shows how dangerous or awful their behavior is? Or do you just love them and accept their behavior as part of who they are?

Here's some advice: "Truth without love isn't real truth, and love without truth isn't real love. And unless they are used together, no real character change is possible."[120] Jesus said the truth will set us free (see John 8:32). But first we must know Jesus, the Son of God, who is not only the embodiment of truth but is also love incarnate.

Truth and love, those two pillars, are joined as one in the person of Jesus Christ, who died on the cross so that we could be free from the bondage of sin and death. We shouldn't fear truth, only the walking away from it.

To God alone be glory!

WE ARE CONTINGENT BEINGS

In the beginning God created the heaven and the earth.
GENESIS 1:1 KJV

It's a very interesting that there is no comma between the words *beginning* and *God* in this verse from Genesis in the King James Version of the Bible. Other translations have added a comma, seeing it as more grammatically correct. But one Jewish scholar says having no comma is correct. It shows that God *is* the beginning. Instead of reading it as there was a beginning and then God created everything, the KJV translation says, "In the beginning God."[121]

This editing choice gives affirmation to another scholar who describes God in this way: "There exists now, and always has existed and will exist, God, a spirit, that is, a non-embodied person who is omnipresent."[122] Philosophers call that "a necessary being." In other words, one that is not contingent on the existence of anything else but is the reason behind existence itself.

We are contingent beings because our existence is based on what has come before us. But acknowledging the need for a necessary Being gets you to believing in God the Father. To believe in the Son and the Holy Spirit, the other equal partners of the Trinity, means having faith that the gospel is that necessary Being's truth for redeeming us contingent souls.

To God alone be glory!

SHARING THE WEALTH

No man can serve two masters:
for either he will hate the one, and love the other;
or else he will hold to the one, and despise the other.
Ye cannot serve God and mammon.

MATTHEW 6:24 KJV

Money is essential in today's world. It has been for hundreds of centuries, which is why it also holds such a danger for us. How much is enough? How much is too much? Many people today would reply, "It's never enough" and "You can never have too much."

God's Word concerning money sometimes makes us feel uncomfortable because money is a tangible path to having a home to live in, food to eat, and clothes to wear, all things we need. And the more money you have the better quality and quantity you can have of those necessary things.

But here Jesus is saying that instead of you becoming a slave to money, of trying to earn more and more of it, be a slave to your heavenly Father. Let him be the thing that rules your heart. That way, you'll always have enough money and you'll always be generous with your wealth. Instead of asking, "How much is enough?" we can now ask, "Who can benefit from my riches?"[123] We "attain God's riches by letting go of our own."[124]

To God alone be glory!

Peace in Praying

"When you pray, go into your room and shut the door and pray to your Father who is in secret. And your Father who sees in secret will reward you."

MATTHEW 6:6 ESV

Praying is such a powerful tool we have and so readily accessible that we sometimes forget it's available to us 24/7. We can communicate with the living God at all times and in all places. The room Jesus speaks of appears to be a physical space in which we pray, but it doesn't have to be. It can be the room in our minds. But Jesus is also telling us about the vast gifts we'll find when we pray.

In fact, one scholar points out that the Greek word for the "room" into which we are to withdraw and pray is *tameion*. It is a room in ancient times used to store treasures. "The implication is that there are treasures already awaiting us when we pray."[125]

Jesus is letting us know that praying is a great treasure in his kingdom. It's how we can tell him all our hopes and dreams, thoughts and fears. We can lie down and rest because we've unloaded our heaviest burdens at Jesus' feet. He is our treasure.

To God alone be glory!

Know the Truth

*I have no greater joy than to hear
that my children are walking in the truth.*
3 John 4 esv

In the 1950s and '60s, most people owned just one television, if any at all, and it usually sat in the living room. There was no internet and no cell phones. They talked to each other in person a bit more, and kids did a lot of playing in the backyard. Many of those same people learned their faith at Sunday school and church, but it was also lived out in the home. Praying at mealtime and bedtime were normal parts of the day. It wasn't high theology, but it was truth. The stories of the Bible were realities that directed their moral decisions.

Today there are many more distractions. Social media has many people chained to their computers and constantly checking their phones. But what's concerning is how young people are learning morality from immoral sources and truth from an industry built on lies. A recent study showed how more than 80 percent of so-called family-themed TV comedies include sexual dialogue taking place in front of children.[126] If children grow up ingesting this kind of narrative, it becomes a fast track to growing in sin without even realizing.

It's an example of the proverbial frog sitting on the stove in a pan of room-temperature water. The frog slowly gets used to the water as it warms over the burner. By the time the frog realizes the water boiling, it is too late; the damage is already done. That's why it's important to set aside time for the living God. Be immersed in God's Word, God's truth. That way, it's easier to recognize when occasions of sin are heating up around you.

To God alone be glory!

A Joyful Earth

Let all the earth fear the Lord:
let all the inhabitants of the world stand in awe of him.
PSALM 33:8 KJV

There's a path to certain joy that is right before our eyes. It's seeing beauty. It's looking at something so amazing that its brightness invades every crevice and crack of darkness creeping into our lives. Being in awe of something makes you treat it with special care, compelling you to respect it and sometimes everything surrounding it.

The next time you're down, think about the wonder and miracle of life, the grandeur of snowcapped mountain peaks, or the expanse of wildflowers in an open field. Then behind it, see the God who created it all and remember that God has never stopped loving you and watching over you. He loves you so much that he sacrificed himself so that you would not have to suffer the ugliness of being separated from him in eternity.

Life is precious. Someone once told me that our very lives are God's way of saying he hasn't given up on us, that he is still here and in charge.

To God alone be glory!

Hope in Sorrow

Great is thy faithfulness.
The LORD is my portion, saith my soul;
therefore will I hope in him.
LAMENTATIONS 3:23–24 KJV

Being sad or downcast doesn't mean being without hope. It's amazing that the book of Lamentations teaches us that even though we might be facing the reality of a painful situation, this sorrow should not leave us lost. It's natural to be sad. It's okay to cry. God has given our frail bodies the ability to shed tears in order to release the tension of sorrows within. But think about this too: sometimes crying can be a sign of inextricable joyfulness at seeing beauty and God glorified.

How interesting that two very different emotions, sorrow and joy, can have the same bodily outlet: weeping. It can't be a mistake. God has built us in such a way that we can always see hope in the midst of sorrow. Jesus' death on the cross seemed like an event of great despair, yet it brought humanity the greatest joy for eternity. Great indeed is his faithfulness.

To God alone be glory!

Dancing All Night

He put a new song in my mouth, a hymn of praise to our God.
Many will see and fear the LORD and put their trust in him.
PSALM 40:3 NIV

Broadway shows are the staple of New York's tourist industry. A woman I know who saw a Broadway revival of one of her favorite musicals, "My Fair Lady," recounts how she hadn't realized the impact it would have to see it live as opposed to watching the movie. One of the show's iconic scenes mirrors God's transformative moments, when he suddenly touches our hearts.

It's the moment Eliza Dolittle finally pronounces the words correctly. It's as if she's been altered down to her very soul. Before then she had endured weeks of grueling vowel exercises and rote repetitions. It all seems a waste, and she's exhausted and feels defeated. Then, in one moment, she gets it, and that moment is exhilaratingly transformational.

Seeing this unfold on stage, the woman realized that's how it can be when we allow God past our defenses and he touches our hearts, when the reality of Jesus' transcendent love reaches deep into our souls. All of our Bible reading and rote prayers take on a whole different meaning. Transforming joy takes away our fatigue and replaces it with unending energy to praise him with songs of joy. Giving us the ability to "dance all night."

To God alone be glory!

WEAPONS OF SPIRITUAL WARFARE

The weapons of our warfare are not carnal but mighty in God for pulling down strongholds, casting down arguments and every high thing that exalts itself against the knowledge of God, bringing every thought into captivity to the obedience of Christ.

2 CORINTHIANS 10:4–5

The Bible is an arsenal of divine weaponry for spiritual warfare. True, we are called to put on the full armor of God, the belt of truth, the breastplate of righteousness, feet fitted with the gospel of peace, and the shield of faith (see Ephesians 6:14–17). We must also have knowledge of our opponent's tactics. In a real physical battle, if your opponent uses tanks and automatic weapons, chances are you'll be severely ill-equipped if you show up with a bow and arrow.

In this natural world, one of Satan's chief tools is deception. Through deception, Satan destroys families by making husbands and wives distrust each other. That distrust causes bickering and arguing, which then create pain and anguish in their children. The most powerful weapon against Satan's schemes is forgiveness. Through forgiveness, husbands and wives reconcile. Through forgiveness, a wayward child is brought back into the loving arms of her parents.

And forgiveness is how Christ defeated Satan on the cross. By being the sacrifice for sin, God forgave us. Satan, the great accuser, lost his power over us. Whatever Satan does now to deceive us, it's only the tactics of a vanquished enemy. Christ is our stronghold. Nothing can change that.

To God alone be glory!

ENCOUNTERING THE LIVING GOD

*"When I saw him, I fell at his feet as though dead.
But he placed his right hand on me, saying,
'Do not be afraid; I am the first and the last.'"*

REVELATION 1:17 NRSVA

Having an encounter with the living God is a world of difference from having information about him. Take, for example, the hearing of great music. The classical composer Ludwig van Beethoven's string quartets are amazing pieces of music for four instruments. But their titles tell you nothing about what they sound like or what you will feel when you listen to them.

Take the "String Quartet in C Major, op. 59, no. 3, II *Andante con moto quasi allegretto*." Its title tells you about its order in the Beethoven lexicon of compositions, opus 59. From the rest of the title, you'll know that it's the second of four movements, that its tempo is moderate but flowing, that it's in the key of C. But all that information never gives a hint of the emotions it evokes as you experience hearing it. To know the music as information is not the same as having an experience of its pleasures.

To know God is much the same. You can know that God is the all-knowing, eternal, ever-present, all-powerful Creator. However, to truly experience the presence of the living God brings you to your knees.

To God alone be glory!

Built to Withstand Hardships

We know that if the earthly tent we live in is destroyed, we have a building from God, a house not made with hands, eternal in the heavens.
2 CORINTHIANS 5:1 NRSVA

Architects build skyscrapers with a certain amount of sway so the structure can flow and move but not strain or break. Over time, the elements of nature—rain, snow, heat, and cold—cause decay and normal wear and tear. But the sway remains intact.

God has built our bodies in much the same way. We have the ability to sway and flow, bend and not break, to withstand the elements of life: hardships and challenges. Jesus referred to our bodies as temples of the living God. In today's verse, Paul refers to our earthly bodies as tents. He's saying that God has given us assurances of a heavenly home.

What this knowledge gives us is the ability to withstand greater and greater strains and stresses. For we need not worry what evil can do to our bodies when we know we will be with the Lord throughout eternity. God is the only architect who can build such a structure.

To God alone be glory!

God's Law Written on Hearts

You shall not bear false witness against your neighbour.
EXODUS 20:16 NRSVA

Today's verse is one of the Ten Commandments sorely forgotten in this culture of legality and hyper litigation. Today it's less about truth than about winning at all costs. It's not about doing right but coming out the victor. Civil laws are not equivalent to God's laws, and just because something is legal by man's standards does not necessarily make it moral in God's eyes.

On this side of the cross, the Ten Commandments should no longer be an external force policing us, as it was when Moses first carved it in stone. But instead, as the prophet Jeremiah said in the Old Testament and reconfirmed in the New Testament, God's law should be carved in our flesh.

The apostle Paul in his words to the Corinthians said, "You show that you are a letter of Christ, prepared by us, written not with ink but with the Spirit of the living God, not on tablets of stone but on tablets of human hearts" (2 Corinthians 3:3 NRSVA). In that way we are to live in a constant state of expressing truth and love; the two operate as inseparable companions. It should be as impossible to break God's law as it would be impossible to stop your heart from beating at will.

To God alone be glory!

Loving Our Enemies

"I say to you, Love your enemies
and pray for those who persecute you."
MATTHEW 5:44 NRSVA

No one said it would be easy to love our enemies. In fact, it's one of the most difficult things for humans to do, to love those who've hurt you or pray for those who've wreaked havoc in your life. And as many theologians will say, it is actually countercultural.

With all the talk in civil society about the Golden Rule of doing unto others as we would want done to us, the actual mode of operation is to lash out at those who've done us wrong. Reverend David Bisgrove said, "There's stuff in the drinking water of the culture." It's vengeance. And that is the cultural directive: "In this world, it's who loves you; stay with your tribe."[127]

The bottom line is, we shouldn't be so quick to find fault in others and think it's an objective judgment. Writer Anne Lamott said, "You can safely assume you've created God in your own image when it turns out that God hates all the same people you do."[128] Jesus understands our hearts, even better than we do. That is why only he is in a position to judge what is their fair treatment. Jesus died on the cross loving those who hated him. It should humble us to truly love our enemies.

To God alone be glory!

Fulfilling God's Plan

I am the first and I am the last; besides me there is no god…
I am the LORD, and there is no other; besides me there is no god.

ISAIAH 44:6; 45:5 NRSVA

Throughout the Old and New Testaments, God is constantly affirming the First Commandment which says, "I am the LORD your God…you shall have no other gods before me." (Exodus 20:2–3 NRSVA). It is both a command and statement of fact. It's saying there are no other gods but God. And that all other supposed gods are only idols that lead us away from the living God and from our true selves. For we are made in God's image.

These days the political landscape is quite ravenous, and even the news is not so much "just the facts" but an evangelizing tool for partisan politics. Politicians have become prophets, while entertainers and media personalities act as preachers and acolytes whose job is to spread the gospel of a party's platform or group ideology.

But God will not be mocked (see Galatians 6:7) nor will he give his glory to another (see Isaiah 42:8). We worship false gods at our own peril. Jesus died for all sinners. And those whose identities are in him are able to breach any political divide.

To God alone be glory!

The Body of Christ

From him [Christ] the whole body,
joined and held together by every supporting ligament,
grows and builds itself up in love, as each part does its work.
EPHESIANS 4:16 NIV

A man I interviewed had lost his legs to a landmine while serving in the armed forces. He spoke emotionally about how upset he got when he heard of some able-bodied person who wanted to take his own life.

The man was certainly upset about the potential loss of life and felt compassionate toward anyone suffering from depression. But he had learned the true value of life only after losing his legs and coming close to death. He said he wished he could tell a person contemplating suicide, "Give me your legs then."

It's a stark reminder that sometimes we take for granted the wonderful things God has given us. Legs, arms, a body…our very lives are all gifts from God. But Jesus reminds us that we are all part of his body. We don't all have the same functions, but we are equally needed and valued in his kingdom. The body of Christ is a wonderful mosaic of all kinds of people, serving Christ with their unique gifts. God also calls us each to help those who may be blind to their gifts to see them in the light of God's glory.

To God alone be glory!

An Order to Our Relationships

Submit to one another
out of reverence for Christ.
EPHESIANS 5:21 NIV

There's hardly a Scripture verse that has been more maligned and misunderstood in our culture today as this one, particularly considering the verses that follow it. The apostle Paul continued his admonition to the Ephesians with a list of how wives should submit to husbands, how husbands should love their wives, how children should obey their parents, how fathers should treat children, and how slaves should obey their masters. It's a directive that rails against the feminist mindset and individualism. But our culture misses the forest for the trees.

What the apostle Paul is saying is that there's an order to life that includes duties to those with whom we are in intimate and close relationships. It's about marriage, parenting, and the work environment. Our sinful nature has always skewed those words to justify many heinous acts, slavery being one of them. Some Bibles use the word *servant* or *worker* rather than *slave* when translating Ephesians 6:5. The point is, the Bible does not and never has endorsed race-based slavery like that of early America.[129]

When Christ is the head of a household, harmony follows: husband and wives are equals with different functions, and children feel secure and confident in their parents' love for them. And when Christ rules in our hearts, we are better employees and bosses. Paul's words should also remind us that we are not alone in this world. Relationships are what drive us and sustain us. The ultimate relationship with Jesus Christ is what saves us.

To God alone be glory!

Ultimate Power in God

*"Now here is the king you have chosen, the one you asked for;
see, the Lord has set a king over you."*

1 SAMUEL 12:13 NIV

There has always been a presence of political power in the world. It's not new to God. For generations, Israel had God as their King. They worshiped the God who brought them out of slavery into freedom. He fed them in the wilderness and quenched their thirst with water from a rock. However, as they drifted away from the source of their salvation, they wanted to have a king just like the nations around them. What the Israelites failed to understand in asking for a king was that "the ultimate power is in God, not political systems."[130]

God never gives up his power just because a certain person or party is "on the throne." It is we who lose power when we bow down to anyone but the Lord. Worship the Lord Jesus, he is the only King with an eternal throne.

To God alone be glory!

Our Thirst Is Quenched

*They soon forgot what he had done
and did not wait for his plan to unfold.
In the desert they gave in to their craving;
in the wilderness they put God to the test.*

PSALM 106:13–14 NIV

Few of us will experience real physical thirst to the point of feeling as if we're near death. In fact, we probably take water for granted because it's so easily accessible. But we do crave other things, and that longing is also a thirst. It's a desperate desire to have something we don't have, and we believe that once that thirst is quenched, life will be happy and joyful. In a sense, we put God to the test. *God, if you'll just give me (fill in the blank), I could be really happy.*

What God knows, and what we may not realize, is that whatever is filling up the blank is the thing we're really worshiping. In our lives we will have seasons of wilderness where we are uncertain about the future. We hunger and thirst for an end to the uncertainty, but it's precisely those times in the wilderness when we draw closer to God and when we can encounter the Living Water, Jesus. He has said that he offers us the kind of water that will eternally quench our thirst.

To God alone be glory!

Nurturing Children of Faith

Fathers, do not provoke your children to anger,
but bring them up in the discipline and instruction of the Lord.
EPHESIANS 6:4 ESV

In recent years, various news outlets picked up on a new trend in parenting of letting children decide if they want to be a boy or girl; parents are calling their newborns "theybies."[131] One expert thought it may be a backlash to society's unrealistic expectations of what it means to be male or female. God didn't create supermodels and uber machismo Marlboro men as our standards of male and female. Yet our culture has created these impossible images. Anyone who has worked in the entertainment industry, where lots of make-up artists and hair stylists are crucial, knows that physical beauty is truly only skin deep.

Babies come into this world as blank slates. The bulk of who they are they learn from the people and experiences around them. But "if instead the parents just let their child grow up as a detached, autonomous self, that's parental malpractice."[132]

Jesus said, "Let the little children come to Me, and do not forbid them; for of such is the kingdom of heaven" (Matthew 19:14). Let the Lord of all creation help you teach your children what it means to grow up to be men and women of faith.

To God alone be glory!

No Editing Out God's Truth

In their case the god of this world has blinded the minds of the unbelievers,
to keep them from seeing the light of the gospel of the glory of Christ,
who is the image of God.

2 CORINTHIANS 4:4 ESV

It's not hard to see how God's glory is being excised from the marketplace, especially in the world of entertainment. For example, in the blockbuster film from the 1990s *Independence Day*, there's a great scene where one of the pilots, played by Harry Connick Jr., gives a mini sermon. At first he seems to joke, saying, "Or as the good reverend would say," then imitating Reverend Jesse Jackson. But it turns into a wonderful pre-battle moment as the pilot expresses his confidence in the mission and its certain victory, readying the hearts of those men who don't know whether they will live or die in the battle.[133]

The scene takes less than thirty seconds. Yet it is edited out of the version you'll see on commercial television. It truly is one of the more poignant and important moments of the film as it helps put into perspective something deeper our hearts need desperately to grasp: life, death, and ultimate salvation. It is unfortunate that TV networks don't see the importance of the message.

As Christians we know that salvation is found in no one else but Jesus Christ by putting our faith in his shed blood. No amount of editing can change that truth.

To God alone be glory!

Our Daily Bread

Jesus said to them, "I am the bread of life;
whoever comes to me shall not hunger,
and whoever believes in me shall never thirst."

JOHN 6:35 ESV

Bread, as well as water, means something different today than in ancient times. We eat bread as an accompaniment to a main meal or as an appetizer. Our frame of reference may also be flimsy white slices with few nutrients. But bread in ancient times was the main meal. It was hearty with grain and barley. Meat was not consumed daily, and vegetables depended on the season. But bread sustained you.

When Jesus calls himself "the bread of life," he really means the source of our daily nutrition. He is the manna, the bread that came down from heaven.

Our physical bodies need food daily. And we need to feed our spiritual selves too. Just like we eat every day to provide fuel for our bodies, so our spirits need to daily ingest the Word made flesh (see John 1:14).

To God alone be glory!

God Knows You Best

"I the Lord search the heart and test the mind,
to give every man according to his ways,
according to the fruit of his deeds."
JEREMIAH 17:10 ESV

Most of us have phones that can track our whereabouts 24/7. As long as the phone is on, it can chart how many miles you've walked, driven, or sauntered. It can also tell you where you've been. All this provides advertisers with information to target your specific likes in retail, restaurants, and entertainment.

We may think it is invasive for a phone to know so much about us. But it could actually be inspiring in that, if a man-made device can know so much about our habits, just think of what an omniscient and omnipotent God knows about us.

Jesus said, "I am the way, the truth, and the life. No one comes to the Father except through Me" (John 14:6). An iPhone may be able to tell you snippets of where you've been, but the God of all creation takes it exponentially further, telling you every detail about your past and present. He also knows where you're headed. What's more comforting, he'll walk beside you all the way.

To God alone be glory!

Our Two Natures

Jesus answered, "Truly, truly, I say to you, unless one is born of water and the Spirit, he cannot enter the kingdom of God. That which is born of the flesh is flesh, and that which is born of the Spirit is spirit."

JOHN 3:5–6 ESV

We have two natures: flesh and spirit. We know that Jesus also has two natures, fully human and fully divine. In the verse above, he talks about our two natures, that we have a physical body and a spiritual self. It is through that spirit that we experience a rebirth.

All of us have been raised in some kind of faith foundation, whether it is a formal, organized religion or informal beliefs on the meaning of life. But Jesus says we all need a rebirth, a baptism of water and the Spirit.

To be reborn is to start fresh like a new babe, full of hope and promise, feeding on the nurturing spirit of a love that surpasses all understanding. Tradition dies hard, but faith in Jesus Christ is a continual fount of water, and feast of the tastiest morsels.

To God alone be glory!

Wording in Grace

The soothing tongue is a tree of life,
but a perverse tongue crushes the spirit.
PROVERBS 15:4 NIV

In any relationship we have the ability to enhance a person's soul, to build them up, and to bring greater joy. We also have the power to crush them, hurt them. We do this a lot through words.

Parents have a greater responsibility when choosing their words because they are setting the pattern of how a child sees himself. Confidence, security, tenacity, love, joy, peace are all the fruits of the spirit (see Galatians 5:22–23) we can instill in a child through the words we say to him or her. At the same time, it is possible to build insecurity, self-hatred, anger, and hostility, just through words. Many parents are unaware of how the words spoken to them by their own parents affect how they speak to their children. Negative traits are easily passed along with positive ones.

The good news is the gospel. The grace, mercy, and love of God through Jesus Christ is like a custom-made corrective brace. He is the Word made flesh, the healing balm that turns a crushed spirit into a tree of abundant life.

To God alone be glory!

Peace in Our Hearts

Peace I leave with you; my peace I give you.
I do not give to you as the world gives.
Do not let your hearts be troubled and do not be afraid.

JOHN 14:27 NIV

If words have power as Scripture says, then these words of Jesus should give us the greatest comfort of all. Not only does he promise to give us a peace that "surpasses all understanding" (Philippians 4:7), but because of that assurance of peace, we can calm our hearts.

That is also the challenge for us, to believe with our hearts what Jesus is telling us. Jesus' words should have the greatest impact because he is the Lord who made the world and established all its precepts, its scientific laws, and its rules. Because he is fully human, he knows what we feel. And because he is fully divine, he provides the cosmic cure for whatever ails us.

He gives us peace, the kind that gives rest, reassurance, and a refuge. It requires nothing except to trust in that peace.

To God alone be glory!

Our Foolishness Atoned For

Fools give full vent to their rage,
but the wise bring calm in the end.
PROVERBS 29:11 NIV

This is one of many verses in the book of Proverbs that delivers practical words of warning about the dangers of uncontrolled rage. There is never a good time for rage. Being wise and calm is always the better path. Calm wisdom brings people closer whereas anger can alienate even the best of friends and divide families.

The book of Proverbs knows us intimately. Proverbs dissects who we are and lays bare our sins for us to see. We cannot hide our envy, anger, bad words, and more when we read Proverbs. We are naturally subversive, lying to ourselves about the state of our own depravity, like our ancient ancestors Adam and Eve. We hide in God's garden, afraid to show our nakedness even to the one who loves and knows us best.

In the end, we are all fools. It is our nature. But it is Jesus Christ's nature that gives us hope so that our foolishness doesn't crush us. He suffered because of our anger and misdeeds so we don't have to.

To God alone be glory!

Pride Destroys, Humility Creates

Pride goes before destruction,
a haughty spirit before a fall.
PROVERBS 16:18 NIV

It's one of the great warnings in the Bible: pride. That's why it's called one of the seven deadly sins. But it could be considered the deadliest because pride is the fuel for the engine of all the great evils.

It is because of pride that we don't forgive and hold resentment against others; pride makes us build walls instead of bridges, cutting ourselves off from enjoying a peace that passes all understanding (see Philippians 4:7). Pride makes us brittle, stiff, and unyielding. Eventually, pride will break us.

But repentance breaks down our prideful defenses. It builds safe passageways not only for us to cross but also for others to approach us. The opposite of pride is humility. Jesus is the ultimate example of humility. He built bridges, pathways, and byways so that our pride could be dismantled.

To God alone be glory!

LETTING GOD'S WORD REIGN

"The eye is the lamp of the body.
If your eyes are healthy, your whole body will be full of light.
But if your eyes are unhealthy, your whole body will be full of darkness.
If then the light within you is darkness, how great is that darkness!"

MATTHEW 6:22–23 NIV

In his book *Escape from Reason*, evangelical theologian and pastor Francis Schaeffer wrote, "People often ask which is better—American or BBC television?" The clever retort was, "What do you want—to be entertained to death or be killed with wisely planted blows?"[134]

It's a funny remark about a serious problem we have today: the influence of television. By now there are several generations that have been raised on the culture provided by what is broadcast through our TVs, phones, and computers. It is the greatest influence on the minds of young and old. The TV has become friend, family member, and spiritual guide whether we like it or not.

How do we counter its influence? We must make sure God's Word has the authority over what we hear and see on the screen. Many believers have said they have often turned shows off because they run counter to God's Word or blaspheme the name of Jesus. May all believers have the strength to do likewise. Jesus is the Light of the World. Fill your eyes with his beauty and live in his resplendent glow.

To God alone be glory!

Reasons to Obey

Therefore let no one pass judgment on you in questions of food and drink, or with regard to a festival or a new moon or a Sabbath. These are a shadow of the things to come, but the substance belongs to Christ.

COLOSSIANS 2:16–17 ESV

There is some debate about whether Christians should be bound by the laws of the Old Testament. The answer many theologians give is "yes and no." There were three kinds of laws in the Old Testament that God gave the Israelites: civil, ceremonial, and moral. Civil laws dictated their daily living, like what they ate and how they washed their garments. These laws helped separate them from the pagan cultures around them. The ceremonial laws had to do with worship, the appointed feasts, and proper ways to approach God. The moral laws were God's commands, like the Ten Commandments.

Most of the ceremonial and civil laws are no longer applicable for Christians because they were for another time in history. But the moral laws still stand. Do not lie or cheat or commit adultery and so on, and stipulations for who you can and should not have "relations" with.

But there's something important about why the ceremonial laws no longer apply; they were foreshadowing Jesus Christ. For example, the Jewish high holy day of Yom Kippur, the Day of Atonement, foreshadowed the atoning sacrifice of Jesus.[135] Jews and Christians are forever linked because of God's plan for redemption. It is our assurance he will never leave us or forsake us!

To God alone be glory!

The Holy Spirit

When they had prayed, the place in which they were gathered together was shaken, and they were all filled with the Holy Spirit and continued to speak the word of God with boldness.

ACTS 4:31 ESV

Many people draw similarities between "the Force," the energy that provided Jedis with their extraordinary abilities, and the Holy Spirit. It's true there appear to be similarities. For instance, much like the Force, "It's the Spirit that gives the Church its life and energy."[136] And, like the Force, the Spirit is personal; the Holy Spirit is our Advocate and helper. It's God's personal presence with us.[137]

But there are some profound differences. The Holy Spirit, as the third person of the Holy Trinity, is omnipotent. He is the power behind creation. He himself was not created but is eternal and the Holy Spirit provides direction to those who walk in faith.

Also, the Holy Spirit is not an unseen energy that humans control. However, it is a force to be reckoned with. He is more faithful, ever-present, and unstoppably powerful than any "Force" that man can comprehend.

So the next time someone says to you "May the force be with you," you can answer, "The Holy Spirit is with me always, and I pray that he will be with you as well."

To God alone be glory!

Tilling the Soul's Soil

*"Your Father knows what you need
before you ask him."*
MATTHEW 6:8 ESV

These were Jesus' words right before he taught his disciples the Lord's Prayer, the prayer that reaches up to God in the most basic and fundamental way. Praying is one of the greatest gifts God has given us to calm our hearts and to come into his presence. Many people have asked, "Well if God already knows what I need, why should I even pray?" That's because praying doesn't change God, it changes us.

God is our heavenly Father, whose desire is to give us all the love we need or want. He knows our needs and knows what's best for us. He also knows something vitally important: the real need underneath the desire we express. So "the question is not whether He [God] is ready to give but whether we are ready to receive."[138]

Prayer readies our hearts to receive. Just as the farmer tills the soil to receive seed, prayer tills the soil of our soul, readying it for God to make us into his garden.

To God alone be glory!

The One Who Sees

[Hagar] called the name of the Lord who spoke to her,
"You are a God of seeing," for she said,
"Truly here I have seen him who looks after me."

GENESIS 16:13 ESV

Hagar is one of the more tragic figures in the Old Testament. She was an unloved servant. She then became the pawn in her mistress Sarah's scheme to circumvent God's plan to give Abraham a son.

Hagar possessed virtually no power and few rights. In her misery, she ran away. But God met her in the wilderness and gave her hope by just letting her know that he saw her. And that's what God became to her, the "God of seeing." She could then withstand anything because she knew God saw it all. The one who is in control of the entire created order also saw one lowly woman's pain and anguish. That knowledge transformed Hagar, and it can transform us as well.

"How would you live, speak, and act differently if you remembered that the Lord God was always observing you?"[139] God has given us something that Hagar didn't have: Jesus. We are assured of his love because he sent his Son to die for our sins and to begin the restoration of the world that's been damaged by our sin. The one who sees is our greatest comfort.

To God alone be glory!

A Luxurious Love

Many are the sorrows of the wicked,
but steadfast love surrounds the one who trusts in the LORD.
PSALM 32:10 ESV

This verse is a gut check. It's a reminder to examine where we put our trust. Is it in God? Or are we trusting in God to give us the thing that we believe will truly save us?

Wickedness doesn't have to be a permanent state. Maybe we wish it could be because that would absolve us of seriously looking at our own actions. Wickedness can be a temporary moment. Even our legal system recognizes a moment of insanity for crimes committed by someone with no history of violent behavior. This sudden change in character tends to creep into our lives when the thing in which we put our ultimate hope is threatened or challenged.

When we are sorrowful over something we don't have or that has been taken away, it's time to do a reassessment of what's truly important. What are our ultimate hopes? What is it that without which life is unbearable? The solution is to put our hopes in the only thing that can save us: Jesus Christ. It's a wonderful thing to stand on the promises of Jesus so that we can truly sit and relax in the lap of a luxurious love.

To God alone be glory!

INTEGRITY FOR LOVE OF GOD

Whoever walks in integrity walks securely,
but he who makes his ways crooked will be found out.
PROVERBS 10:9 ESV

What is integrity? Is it only being honest about your sin? Or is it behaving in a godly way? There's a great scene from an old movie, *Please Don't Eat the Daisies*, in which the wife is angry because she suspects that her husband may be having an affair. Her husband is an intellectually gifted theater critic. So the wife concludes that simple men try to hide their indiscretions, but those "egg heads," the smart guys, tell you you're reacting irrationally when they admit their wrongdoing.

Make no mistake, the dictionary defines *integrity* as being moral and honest. Changing the meaning of a word in your mind doesn't make actions any less sinful in the eyes of God. But at the same time, being afraid of being found out should not be a reason to avoid indiscretions. For "if the only motivation for honesty is fear, it is inevitable that you will be dishonest in those situations where there is no fear or possibility of detection."[140]

The greatest motivation is to live to please the Lord. His love for us motivated him to die on a cross so that we would be brought into the arms of the Father. Whatever we do, we should do for the glory of God (see Colossians 3:23).

To God alone be glory!

JONAH AND GOD'S GREAT MERCY

The LORD appointed a great fish to swallow up Jonah.
And Jonah was in the belly of the fish three days and three nights.
JONAH 1:17 ESV

One of the most famous stories in the Old Testament is Jonah and the whale. For modern folks, the account of a man being swallowed whole by a "great fish" and remaining in its belly for three days and three nights seems improbable. However, historians know Jonah was a real person who prophesied under Jeroboam II, king of Israel. We also know that Jesus speaks of Jonah and relates the prophet's encounter in the stomach of the whale with his own impending death and resurrection.

It is in Jonah's fleeing from God that we can see ourselves reflected best. Jonah was a prophet who became angry when God wanted to show mercy to people Jonah thought deserved severe judgment. "At the very end he says, 'this is the reason I fled because I knew you were a merciful God and I hate that about you.'"[141]

God called Jonah to preach repentance to the Assyrians in Nineveh, the equivalent of a terrorist state. But Jonah fled from the task, not wanting his enemies to reap the benefit of God's mercy. This relates to us today since "we'd like to write entire groups of people off, those countries, those races or even that political party."[142] We want them to be judged not saved. The story of Jonah helps us understand that God has compassion for all of us and never sees anyone outside the possibility of redemption. We're called to do likewise.

To God alone be glory!

Feeding Your Foes

To the contrary, "if your enemy is hungry, feed him;
if he is thirsty, give him something to drink;
for by so doing you will heap burning coals on his head."
ROMANS 12:20 ESV

The apostle Paul is quoting verbatim here a passage from the book of Proverbs in the Old Testament. It is one of the many branches to the tree of forgiveness in the Bible. There's one difference between what Paul says and the verse in Proverbs. The Old Testament version ends with the words "and the Lord will reward you" (25:22). Paul leaves this phrase out. Is it because he forgot the rest of the verse? Likely not. He leaves it out because on this side of the cross, we have received our promised reward, redemption through Jesus Christ.

Forgiveness is a rather complex requirement that involves more than just saying, "I forgive." It also requires sacrifice, a move that blesses the person who's wronged you, which can be painful and costly and is why we should be even more grateful for Jesus dying on the cross.

If one person who wrongs us causes us a lot of pain and anguish, how much more pain has God endured through an eternity of wrongs committed by gazillions of beings made in his image? If God can give us food and drink when we sinful beings hunger and thirst, we can do likewise to those who've wronged us.

To God alone be glory!

Serenade Him

*I will sing of the steadfast love of the Lord, forever;
with my mouth I will make known your faithfulness to all generations.*

Psalm 89:1 esv

There's nothing like a wonderful love song. Singing is a way our heart expresses its deepest feelings. Music gives voice to what seems impossible to express with mere spoken words.

It's no wonder God tells us to sing to him. In fact, God has commanded us to sing to him. It's not because his ego needs pumping up or that he's filled with jealous envy. It's because singing to God benefits us.

In singing, we praise. And what we praise we will emulate. Praising God through song changes us into souls eager to please our maker. Lifting our voices to what Jesus has done for us burrows all that goodness down to our very bone and sinew. Yes, a good love song is a hymn to him.

To God alone be glory!

WALKING BY FAITH

We are always of good courage. We know that while we are at home in the body we are away from the Lord, for we walk by faith, not by sight.
2 CORINTHIANS 5:6–7 ESV

The world we live in is a constant assault of visual and audio stimulation, all clamoring for our attention. It's hard not to be drawn toward the many sights and sounds, all designed for our minds to ingest. But the apostle Paul helps us understand that there is another world, a world of the Spirit, that has greater authority over us; that is the world of faith, what we worship.

To walk by faith means "living all of one's life based on confident trust in God's promises for the future."[143] It's the confidence that says, "I do not know what the future holds, but I know who holds the future."

If God can take what seemed like the worst tragedy, Jesus brutally dying on a cross, and turn it into the salvation and redemption of the world, he can certainly turn any of our sorrows into joy. The future is in God's hands. It is his power, his mercy, his grace.

To God alone be glory!

Singing through Sorrow

My soul is weary with sorrow;
strengthen me according to your word.
PSALM 119:28 NIV

There are just some heartaches that only music can soothe, that only the great songs of the church can remedy. The voice is the most expressive instrument on earth, giving passion to the full scope of human emotions. It's no surprise that some of the greatest music of the church was written by people broken with grief, sorrow, or torment.

"Precious Lord, Take My Hand" was written by Thomas A. Dorsey, a gospel church music leader, after learning that his wife died in childbirth and the baby boy died a few hours later. "It Is Well with My Soul" was written by Horatio Spafford as he crossed the same spot over the Atlantic where his wife and four daughters' ship had sunk. Only his wife survived. And the words of "Amazing Grace," one of the greatest hymns of the church, come from the pen of John Newton, a once brutal slave trader, as he came to grips with a love that surpasses all understanding and the realization that he was not just forgiven but unconditionally loved.

Grief is entwined in life. But the prophets assure us, "The battle is the Lord's" (1 Samuel 17:47). And he has given us the victory. So sing his praises.

To God alone be glory!

The Fabric of Our Lives

In the beginning God created the heavens and the earth.
GENESIS 1:1 NIV

Back when they taught such things in school, one of the first things young women learned in sewing class is that all fabric has something called a *nap*. A nap is the grain of the material that flows in a certain direction. It can actually make the fabric appear to be a different shade, depending on if it's right side up or upside down. Velvets are a good example of fabric with a very visible nap. The nap requires the seamstress to cut pattern pieces in the same direction.

God has also created the fabric of this world with a nap; he has "created us, so there is a 'fabric' or 'grain' to the universe."[144] What this means is that there is a way that things work best. But we also know that our ancient ancestors spoiled our understanding of how things should work. Every day is a good day to reflect on how God sacrificed his only Son to bring us back into the fold of his perfect fabric.

To God alone be glory!

FITTED FOR GOD'S GLORY

We are God's handiwork,
created in Christ Jesus to do good works,
which God prepared in advance for us to do.
EPHESIANS 2:10 NIV

Sewing, like many creative ventures, can be very satisfying as you see a beautiful piece of fabric transformed into a wonderful garment that fits perfectly. But it takes time and effort to create the garment. It often takes more time or patience than the seamstress anticipated, and bolts of unused fabric start piling up.

The stored raw materials of potential garments sometimes seem like our own feeble efforts to be a better person, a more loving wife, a more diligent employee, all the raw materials of God's good gifts we all possess.

It's a reminder of the cost of receiving good gifts. "The price is that we must be changed."[145] We must allow ourselves to be taken off the shelf, cut into a pattern of God's choosing, fashioned according to his standard of beauty and rightness, not our own. But in the end, we will have a garment that fits us perfectly.

To God alone be glory!

Words to Live By

*Avoid godless chatter, because those who indulge in it
will become more and more ungodly.*

2 Timothy 2:16 niv

We all like to engage in some lighthearted banter. But this verse reminds us that even the most offhanded remark meant to add color and comedy to a gathering can have lasting and devastating effects.

The Bible warns us to always speak with the best of intentions, to build up those around us, to heal and not to hurt, to be a balm instead of a battering ram. Words always have a target, and they always land somewhere. Even words spoken alone and in the dark or only to ourselves become like tape recorders that reinforce beliefs.

If our words have such power, think about how much power Jesus' words have. He only spoke truth and words for the saving of souls, for the transforming of hearts and minds. His words are words to live by.

To God alone be glory!

Acts of Kindness

Whoever is generous to the poor lends to the LORD,
and he will repay him for his deed.

PROVERBS 19:17 ESV

A news story from several years ago told how a pizza shop manager drove three hours to bring a dying man his favorite pizza. The family had only asked that he send a nice card with words of comfort. Instead, after he closed the shop for the night, the manager drove during the wee hours of the morning to give the man something no one else could give him.[146]

In monetary costs, it was a pittance, nothing really. But to a man whose life was close to ending, it was a priceless offering. Sometimes all it takes for us to build up God's kingdom is to give something to someone only we can give. Maybe it's a phone call, an encouraging word, a hug, or even a favorite meal.

Jesus calls us to be the conduit through which his kingdom flourishes. Performing random acts of kindness is one small step in a vast landscape of healing in a wounded world.

To God alone be glory!

Exposing Our True Heart

Where your treasure is,
there your heart will be also.

MATTHEW 6:21 ESV

A woman had a fairly large sum of money stolen from her office. Her initial reaction was to feel violated and horribly wronged. Then in righteous anger, she quoted the words of Exodus, "Thou shalt not steal!" But then later she remembered the words of Jesus when he talked about forgiveness and what was truly in her heart. The money was relatively little in the scheme of her income. She was still able to pay her rent and buy food, clothing, and even frivolous things. Then she began to think that perhaps the person who took the money really needed it. She didn't know but realized the thief's reasons were between them and God.

What the woman realized in her moment of outrage was that what had truly been defining her came to the surface—she had let her wealth, her position, and even her supposed good nature all determine who she was. And it wasn't good.

Jesus wants us to let him define who we are. "His teachings remain paradoxes until our hearts are so purified that we see that our true good is beyond the goods that are obtainable by power, money, and intellectual endeavor."[147]

To God alone be glory!

Mighty to Heal and Save

*Great crowds came to him, bringing with them the lame,
the blind, the crippled, the mute, and many others,
and they put them at his feet, and he healed them.*

MATTHEW 15:30 ESV

A woman had surgery to relieve some scarring that occurred after a C-section. She had been in a lot of physical pain but never outwardly showed it. After the surgery, she felt so much better, and the pain was gone. She said she hadn't even realized how much pain she had been in until it was no longer there. Her doctor told her that chronic pain becomes hard to detect after a while. It becomes a new normal. She felt so much better afterward and didn't know how she had managed regular life routines with the pain.

That can be true of any of us. We don't always know the pain we are in. But God, the Great Physician, the Healer, knows not only of our pain but also how to take it away. He suffered greatly on a cross, taking the cosmic pain, so that we won't have to. He is mighty to save.

To God alone be glory!

God's Way Brings Freedom

I will run the course of Your commandments,
for You shall enlarge my heart.
PSALM 119:32

Restrictions and commands sometime feel limiting and without freedom. But the psalmist makes a direct connection between "commands" and freedom; he says God's law equals freedom.

A good example is marriage. The old conventional rules say we shouldn't have sex outside of marriage. Very few people follow that today, let's be honest. But when you look at the reasons behind the rule, it starts to make more sense.

We are made to form life-long relationships in marriage. Sex helps form that bond of life-long intimacy. However, by having sex outside of marriage, with perhaps several different partners, what we're doing is separating sex from love. It's like the weakening of heavy tape. It loses its stickiness after ripping it off and applying it again and again. It can no longer do what it was meant to do.

We can see now that the commands from God are meant for our well-being, "not to limit freedom." One of the best things we can do is "look for God's promises in every one of His commands."[148] His commands are not always easy. If that were so, Jesus would never have had to die on a cross to save us from our sins. But because of God's great love for us, we can always learn to love again according to his plans, not ours.

To God alone be glory!

Voting for God's Will

Submit yourselves to every ordinance of man for the Lord's sake, whether to the king as supreme, or to governors.
1 Peter 2:13–14

We don't serve emperors and princes in America. We elect our civic leaders. It's a duty as well as a privilege because in this world there are still communities and countries where voting your conscience means risking your life. We are called to be participants in the civil government. But as believers in the saving grace of Christ Jesus, we must also pay close attention to the Lord's teaching as we cast our vote.

The Bible is a wonderful treasure trove of loving directives for us and has something to say about all aspects of our lives, how we should and should not live. And if Christianity is true, objectively true, then it's true for all of humanity and is a blessing as well.

So with boldness, we can vote on what kind of community leaders we want, to create a collective home in line with God's good and perfect will.

To God alone be glory!

Growing the Kingdom of Heaven

Another parable He put forth to them, saying: "The kingdom of heaven is like a mustard seed, which a man took and sowed in his field"…Another parable He spoke to them: "The kingdom of heaven is like leaven, which a woman took and hid in three measures of meal till it was all leavened."

MATTHEW 13:31, 33

These two parables both describe the kingdom of heaven but in different ways. In one, Jesus says the kingdom is like a small seed that blossoms into a huge tree. The other parable involves the making of bread. The message of both is that the kingdom of heaven is a process. It's not something that we can purchase in a store or order online. We can't obtain it and then put it on a shelf to use when it suits us. The kingdom of heaven is the fundamental source and identity of who you are.

Within a seed is the entire DNA of the tree. In the yeast is the fullness of the bread's purpose. If there's no yeast, the bread is flat; it will not rise. If there's no seed, there is no tree. The mustard seed is extremely small, and only a small amount of yeast is required to make a large loaf. You never see the seed when the tree grows. You never see the yeast when bread is baked. You only see their effects. We are called to let the kingdom of heaven grow in us and let its effects transform the world.

To God alone be glory!

WISDOM'S WORTH

How much better to get wisdom than gold!
And to get understanding is to be chosen rather than silver.
PROVERBS 16:16

Recently a couple went on a road trip to Newport, Rhode Island, to see the summer mansions from the Gilded Age. It is an incredible display of wealth from the movers and shakers of the late nineteenth and early twentieth centuries. Despite having almost all the money in the world, many of the mansions' owners had tragic stories of loss and heartache. Their wealth did not protect them against depression, deception, or sudden death.[149]

Gilded Age is a phrase coined by Mark Twain as more of an insult. Gilding something in gold means laying a thin layer of gold over a common substance. Twain was saying that on the surface, there was lots of glitter and beauty, but underneath, the people and their lives were quite common, perhaps even possessing a poverty of the soul.

The greatest value we have is God's redeeming power through faith in Jesus Christ. Scripture tells us that although he had a simple birth in a manger surrounded by hay and animals, he was born to be the King of kings and Lord of lords. God in his wisdom reminds us that all that glitters is not gold, and what's golden doesn't always glitter.

To God alone be glory!

TREASURED VESSELS

We have this treasure in jars of clay to show
that this all-surpassing power is from God and not from us.
2 CORINTHIANS 4:7 NIV

The town of Megiddo in Israel is the ancient city in the book of Revelation known as the location of the final battle called Armageddon. Currently, there's an archeological dig taking place there. The dig, however, is also interesting for other reasons. There are thousands of shards of broken pottery everywhere.

Clay pots were used for every kind of household need, cooking, washing, eating. It was the cheapest and most widely available kind of vessel. But it was also fragile and easily broken. In fact, because of the Mosaic clean laws, unclean or impure clay vessels were broken on purpose so they would not be reused. No one would put anything of real value in a clay pot.

So it is all the more astounding that Paul calls us "jars of clay," showing our insignificance. Yet God has put treasures in us, his image, showing our greatness. Only Christianity makes sense of these "two realms, the natural and the divine."[150]

To God alone be glory!

Let God Take Charge

Let us then approach God's throne of grace with confidence, so that we may receive mercy and find grace to help us in our time of need.
HEBREWS 4:16 NIV

Grand pianos are heavy and pretty delicate at the same time. When you move them from one home to another, you must make sure a specialized company does the job. They'll know how to remove the legs, secure the lid, protect the wood from scratches, and ensure no damage to the delicate soundboard. Then they'll have to lift it. All the piano owner must do is get out of the way and let the pros do their job.

In so many ways, God is like those professional piano movers. He knows exactly what to do and how to do it. He knows how to bind up our wounds and protect our vulnerable parts. And what's more, he has already done the heavy lifting. He sent his Son to die on the cross, to open heaven's gates for us, a portal to our eternal home.

The only thing left for us to do is get out of the way and let God do his work. Let the professional move your life and fight your battles.

To God alone be glory!

Praising Changes Us

He predestined us for adoption to himself as sons through Jesus Christ…
to the praise of his glorious grace, with which he has blessed us in the Beloved.
EPHESIANS 1:5–6 ESV

Worshiping God is not always a matter of emotion. Sometimes we're in a bad mood and find it hard to lift our voices to him. But Reverend David Bisgrove said something really important that will help. Remember that actions will change our feelings. By praising God no matter our mood, we will be lifted up, "You feel as you worship, not worship as you feel."[151]

Second, when we worship, we are not performing a religious ritual. We are communing with God. Doctrine and theology are ways to understand our faith, but the core is the communion with Christ.

Just like the psalmist asks, so, too, can we ask, "Give me an undivided heart, that I may fear your name" (Psalm 86:11 NIV). And *fear* here doesn't mean to be afraid of. It means to be in awe of, to bow down to. To praise God, to worship him, brings us closer to the one who knows and loves us best.

To God alone be glory!

No Fear of This "Evil Age"

*The Lord Jesus Christ…gave himself for our sins
to deliver us from the present evil age.*
GALATIANS 1:3–4 ESV

If you have more than one cat, you know cats get into little fights that can escalate into full blown brawls. It's quizzical. Why should they fight when they are all well-fed, enormously loved, and totally safe from harm? However, people behave in much the same way even though they're well-fed, loved, and safe from harm, thanks to God's good gifts.

The apostle's letter here makes sense of cats' behavior as well as ours. It's a good news and bad news situation. The good news is Jesus Christ died for our sins. He has defeated death and Satan. The bad news is that we still live in the overlap of the ages where Satan is still working to harm us and draw us away from the living God. That is why the apostle Paul says we are living in an "evil age." "This 'evil one' is called 'the god of this world,' and his main aim is to blind people to truth."[152]

Satan, however, is in the death throes of a defeated enemy. He's lost the battle, but he's still dangerous, like a wounded bear. God's good news, the gospel, assures us that he has "not abandoned this sin-wracked world" and says, "I am still richly present."[153]

To God alone be glory!

Who Is Jesus to You?

He said to them, "But who do you say that I am?"
Simon Peter replied, "You are the Christ, the Son of the living God."
MATTHEW 16:15–16 ESV

All of us at some point in our life are faced with the question of Jesus. In this Scripture above, Jesus is asking his disciples, but he could well be asking it of us today and throughout history: "Who do *you* say that I am?"

We must be sure of how we answer because our whole life hinges on who we think this Jesus is. For Peter it was clear. And on that sure foundation of knowing who Jesus is, Christ built his church, of which all believers are part. Jesus makes claims that no other religious leader throughout history made. He claimed to be God. Buddha never made such claims; neither did Mohammed.

Jesus also said that "all authority in heaven and on earth has been given to me" (Matthew 28:18 NIV). That's a pretty bold statement. That's why C. S. Lewis wrote famously that Jesus was either a liar, a lunatic, or Lord. To quote Lewis directly: "You can shut him up for a fool, you can spit at him and kill him as a demon or you can fall at his feet and call him Lord and God, but let us not come with any patronizing nonsense about his being a great human teacher. He has not left that open to us. He did not intend to."[154] Who do *you* say that Jesus is?

To God alone be glory!

LIGHT OF THE WORLD

"Because of the tender mercy of our God, whereby the sunrise shall visit us from on high to give light to those who sit in darkness and in the shadow of death, to guide our feet into the way of peace."
LUKE 1:78–79 ESV

The star of Bethlehem is mentioned only in Matthew's gospel. However, Luke has given us his own version of it: light dawning like a sunrise. Where the star in Matthew's version that led the magi to the tiny baby Jesus in a manger is concretely a physical presence, Luke has given us a rendering that expands it into the metaphysical realm and beyond.

This Light of the World is so bright and radiant that it rids the world not only of physical darkness but also darkness of spirit, of pain, of fear, of anxiety. This Light is a kind of glow like no other, penetrating down to our very bone and sinew and synapses in our brains. This is a Light that scientists cannot exam in a laboratory or see with a telescope. It's a Light we can begin to get glimpses of by opening our hearts to its presence.

It is by this Light that we see all other lights more clearly, "for with you is the fountain of life; in your light do we see light" (Psalm 36:9 ESV). Jesus, the Light of the World.

To God alone be glory!

Looking Up to the Lord

Praise be to the LORD, the God of Israel, from everlasting to everlasting.
Let all the people say, "Amen!"
PSALM 106:48 NIV

If you visit New York City, the best way to experience it is by walking. The city is so densely packed with buildings, shops, and stores jammed close together in a grid-like pattern that you could travel twenty blocks and still miss a great deal.

Case in point: A tourist walking down 5th Avenue passed right by the Empire State Building not even realizing it was the iconic building of the city's skyline where King Kong fought off airplanes. From a skyline view, the ESB lifts majestically into the air. But from street level, it's easy to miss because the buildings are all huddled together. But by looking up, you can clearly see its soaring power and greatness.

Sometimes we're so immersed in "godly" affairs that we can miss the greatness of God. We go to church and Bible study, but then all of that can become routine, and we forget that Jesus is King. If we look up, away from ourselves, we can see fully his greatness. Sometimes all that we need to do is to gaze upon that greatness…and give him praise.

To God alone be glory!

The Power of God's Love

It is by grace you have been saved, through faith—
and this is not from yourselves, it is the gift of God.

EPHESIANS 2:8 NIV

We constantly need to be reminded of two things about God: that God is God and we are not and that God is love. Although we are made in God's image, how we love is a reflection, not the source. Sometimes that reflection gets distorted by what we do but not by God. The power of God's love is that no matter what we do, his love is still available to us. It doesn't always feel that way at times, but that's only because we tend to base our identities on how we feel and not on what God has done for us through Jesus Christ.

The apostle Peter was a complicated fellow but, in many ways, quite simple. He was just like us. He loved Jesus but mistakenly put his hope in how he felt. "Peter was basing his self-worth on his love for Jesus instead of Jesus' love for him."[155]

If we base our identities on our actions and how much we care for God, we begin to form God in our image, and not only does this distort our reflection, but we may also lose sight of God altogether. Jesus was patient with Peter and gently corrected his vision. He can do the same with us if we let his love guide us.

To God alone be glory!

Our True Home

Our citizenship is in heaven. And we eagerly await a Savior from there, the Lord Jesus Christ, who, by the power that enables him to bring everything under his control, will transform our lowly bodies so that they will be like his glorious body.

PHILIPPIANS 3:20–21 NIV

There's a lot of political talk about borders and boundaries and who has the right to enter the country and how. While the Bible holds up civic leaders and laws as something we must respect and obey, it knows our real home is somewhere else. Our heavenly home is where we came from, and it is what we really long for. All other earthly dwellings are mere shadows, weak hints of our ultimate home.

We live now in the overlap of the ages where God is making all things new through the transforming love, the amazing grace and mercy of Jesus Christ. Our ultimate citizenship is with him in the heavenly realms. It's our native land, whose only boundaries are belief and faith in his saving grace.

The only passport we need is prayer, the required visa is a vision of his resurrection, and the golden ticket is the opening of our hearts to his transforming love. All are welcome. Bow down and worship the living God.

To God alone be glory!

Lifted to the Maker of Hills

I will lift up my eyes to the hills—from whence comes my help?
My help comes from the LORD, who made heaven and earth.
PSALM 121:1-2

For those who are big fans of the movie *The Sound of Music*, you'll recognize the first part of this Bible verse. It is from the climactic moment when the Mother Abbess gives Maria her final words of comfort and hope as they desperately flee Nazi soldiers. She says, quoting the New King James Version, "Remember Maria, 'I will lift up mine eyes unto the hills, from whence cometh my help.'"[156]

It does sound as if the hills are her hope. But the actual verse ends in a question mark. Maria, as a former nun-to-be, would know this. Movie watchers may not. Maria would know that her help comes from God the Creator, not creation. As Eugene Peterson writes of this psalm of ascent: "It rejects a worship of nature, a religion of stars and flowers, a religion that makes the best of what it finds on the hills; instead it looks to the Lord who made heaven and earth."[157]

Sometimes we look to created things as our ultimate salvation, even beautiful mountains and fields. For modern folk, we tend to look toward a job, a relationship, a new pair of shoes, or a fancy car. These are all wonderful things that we should definitely be thankful for. But we must always look past the gift and offer our ultimate worship to the gift giver.

To God alone be glory!

The Knowledge in God

Both of the Father and of Christ,
in whom are hidden all the treasures of wisdom and knowledge.
Colossians 2:2–3

We can acquire knowledge through education and diligent study; it is primarily information. But we gain wisdom through life lessons. We find wisdom through experiences. For us, as Timothy Keller said, "Wisdom… is knowing what to do in the many situations where the moral rules don't apply."[158]

Think of the vast amount of knowledge that is in the world, in all the disciplines and academic pursuits known by humanity down through the ages. All the philosophers, the great thinkers, from architecture to zoology, mathematics to music. Combine all the knowledge and wisdom of the world, and it still cannot surpass that of Christ, in whom all these treasures are hidden.

We bow down before him because first, he is the risen Savior. And second, because he is all wise and all knowing. The knowledge and wisdom of Jesus Christ is nothing else but amazing.

To God alone be glory!

Living Out the Gospel

The fear of the LORD is the beginning of wisdom;
a good understanding have all those who do His commandments.
His praise endures forever.

PSALM 111:10

Catholic bishops in the United States meet twice a year for their general assembly. The gatherings are usually just housekeeping and administrative topics that would bore to tears the general public. But one year, not too long ago, it was anything but business as usual. They were trying to take decisive action on the abuse crisis assaulting the church. This is Satan's most demonic attack on the body of Christ.

While the top priority is caring for the victims of abuse, another pressing issue is getting at the root cause. How could people responsible for shepherding flocks of the faithful embody the evil they preach against? Many devout clergy and laypeople recognize it quite plainly as a failure to live out the gospel. Once we take our eyes off Jesus, his beauty, mercy, and justice, our baser natures take over.

God understands our sinful natures. And he also knows our foundational need for love, our need to be loved and to give love. Making God, through Jesus Christ, our first love orders all our other loves. To "fear" the Lord is to be in awe of him. It is the beginning of wisdom. That is what's required for living out the gospel.

To God alone be glory!

Jesus, the Perfect Word

The law of the LORD is perfect, refreshing the soul.
The statutes of the LORD are trustworthy, making wise the simple.
PSALM 19:7 NIV

If we are not tethered to the Bible, something else will be our go-to reason for everything. It's God's Word that compelled the founding fathers to frame the Declaration of Independence to justify our freedoms and rights. They knew that our founding documents could only work if people ultimately lived under God's laws first. So the Bible is the foundation of the United States Constitution too.

Think about Jesus' words of turning the other cheek (see Matthew 5:39). They must be the operating principle, tacitly present and undergirding the First Amendment of freedom of speech. Without that, hate speech becomes anything you say it is, measured only by the litmus test of your feelings.

We are not perfect beings. But God's Word makes it possible for us to at least know what perfection looks like. It is God's Word made flesh. It is Jesus, the perfecter of our faith (see Hebrews 12:1–3).

To God alone be glory!

℞EALITY ℭHECK

Jesus said to those Jews who believed Him,
"If you abide in My word, you are My disciples indeed.
And you shall know the truth, and the truth shall make you free."

JOHN 8:31–32

In a woman's office there is a full-length mirror, which she calls "the thin mirror." Its reflection makes anyone look about ten to fifteen pounds lighter. It's quite flattering! The problem is it doesn't show the true impression. When she tried on some winter clothes that she hadn't worn in a while, the truth of the few extra pounds she had gained was evident. The distorted mirror allowed her to avoid the truth about her overeating and consuming the wrong things. The clothes, however, forced her to face reality.

That is what it's like to know God. We are made in his image. But sometimes we distort the image to make ourselves look better than we really are. We all like to believe we're a good person who may slip up once in a while on minor things, but when we read God's Word and look at the beauty of Jesus, then we will see clearly the truth of who and what we are meant to be. The truth doesn't have to hurt. It makes us free to live life to its fullest.

To God alone be glory!

To Be Thankful

In everything give thanks;
for this is the will of God in Christ Jesus for you.
1 THESSALONIANS 5:18

Being thankful is not just something you do; it's a way of being. And it's a lot more difficult than it sounds. This time of year, we all get those colorful catalogues of beautiful decorations for the home or gifts of every kind to buy, and we may enjoy leafing through them and daydreaming about which items we would like to have. Do you ever wonder if God sees that as being ungrateful for what he has already given us?

Here's an exercise. Before opening those catalogues, say to the Lord, *I want to thank you, Lord, for my home, for family, for friends.* Thank him for every wonderful thing in your life. For the beauty of music, of a cozy evening with a good book. *Lord, there's so much to thank you for that it's almost overwhelming.*

Looking at the good things God has given us is like brightness dispelling the dark clouds. A life of thankfulness is a life of pure joy. Most of all, thank him for Jesus Christ. Thank him for loving us so much that he was willing to die to save us all.

To God alone be glory!

The Good of Pain

We know that all things work together for good to those who love God,
to those who are the called according to His purpose.

ROMANS 8:28

Does this verse apply to toothaches? It's a valid question. What good can come from a toothache? Sometimes we forget that even in small doses of personal pain, God is with us if we call on him. *Jesus, be with me and help me make it through this struggle.* Pills mask the pain of a toothache but don't take away the reason for it.

Each of us has a unique testimony based on our own path in life. But in our human struggles, we are forever connected to the community of God's creation. Pain, no matter how small or great or whether it's physical or spiritual, binds us together, makes us one. It also helps us understand and sympathize with others who experience the same things, even toothaches.

We have confidence when we turn to Jesus because we know he has experienced pain and suffering. He understands our pain. He's there to help us in our trials.

To God alone be glory!

The Testing of Faith

What good is it, my brothers, if someone says he has faith but does not have works? Can that faith save him?...So also faith by itself, if it does not have works, is dead.

JAMES 2:14, 17 ESV

The Willis Tower in Chicago is one of the tallest buildings in the Western Hemisphere. It stands 1,450 feet high and 110 stories above the ground. On the 103rd story is the Skydeck ledge, a completely glass enclosed structure, including a glass floor.

Stepping out onto the glass, visitors experience a kind of floating in the air. It can also be scary. While intellectually visitors know the glass won't break, there's still a bit of skepticism about its soundness. The bottom line, though, is that the only proof that the glass can hold you is stepping out onto it, putting your full weight on it. Some people refuse to trust, giving in to their fears.

In the same way, God wants us to trust him, to put our faith in his ability to hold us up through uncertain times. Life is full of glass floors, where we must step out in faith, trusting that a job will come, a bill will get paid, a marriage can be repaired. It is trusting that regardless of how uncertain or unstable a situation appears, there's a great God who will hold us up. "Faith is the substance of things hoped for, the evidence of things not seen" (Hebrews 11:1 KJV).

To God alone be glory!

USING YOUR GIFTS

*As each one has received a gift, minister it to one another,
as good stewards of the manifold grace of God.*

1 PETER 4:10

In our everyday lives, some of us are bosses, and some of us *have* bosses. But regardless, God reminds us that we are all servants living under authority. Even the wealthiest among us are concerned about stockholders and customers. But we are all servants of the living God and stewards of the gifts he has given us. Our talents are not for the purpose of showing off and glorifying ourselves. They are a means of worshiping the Creator.

Jesus is our most excellent model. Jesus never used his abilities to exert raw displays of power—no leaping tall buildings at a single bound, no destroying enemies with a laser beam. Instead, he used his powers to heal the sick, to give the blind sight, to make the lame walk. He used his power to serve and not be served.

As we prepare to enter the Advent season, let us be thankful for our gifts, whatever they may be, and use them to help bring hope and healing to a hurting world.

To God alone be glory!

FAITH IN THE FUTURE

You see that faith was active along with his [Isaac's] works,
and faith was completed by his works.

JAMES 2:22 ESV

Stepping out in faith is like opening door number three on a game show. Except with God, it's always the winning door. If I believe that God will supply all my needs according to his riches in glory as the Scriptures say (see Philippians 4: 19), how do I move out into the world believing that? How do my countenance and attitude change?

It's like Christmas Eve. There's excitement knowing there will be presents under the tree. Faith in that changes how you anticipate the next day. It's as if you already have it. We can have the same Christmas faith every day, believing that we have "evidence" of what we do not see or presently have in our lives (see Hebrews 11:1), a new job, a new house, a relationship mended, or a future spouse.

Faith is only completed by how we act. It means not worrying, seeing the glass half full. Jesus was able to endure the cross for the joy that was to come (see Hebrews 12:2). A joy that would give us all eternal peace. Have faith in the wonders that God has prepared for you.

To God alone be glory!

God with Us

The Lord Himself will give you a sign:
Behold, the virgin shall conceive and bear a Son,
and shall call His name Immanuel.

ISAIAH 7:14

If there's one thing this verse from the prophet Isaiah helps us understand, it is that God is in the business of transforming lives. All lives. Isaiah foretells of a lowly Jewish peasant girl, whose womb will hold the Son of the living God. From the moment of conception by the Holy Spirit, it will be this young woman's body that protects, nurtures, and sustains the life of a baby that will save humanity.

Immanuel, meaning "God with us," is not just a wonderful Christmas story. It's proof of God's love for us and evidence that he will never abandon us. The Creator of the universe has put himself in our world in order to transform us and it.

As Bible scholar N. T. Wright put it, "How can you live with the terrifying thought that the hurricane has become human, that the fire has become flesh, that life itself came to life and walked in our midst?"[159] Know this: there is nothing, no problem, no hurdle, no impossible situation that is too difficult for God. Welcome, Advent season.

To God alone be glory!

The Quiet Battle

Yet I will rejoice in the Lord,
I will joy in the God of my salvation.
HABAKKUK 3:18

The devil's greatest fear is that you will endure hardship and still be faithful to God, still pray, still worship, still do God's will. That word *yet* in the Scripture verse above holds a mountain of faithful possibilities. It is so small but sends the devil quaking.

C. S. Lewis, in his book *The Screwtape Letters*, imagines the voice of Lucifer himself (Screwtape) as he cringes at the fight that is ahead when God's faithful endure. He knows why God, whom he calls the Enemy, allows them to sometimes suffer. Here's a sample: "Our [the devil's] cause is never more in danger than when a human, no longer desiring, but still intending, to do our Enemy's [God's] will, looks round upon a universe from which every trace of Him seems to have vanished, and asks why he has been forsaken, and still obeys."[160] If we stumble, God is there to catch us. We may have a scraped knee, but it will heal, and we will learn to walk and run in the process.

Jesus sweated blood on his path to the cross. He bore all our stumbles, our sins, so that God could continue to pick us up and set us on our way again. He is ever faithful, always present. Be assured of that.

To God alone be glory!

NEVER FORGOTTEN

In peace I will lie down and sleep,
for you alone, LORD, make me dwell in safety.
PSALM 4:8 NIV

A journalist I interviewed divulged that in his job, one of the most feared email subject lines from the boss is: "Did you see this?" He said it always managed to roil the stomach because it invariably meant he missed something important or something huge happened while he was sleeping or distracted with other activities. Either way, he knew that such an email was going to upset the normal course of the day.

We like to think of the peace that Jesus is offering as a kind of ethereal, other worldly rest that has no bearing on the stress of our daily life. But we would be wrong to think that way. We have to get out of the mode of believing that God doesn't care about the details of our daily grind. He does care. If it's a concern to you, it's a concern to God.

When those kinds of emails come or any kind that may be upsetting to you, learn to say, *Jesus, help me. I trust that you will guide me through whatever it is that's ahead.* That is the peace he gives. We are assured that we are never alone and never forgotten.

To God alone be glory!

A Prophetic Headline

"You, Bethlehem Ephrathah,
though you are little among the thousands of Judah,
yet out of you shall come forth to Me the One to be Ruler in Israel,
whose goings forth are from of old, from everlasting."
MICAH 5:2

In journalism, it's crucial to answer the all-important five *W*s in the first paragraph of a story: Who, what, when, where, and why? The reader understands the whole piece with those few facts. Though written centuries before Jesus' birth, Micah gives us four out of the five *W*s in this verse. It's one reason this verse from the Old Testament can be considered the single most important prophetic statement concerning the coming Messiah.

Who? A divine being that is outside of time and space.

What? Micah tells us that this little town, although small, is destined for greatness.

Where? There's no doubt this is the Bethlehem that is a few miles southwest of Jerusalem. It's the Bethlehem of the tribe of Judah and not the one of Zebulun.

Why? The answer is in the name of the town. *Bethlehem* means "the House of Bread." It would be the birthplace of the Bread of Life. And *Ephrathah* means "fruitful." The kingdom will have no end.

The only thing missing from Micah's headline is "When?" But we can answer that. Two thousand years ago.

Today this once-tiny country town is filled with conflict between Palestinians and Israelis, with Christians often caught in the middle. But pilgrims can still visit, and it's worth the effort to know that you've walked the spot of earth where Jesus, the Light of the World, was born.

To God alone be glory!

PREPARE FOR THE LIGHT

The people who walked in darkness have seen a great light;
those who dwelt in the land of the shadow of death,
upon them a light has shined.

ISAIAH 9:2

Darkness not only brings visual blindness, but it can also be a form of intellectual and spiritual blindness. A middle-aged woman expressed how when she was in her early twenties, she thought often about God but would not read his Word or seek his counsel. She admitted being blinded by her wish to create God in her own image. She wanted a God she could control. She was living in darkness and didn't even know it. That is the insidiousness of darkness: it can mean not knowing what you don't know.

In the verse above, the great prophet Isaiah is saying that all of humanity was in that kind of darkness. It was as if they were living in perpetual nighttime. Darkness was all around, so much so that light was a barely imagined state and, of course, never realized.

Now as Advent begins, we can relive that dawning of not just a new day but also of a new epoch. The moment Light came into the world. A new relationship with everyone and the entirety of creation.

To God alone be glory!

Payment in Fullness

"I will forgive their iniquity,
and their sin I will remember no more."
JEREMIAH 31:34

The holiday season can be a strain on finances, but it doesn't have to be if we remember what the birth of Jesus brings to us. Imagine having racked up credit card debts of thousands and thousands of dollars, more than you could pay off in a lifetime because of accruing interest. Now imagine that a friend of yours who just won the lottery comes to you and says, "I will not only pay off all your credit cards, but I will also give you an income that will last the rest of your life so that you never have to worry about debt again."

Just imagine the elation you would feel. You'd be forever grateful to that friend, wouldn't you? Now, thank Jesus Christ because that is exactly what he has done for us. He paid off a debt we couldn't possibly absolve in several lifetimes while giving us a new life free of debt. This is what the birth of Jesus means, receiving the greatest gift ever imagined.

To God alone be glory!

He Calms the Storms

[Jesus] arose and rebuked the wind, and said to the sea,
"Peace, be still!" And the wind ceased and there was a great calm.
MARK 4:39

Meteorologists know how to predict storms. Scientists have learned to measure the natural signs from barometer readings, air pressure, and doppler radar to create warning systems for daily climate conditions. Those tools help us know whether to bring an umbrella or prepare for catastrophic occurrences like hurricanes and tornados.

But there are very few early warning devices for the storms of life. Lost jobs, deaths, broken relationships. These are the storms we encounter that are part of the human condition from which none of us can escape.

Be assured that God's Word tells us that Jesus calms the storms by saying simply, "Be still!" Because he calmed the wind and the waves, we can have faith that he can calm the storms of our lives as well.

To God alone be glory!

GRACE SO WONDERFUL

*By grace you have been saved through faith, and that not of yourselves;
it is the gift of God, not of works, lest anyone should boast.*

EPHESIANS 2:8–9

There are very good reasons why we cannot be our own lord and savior. Perhaps the biggest reason is that God in his wisdom didn't make the world that way. There are tell-tale signs of why we aren't good at being God. Most of us, if not all of us, don't have the ability to administer grace. Yes, grace.

We want to judge and not be judged, to demand repentance and forgiveness from others but never imagine that we would need to do the same for anything we've done or words we've spoken. It is not until we are confronted with our own sins that grace and mercy become treasures, and our repentance flows as streams of tears. The amazing grace we feel is overwhelming.

It is then that we realize how wonderful it is *not* to be God. We instead have the joy of worshiping God, praising him for writing himself into our story, becoming flesh. This Advent season, open your heart to his amazing grace.

To God alone be glory!

DIVINE LOVE

He who does not love does not know God,
for God is love.

1 JOHN 4:8

What does it mean to love God? How does it play out in our day-to-day life? It means that all earthly loves should benefit from our loving and serving God. It means knowing how to love our husbands and wives as we should in a covenantal marriage. It means loving parents honorably, loving the stranger who also is made in God's image, respecting the coworker, and protecting the children.

Earthly loves are opportunities to reflect the fundamental love we're hungering for. For it takes all those relationships to express the love we have for God. "By loving Him more than them we shall love them more than we now do."[161]

Love is the "Divine energy" binding us all together. God loves us not because we deserve it but because he is love.[162] To strip himself of his majesty, to be born poor and in a lowly barn, to become weak and vulnerable so that we could become strong and eternally secure…that is love.

To God alone be glory!

MUSCLING FAITH

Beloved, do not think it strange concerning the fiery trial which is to try you, as though some strange thing happened to you; but rejoice to the extent that you partake of Christ's sufferings, that when His glory is revealed, you may also be glad with exceeding joy.

1 PETER 4:12-13

Muscles verses magic. We know the difference. It takes muscle to move a couch or lift a heavy sack of groceries. Magic is an illusion, meant to amaze and visually elude. Muscle strength can be a spiritual condition as well. Just like the physical version, it has to be tested with a counterweight in order to be strengthened. There is no magic version of faith for us.

How do you have great faith? Difficult times will increase your ability to trust in God's ability to bring you through. How do you get patience? Certainly not by demanding it but by being confronted with trying times or people. A child having a meltdown can try the patience of a saint.

The bottom line, "The true test of a person's strength or mettle is adversity; almost everyone can survive the good times."[163] We take for granted Jesus enduring the cross, being beaten, his body nailed to the wood. But what faith and patience it must have taken! "For the joy that was set before Him" (Hebrews 12:2), of saving us, it was worth it.

To God alone be glory!

Mary Was Tuned in to God

*Now in the sixth month the angel Gabriel was sent by God to a city of
Galilee named Nazareth, to a virgin betrothed to a man whose name was
Joseph, of the house of David. The virgin's name was Mary. And having
come in, the angel said to her, "Rejoice, highly favored one, the Lord is with
you; blessed are you among women!"*

LUKE 1:26–28

Today's Information Age began with the discovery of the radio wave.
Radio waves travel at the speed of light. When they arrive at a receiver
antenna, it makes electrons vibrate inside it, producing an electrical
current that recreates the original signal. The transmitter and receiver are
very often similar in design.[164] We understand it in the tech world, but
ancients understood that same concept in the spiritual realm.

For example, how was Mary able to discern that an Angel of the
Lord was speaking to her? How would God be sure that this humble but
devout peasant girl would recognize that it was a servant of the living God
who approached her and not some demon? It's because Mary was tuned in
to God's frequency all her life, studying his Word, obeying his laws.

In Nazareth, the Basilica of the Annunciation commemorates this
moment when Mary receives the visit from the angel Gabriel. On a long
wall of the church are mosaics of the Madonna and Child from scores of
nations. Black ones, white ones, Asian ones, African, Native American,
Spanish, German…all in their native dress honoring Mary, the mother of
Jesus. Although Mary was a young, Jewish girl, all cultures claim her, love
her, and adore her as the blessed virgin, the mother of God.

To God alone be glory!

A Season of Transformation

The angel said to her, "Do not be afraid, Mary, for you have found favor with God. And behold, you will conceive in your womb and bring forth a Son, and shall call His name JESUS. He will be great, and will be called the Son of the Highest; and the Lord God will give Him the throne of His father David… For with God nothing will be impossible."

LUKE 1:30–32, 37

The miracle of this moment is, well, momentous. And yet the words explaining it are very simple and almost matter of fact. It reads almost like a very dry report or press release, with only the salient information present. Later there will be choirs of angels and trumpets. But now, it's "just the facts, ma'am."

While all the four Gospels recount Jesus' ministry, crucifixion, and resurrection. Only two Gospels, Matthew and Luke, give us glimpses of the birth narrative. Only in the Gospel of Luke do we get Mary's point of view and her interaction with her older cousin Elizabeth, who, although past the age of childbearing, was pregnant and would give birth to John the Baptist. The key phrase here is that, with God, all things are possible. And because the angel Gabriel says it in such a business-like manner, he's not asking for emotion here; he's not creating tension by speculating if God will do what he promised. He's making a statement. It will be.

This Advent season, we are asked to accept that if God can create this miracle of making himself into a tiny, vulnerable baby, then all things are possible. This season is about transformation.

To God alone be glory!

The Hope in New Birth

For unto us a Child is born, unto us a Son is given; and the government
will be upon His shoulder. And His name will be called Wonderful,
Counselor, Mighty God, Everlasting Father, Prince of Peace.

ISAIAH 9:6

There is so much promise when a child is born. Every time a new life is conceived, there is joy at the potential that this brand new being holds, a plethora of amazing future possibilities.

But even if a child is conceived in less than perfect conditions, there's still the promise of the unpredictable. A successful man talked easily about how he was conceived in rape. It's one of the most horrible of injustices, a violation of a person's body. And yet that man grew to be a minister, a journalist, and a talented singer. God turned what was horrific into something wonderful.

The Virgin Mary, a betrothed but unwed woman, could look to Isaiah's prophetic words for comfort even when the culture around her was less than believing of the divine nature of the child she carried. And we, too, can look to those same words to be assured that all lives matter and hold within them the possibility of making the world a better place.

To God alone be glory!

SHOUTING OUR BLESSINGS!

Come and hear, all you who fear God,
and I will declare what He has done for my soul.

PSALM 66:16

There are two terms in Christian doctrine that are key to understanding who we are in Christ Jesus: justification and sanctification. Sometimes the distinction is hard to grasp, "but they are different. One is an instantaneous declaration: not guilty. The other is an ongoing transformation."[165]

When we accept Christ as our Lord and Savior, God, the great judge, lets Jesus bear the wrath of our sins, and they are instantly taken away. But the change in us happens over time. We're still going to be tempted and tried. We're still going to make mistakes. But over time, there's a change. And God is walking along with us on the journey.

Just think and ponder the amazing things God has done for you, how he has saved you, loved you, protected you. When we really, truly, count our blessings, we must shout with our whole being, "Come and hear! Let me tell you what he has done for me!"

To God alone be glory!

Mary Said Yes

Mary said, "Behold the maidservant of the Lord!
Let it be to me according to your word."
And the angel departed from her.
LUKE 1:38

Through her fear, not knowing what would happen, Mary trusted God. She didn't say to the angel Gabriel, "Well, show me your credentials, and I'll get back to you in a few days." She also didn't say, "Well, what do I get out of it?" She did not think of earthly praise or platitudes. She simply said, *yes*.

Modern people today aren't the only skeptics. There were plenty in Mary's day as well. For her to say *yes* took a strength and faith few of us possess. We also have opportunities to answer God's call to obedience. When God asks us to "feed the hungry," we can answer, "Yes." When he says, "Forgive your brother," we can answer, "Yes." And when God says, "Trust in me," we can say again, "Yes."

In small and large ways, we can echo Mary's words, "Let it be to me according to your word." During the Advent season, we can strive to bring peace on earth by doing something that is oh so simple if we would follow Mary's example and say, "Here I am, the servant of the Lord."

To God alone be glory!

WORD BECOMES FLESH

It happened, when Elizabeth heard the greeting of Mary, that the babe leaped in her womb; and Elizabeth was filled with the Holy Spirit. Then she spoke out with a loud voice and said, "Blessed are you among women, and blessed is the fruit of your womb!"

LUKE 1:41–42

Today's verses speak of the joy and excitement that Elizabeth and Mary shared over the future birth, life, and glory of Jesus, and they pair so naturally and powerfully with John 1:14: "The Word became flesh and dwelt among us" (ESV). These verses come from two different Gospels and, in a sense, speak of Jesus at two different stages of his humanity. And yet they so clearly belong together.

When the apostle John writes of the Word becoming flesh, we tend to see Jesus as an adult in his ministry. But this verse testifies to the fact that Jesus' "flesh" began life at the moment of conception—conception by the Holy Spirit.

The Word, the Logos, the totality of existence itself took on human form in the same way we all did—as an embryo growing inside his mother's womb. When Elizabeth encountered her pregnant cousin Mary for the first time, she was filled with the knowledge of Jesus' glory because the Holy Spirit revealed it to her. There's something incredible at work here. Although John's Gospel doesn't explicitly give us a birth narrative, it is every bit implied and bears repeating: "The Word became flesh."

To God alone be glory!

MAGNIFY THE LORD

*Mary said: "My soul magnifies the Lord,
and my spirit has rejoiced in God my Savior."*
LUKE 1:46–47

Mary is a wonderful and holy vessel. And yet she was just like all pregnant women. The Gospels never tell us if she had any of the normal challenges pregnant women encounter. Did she have morning sickness or food cravings? Did she ever have doubts about what kind of life she carried inside her. Was she afraid of the social, legal, and religious backlash of being "in the family way" before being officially wed? We will never know. Luke's Gospel doesn't say. The Gospel narratives only relate to us the most important and crucial information that will help lead us to transformed lives.

Mary's response during these months of pregnancy gives us an image of what it means to trust in God Almighty. In fact, she went beyond trust. While all the conditions surrounding her pregnancy went against the grain of her cultural norms, the worship of God took such precedence in her heart, soul, and mind, that all other earthly concerns became insignificant.

I am poor: My soul magnifies the Lord.

I am alone in the world: My soul magnifies the Lord.

I am frightened: My soul magnifies the Lord.

I fear the future: My soul magnifies the Lord, and my spirit rejoices in God my Savior.

We are called to order our life in exactly the same way.

To God alone be glory!

GOD IS IN CHARGE

It came to pass in those days that a decree went out from Caesar Augustus that all the world should be registered.

LUKE 2:1

Have you ever noticed how man's political moves tend to fall right into God's plan? Although Jesus grew up in Nazareth and was known as a Nazarene, he was born in Bethlehem. All Israel's prophets knew the Messiah would be born in the City of David, Bethlehem. The implication is that it would be his hometown. Ah, but God's plans are always so different from our own, and his purposes are sometimes contrary to ours.

Why would a political figure call for a census? In ancient times taking a census was part of being powerful. It meant trusting in a political system, in the number of subjects under your rule. For instance, we're told how King David severely sinned by taking a census of able-bodied men in Israel who could fight. Even his commander in charge knew it was a great sin and objected, but David still carried out the order. Taking a census was a sign that David was putting faith not in God but in his own strength, the strength of his army. David repented, knowing that he had blasphemed against God.

Here in Luke, a political figure showed the same inclination by calling for the census. Of course, he showed no remorse because Herod did not know God. Yet it was this historical act that moved all of God's plans precisely where he wanted them. It just shows how much in charge we humans are not.

To God alone be glory!

There Is Always Room

All went to be registered, everyone to his own city. Joseph also went up from Galilee, out of the city of Nazareth, into Judea, to the city of David, which is called Bethlehem, because he was of the house and lineage of David, to be registered with Mary, his betrothed wife, who was with child. So it was, that while they were there, the days were completed for her to be delivered.

LUKE 2:3–6

From a news perspective, this whole national registration and census would have been a lead story. Imagine tens of thousands of people traveling for weeks, if not months, to officially give their name, address, and what would be the equivalent of a social security number to a government official. Try to envision the typical man-on-the-street interviews with tired families telling the reporters how far they'd come and how long the journey the return trip. Even a few would grumble about the current politician who ordered the census in the first place, "Who does he think he is?"

Yet one story that we now know was the climax of the whole event went unnoticed for centuries. The holy couple, Joseph and Mary, also made the journey to their ancestral home, Bethlehem, to register.

Many scholars say it's likely they had not intended to stay until Mary gave birth. But traveling back then took so much time, and her pregnancy advanced so much further than they anticipated during the trek that making the return trip to Nazareth would have been far too dangerous. Needless to say, all God's plans and prophetic predictions were now in place. No room at the inn? No problem.

To God alone be glory!

LETTING YOUR LIGHT SHINE

"Let your light so shine before men,
that they may see your good works
and glorify your Father in heaven."
MATTHEW 5:16

If you have a gas stove, you know there's always a pilot light burning. It's a tiny flame you never see that ignites the burners when the stove's knobs are turned on, allowing the gas to flow.

At the moment we were conceived, God put in each one of us his pilot light, the spark of creation. In fact, scientists have detected such a spark. It's some kind of chemical reaction, but a spark all the same. However, God doesn't force us to burn only for him. We have a choice of whether to turn up the blaze for his glory or toward something or someone else.

There's something very interesting about pilot lights. Even when the flame goes out, the fuel is still present. You can smell the noxious gas fumes, which in a stove is dangerous. God's fuel for the flame he put in each one of us never goes out. It's always there, always flowing. His sweet scent is all around us ready to ignite the fire for him if we just turn toward him, opening up those fuel lines of faith. He sent himself, in Jesus Christ, to be our flame and our fuel. Let his Light shine.

To God alone be glory!

Resting in God's Light

For You will light my lamp;
the Lord my God will enlighten my darkness.
PSALM 18:28

At times, all our own resources are exhausted. Our mind is tired; our bodies are worn out; and the paths once wide open to us have narrowed and seem impassable. There may be physical sunlight, but we feel surrounded by darkness, and it's hard to find our way through. God has assured us that he is the Light we must look to for all our needs and the rest that brings relief from the toils and tribulations of life. Because in him, there is no darkness.

Jesus on the cross suffered the ultimate cosmic darkness, separation from God. But his birth, death, and resurrection brought the ultimate light into the world and intimate closeness to God. It means that in our earthly hours of darkness, we can turn to God for comfort, yes, but also just to know that he is handling it. He is fighting the battle, and all we need to do is rest.

To God alone be glory!

THE ULTIMATE SMACKDOWN

We do not wrestle against flesh and blood, but against principalities, against powers, against the rulers of the darkness of this age, against spiritual hosts of wickedness in the heavenly places.

EPHESIANS 6:12

There's a lot of wrestling going on in the spiritual world. It's the world of our mind's eye. It's the place deep inside us where all our decisions are made. The place where we choose what to do and how to do it. And we endeavor each day to free ourselves from the chains that bind us.

But are we certain where those chains come from? The yoke of slavery is what God freed the Israelites from in Egypt, and the yoke of sin is what Jesus Christ's death and resurrection freed us from on the cross. What we still must grasp is that while God has set us free, our only true freedom is whether we choose to bow down and worship him.

The world is still fallen, and "there is no autonomy in the fallen world. We are governed by sin, or governed by God."[166] There are many choices available in the world today. But only one choice—to follow the Man who calmed the sea, who made the blind see and the lame walk— gives the ultimate smackdown to the forces we wrestle with.

To God alone be glory!

The Father Who Stays

Joseph her husband, being a just man, and not wanting to make her a public example, was minded to put her away secretly. But while he thought about these things, behold, an angel of the Lord appeared to him in a dream, saying, "Joseph, son of David, do not be afraid to take to you Mary your wife, for that which is conceived in her is of the Holy Spirit."

MATTHEW 1:19–20

What a man! Put yourself in Joseph and Mary's world, a patriarchal society where a woman had very few rights and her status depended on her purity and her ability to bear children. Finding out that his intended was pregnant, and not by him, Joseph was within his rights to walk away from the relationship or even to have Mary stoned. But he didn't.

Today, thousands of children grow up without fathers as many men put their needs ahead of the needs of the child or the mother. It has created devastation in the lives of millions of children. Statistics show that children with absent fathers are more likely to do drugs, commit crimes, or drop out of school.

It takes strength to be a father, to protect a child from the world, and teach them to love God. Joseph appears only a short time in the biblical narrative. But his influence lasts an eternity.

To God alone be glory!

God's Precious Family

*A man shall leave his father and mother and be joined to his wife,
and they shall become one flesh.*

GENESIS 2:24

Families aren't perfect. Even the perfect life Adam and Eve had with God in the garden of Eden became marred through sin, the fall from grace. But it doesn't negate the fact that as imperfect as families are, "God…created us to thrive best in families."[167] Mother and father, sisters and brothers, aunts and uncles, grandparents and in-laws. These are the people tasked with doing God's work of raising us, molding us, loving us.

"For those without a family, there is God's family, the Church, united by the common 'life blood' of the Spirit."[168] The people who make up families aren't perfect, but Jesus is. Families don't always understand you, but Jesus does and intimately so. Families can't always be there when you call, but Jesus can. Through his Word, Jesus is but a breath, a sigh, a moment away.

God gives us earthly families to give us the love and nurturing we all need. But through the "life blood" of Jesus Christ, we have a wholly different kind of family that will always be there. DNA has its limits. But the blood of Jesus has created in us a divine DNA whose strength will never perish.

To God alone be glory!

WE LIVE IN GOD'S WORLD

*"In Him we live and move and have our being,
as also some of your own poets have said,
'For we are also His offspring.'"*
ACTS 17:28

Sometimes maybe God is humored by our belief that we're in control of our own lives. That we are the center of our own universes. Perhaps the selfie is a manifestation of that tendency. In the end, though, we are living in God's world, in the world he created. It's good to have that perspective just to understand that all we see, and even the parts we don't see, all belongs to God.

That is not to say we don't have free will. We are active agents in the landscape of our journey through life. But we move in and through a world created by God. He has made the world with a certain order to it. When we go against that order, life can get out of balance.

The fallenness of this world required God to get ahead of the game, so to speak. Jesus is the game changer. He is the part of the triune God who makes all things new. Order is restored. Life is back in balance.

To God alone be glory!

Jesus Is the Only Way

Beware lest anyone cheat you through philosophy and empty deceit, according to the tradition of men, according to the basic principles of the world, and not according to Christ.

COLOSSIANS 2:8

It's so important to be very careful about what we ingest intellectually. Ideas have power. Many beliefs are based on commonly held views that are not often tested against God's Word.

Not too long ago, a politician said all the prayers of all religions go to the same place, the same deity. The problem is, many religions, though they may agree on certain social issues, widely disagree on fundamentals, and some have contradictory doctrines. Jesus said, "I am the way, the truth, and the life" (John 14:6). It's a bold statement about the nature of truth that no other religious figure claimed. It gives believers incredible confidence to worship him. But it means that if he is the way, other religious figures are not.

The Gospel of John claimed Jesus is God's Word made flesh and dwelling among us (see John 1:14). He's not just a concept or a philosophy. He is a person with all the answers to life's most pressing problems.

To God alone be glory!

Sorrow in the Midst of Joy

Trust in the Lord with all your heart,
and lean not on your own understanding.

PROVERBS 3:5

This time of year, despite all its joy and merriment, can be very stressful and sometimes painful, especially for people who have suffered a great loss or disappointment. The death of a loved one, the ending of a relationship, or the loss of a job can make it so challenging to trust in God.

Author Lysa TerKeurst has wonderful words of encouragement for those struggling. She says, "Disappointment isn't proof that God is withholding good things from us. Sometimes it's His way of leading us Home."[169]

For most of us the holidays will be filled with joy and good things. But Jesus wants us to keep a close and keen eye out for the broken-hearted, for the mournful, for those who have lost their way and perhaps need a hand to guide them. That is what Jesus did when he first walked the earth. If peace and goodwill are the hope for this season of the Savior's birth, then each of us can be a light, heralding its meaning. As we give gifts, remember that the greatest gift has already been given. Advent is here. Prepare ye a place for him.

To God alone be glory!

A Christmas Carol's Faith

Grace to you and peace from Him who is and who was
and who is to come, and from the seven Spirits who are before His throne.

REVELATION 1:4

No doubt many people will be watching adaptations of Charles Dickens' classic story *A Christmas Carol* this day. Many people have their favorite version. But did you ever realize the foundations of faith that are coursing all through the story, like the meaning of the miserly Scrooge's first name, Ebenezer? It means "stone of help." (See 1 Samuel 7:12.) It's from the Old Testament. Ebenezer was the name of the stone the Israelites placed in special places to remind them of how God had brought them through.

And why are there three ghosts in Dickens' story? The spirits of Christmas past, present, and future? Technically there are four, including the ghost of Marley. They represent the four lessons of Advent in the Church of England. Another theme in the story is that it's the poor people who are rich in faith and quite joyful in their lives, like Bob Cratchit, Scrooge's clerk. But the wealthy are often discontent, angry, or miserable like Scrooge himself. Dickens witnessed this in his own life. His grandfather, a servant in a big estate, was happy in his role in life and lived within his means. But his father wanted more, and although he made a good living, he often lived beyond it and wound up in debtors' prison. [170] This Christmas let Christ reign in your life. And while presents under the tree are nice, let Jesus' presence be born in your heart this Holy Night. He is the greatest gift you will ever receive.

To God alone be glory!

Joy to the World

*"I will put enmity between you and the woman, and between your seed
and her Seed; He shall bruise your head, and you shall bruise His heel."*

GENESIS 3:15

Merry Christmas! Today, we celebrate the start of the fulfillment of this
verse in Genesis, the first book of the Bible. Yes, on Christmas Day, when
we welcome the birth of Jesus, this prophecy begins to unfold. It's a time
to harken back to the garden of Eden and the fall from grace when Eve, in
defiance of God's edict, was tempted by Satan and ate the forbidden fruit.

We should never lose sight of God's grand narrative, of his plan to
redeem a fallen world. That is what Jesus, the Word made flesh, is for us
this day. Even in that manger in Bethlehem, we see the past problem of
inherited sin, of a present struggle of hard times, and the future of nails
holding him to the cross.

But oh! The resurrection is coming too. All this is contained in that
tiny baby, born of a woman, helpless yet hopeful, small yet larger than life,
vulnerable yet soon to be victorious. Yes, God has a plan. And it is fulfilled
today. Joy to the world!

To God alone be glory!

Go Tell Everyone!

*The shepherds returned, glorifying and praising God
for all the things that they had heard and seen, as it was told them.*

LUKE 2:20

A woman said her mom used to play a Christmas album that was a favorite of the family. On the record jacket was an illustration of a little drummer boy. On the back of the jacket were printed the words to all the carols so listeners could sing along.

It's how the family memorized many of the Christmas hymns. The child would beg her mother to put the record on and keep playing it over and over. A favorite song on the album was "Go Tell It on the Mountain." This is the shepherd's song. It means they believed! They had sought with their hearts and then they believed with their minds. The shepherds, unbeknownst to even themselves, were the first evangelists. News like this just can't be contained; it must be spread.

Christmas is not a private affair to celebrate among only those who believe. It is a time to share the good news that Jesus is born. Go tell it on the mountaintops! From the highest peaks so that everyone may know and believe and be transformed. Merry Christmas!

To God alone be glory!

Looking for the Christ Child

After Jesus was born in Bethlehem of Judea in the days of Herod the king, behold, wise men from the East came to Jerusalem, saying, "Where is He who has been born King of the Jews? For we have seen His star in the East and have come to worship Him."

MATTHEW 2:1–2

By now all the presents have been opened, and there may be only leftovers from Christmas dinner in the fridge. But it is still Christmas. For the wise men who traveled long distances, the journey to find the newborn babe was their life's ambition. Their eyes and ears, hearts and minds were trained to search for this promised King, newly born. That he was in a manger, the poorest of conditions surrounding him, made no difference. They gave him gifts of gold, frankincense, and myrrh, bowing down to his glory.

It is an example of how weakness does not mean worthless. In our society today, we associate wealth with wisdom and earthly power with what should be praised. But Christ being born in the most rudimentary conditions is a reminder to us to pay closer attention to those whose voices are faint or even silent, the quiet cries of the indigent, the poor, the aged, and the unborn. "A society is as strong as its care for its weakest members."[171]

Christmas is about God giving us the greatest gift of all time. And so many times, the best gifts come in the most unlikely packaging. But like the Christ Child, they are priceless.

To God alone be glory!

The Golden Rule

"Whatever you want men to do to you, do also to them,
for this is the Law and the Prophets."

MATTHEW 7:12

This is the Golden Rule. There's no better, everyday testing of this sacred directive than an encounter with a telemarketer and the cold calls from strangers wanting to sell us something we probably don't want and most likely don't need. As a good exercise, the next time you're impatient or rude to one of those callers, say to yourself, *What would it feel like if I were earning a living, paying rent, or putting food on the table by calling strangers in a cheery voice about the benefits of a product? And then being hung up on, sworn at, yelled at...?*

Jesus didn't qualify his words. He didn't say to treat others as you would want to be treated except for (fill in the blank). Our tendency to make our judgments worth more than God's edicts is one of the sins for which Christ died. It's one of the countless ways we put ourselves in God's place, which is our foundational sin.

But it's also a way we can see the beauty and joy of Christmas. Jesus is here, so let him be the judge. Jesus is born, so let him be your blessing. Jesus lives! So let him be your joy in life. And be kind to those telemarketers, knowing God cares for them the same as he does for you.

To God alone be glory!

ᴮELIEVING ᴵs ᔕEEING

[Simeon] took Him up in his arms and blessed God and said: "Lord, now You are letting Your servant depart in peace, according to Your word; For my eyes have seen Your salvation which You have prepared before the face of all peoples, a light to bring revelation to the Gentiles, and the glory of Your people Israel."

LUKE 2:28–32

If the message of Christmas is anything, it's the knowledge that life is forever changed. The birth of Jesus is the climax of human existence. All other historical activity up until this point has been preparation for this moment in time. For the Lord of history, who controls all things in heaven and earth, has written himself into our story.

It's as if Shakespeare wrote himself into his play *Hamlet* or Jane Austen transcended her written pages of *Pride and Prejudice* and introduced herself to Elizabeth Bennet. Christmas says the author of existence itself has joined the journey of mankind to correct its course, to get us back on the proper trajectory, one that leads us to him.

The priest Simeon, in his way, knows all of this. To hold in his hand the baby Jesus is to hold the great I AM. That is why he is at peace, perfect peace. The balance of life, which we all strive for, can now be grasped. The only thing for us to do now is believe.

To God alone be glory!

MIRACLES OF BIRTH

When they had departed, behold, an angel of the Lord appeared to Joseph in a dream, saying, "Arise, take the young Child and His mother, flee to Egypt, and stay there until I bring you word; for Herod will seek the young Child to destroy Him."

MATTHEW 2:13

The saga continues. While Christmas is about peace and joy, it is also about a tiny baby upsetting the political landscape. The holy family had to flee. They had a price on their heads the minute Jesus came into the world. Herod typified a lot of rulers down through the ages who have tremendous egos and see themselves as gods to be worshiped. There is no room for the real God in their world.

Even in their escaping from the clutches of evil, Mary and Joseph had practical concerns, like feeding a newborn baby. And in Bethlehem today, there is a chapel that marks the spot where Mary first stopped to breastfeed the tiny baby Jesus on their journey to Egypt. It is called, for that reason, the *Milk Grotto*. On the walls of the cave is a white substance that the priest there says is the miracle of the place. It is Mary's breast milk. And it is scraped off continually and offered to women who've had trouble conceiving a child. The priest's office walls are filled with photos of couples who were barren who then conceived and bore children.

This is the goodness of Christmas, that even in the midst of hardship, of upheaval and uncertainty, there can still be new life, new and abundant life.

To God alone be glory!

Saved by Grace

Of His fullness we have all received, and grace for grace.
For the law was given through Moses,
but grace and truth came through Jesus Christ.
JOHN 1:16–17

There is no better time to reflect on God's amazing grace than on the last day of the year. Even those of us who have been saved by putting our faith in Jesus Christ still sing the song "Amazing Grace" knowing how totally inept we are at saving ourselves.

We are all sinners who can look to our past and see how grace saved us—in our long past, in just this past year, and this very day. All the times we've been a less than the perfect person. God has given us enough wisdom to know that we will never be perfect, that our sin of selfishness and self-righteousness is always before us.

We need God's amazing grace that he provided through Christ crucified. Thank you, Lord. For it is by grace all of us have been saved. (See Ephesians 2:8.)

To God alone be glory!

Acknowledgments

It's difficult to thank all the people who have helped birth any writing project. I wish to thank countless friends who have been partakers of a plethora of faith-filled conversations and prayers. Thank you for helping me see the Living God through your spiritual journeys.

I'd like to thank the folks at BroadStreet Publishing, whose dedication and gentle prodding helped move this effort forward.

I owe so much to the late Dr. Timothy Keller, who passed away just as the manuscript for this devotional was in its final stages. Dr. Keller opened up a deeper and wider understanding of the gospel of Jesus Christ for me and countless others. Without his profound theological insights, I never would have written *Lighthouse Faith* or *Light for Today*.

Finally, I'd like to thank my family: my sisters, brother, nieces, nephews, and, of course, my supportive husband, Ted. And to our four-legged creatures who fill our home and are constant reminders that God has made us stewards over his creation.

To God alone be glory!

Endnotes

1   Timothy Keller and Kathy Keller, *The Songs of Jesus* (New York: Penguin Publishing Group, 2015), 315.

2   Oswald Chambers, *My Utmost for His Highest* (Grand Rapids, MI: Discovery House Publishers, 2012), November 14.

3   Eugene H. Peterson, *A Long Obedience in the Same Direction* (Downers Grove, IL: InterVarsity Press, 1980), 96.

4   Peterson, *A Long Obedience*, 132.

5   J. I. Packer, *Knowing God* (Downers Grove, IL: InterVarsity Press, 2021), 25.

6   Peterson, *A Long Obedience*, 153.

7   Peterson, *A Long Obedience*, 195.

8   Herbert Schlossberg, *Idols for Destruction: The Conflict of Christian Faith and American Culture* (Wheaton, IL: Crossway Books, 1990), 12.

9   Eugene H. Peterson, *Every Step an Arrival* (Colorado Springs, CO: WaterBrook, 2018), 14.

10 C. S. Lewis, *Weight of Glory* (Grand Rapids, MI: Zondervan, 2001), 167.

11 Neil Postman, *Amusing Ourselves to Death: Public Discourse in the Age of Show Business* (London, England: Penguin Books, 2005), 14.

12 Vern S. Poythress, *The Shadow of Christ in the Law of Moses* (Phillipsburg, NJ: P & R Publishing, 1995), 73.

13 Peterson, *Every Step an Arrival*, 26.

14 Timothy Keller and Kathy Keller, *God's Wisdom for Navigating Life: A Year of Daily Devotions* (New York: Viking Press, 2017), 35.

15 Keller, *God's Wisdom*, 32.

16 Jonathan Edwards, *The Works of Jonathan Edwards, Volume One*, Christian Classics Ethereal Library (Avon: The Bath Press, first published in1834), preface, https://www.ccel.org/ccel/edwards/works1.vii.i.html.

17 Pastor Tommy Nelson, "The Melancholy Flight" (sermon, Denton Bible Church, Denton, TX, February 9, 2014), https://dentonbible.org/sermon/the-melancholy-flight/.

18 Saint Augustine of Hippo, *The Confessions* (San Francisco: Ignatius Press, 2012), 416.

19   Charlie Johnson, "Love and St. Augustine's Weight Problem," *Sacra Pagina* (website), February 17, 2012, https://sacredpage.wordpress.com/2012/02/17/love-and-st-augustines-weight-problem/.

20   Saint Augustine, *The Confessions*, 3.

21   Rev. David Bisgrove, "A Movement of Conversions: Simon the Magician" (sermon, Redeemer Presbyterian, New York, NY, January 13, 2019).

22   Rodney Stark, *Why God? Explaining Religious Phenomenon* (West Conshohocken, PA: Templeton Press, 2017), 14–15.

23   Poythress, *The Shadow of Christ*, 113.

24   Keller, *The Songs of Jesus*, 14.

25   Keller, *The Songs of Jesus*, 164.

26   Keller, *God's Wisdom*, 55.

27   C. S. Lewis, *The Problem of Pain* (Grand Rapids, MI: Zondervan, 2001), 47.

28   This information came from several sources of interviews and books. However, there is an article from the American Speech-Language-Hearing Association that may succinctly address this: "Effects of Hearing Loss on Development," Audiology Information Series, The American Speech-Language-Hearing Association, accessed on May 18, 2023, https://www.asha.org/siteassets/ais/ais-hearing-loss-development-effects.pdf.

29   Keller, *The Songs of Jesus*, 20.

30   Keller, *God's Wisdom*, 61.

31   Charles H. Spurgeon, "Abundant Pardon: A Sermon Delivered on Lord's-Day Morning, September 27, 1847," in *The Metropolitan Tabernacle Pulpit: Sermons Preached and Revised by C. H. Spurgeon during the Year 1874* (London: Passmore & Alabaster, 1875), 549.

32   Melissa Gomes, "Fasting Faithfully: A Discipline of Devotion and Trust," Intimaseed (website), accessed February 17, 2023, https://intimaseed.com/how-to-fast/.

33   Oswald Chambers, "God First," My Utmost for His Highest (website), May 31, 2022, https://utmost.org/classic/god-first-classic/.

34   Miroslav Volf, *Exclusion and Embrace: A Theological Exploration of Identity, Otherness, and Reconciliation* (Nashville, TN: Abingdon Press, 1996), 96.

35   Volf, *Exclusion and Embrace*, 98.

36   J. R. R. Tolkien, *The Lord of the Rings: The Return of the King* (New York, NY: The Random House Publishing Group, 1973), 246.

37   Peterson, *Every Step an Arrival*, 64.

38   Keller, *The Songs of Jesus*, 105.

39   Peterson, *Every Step an Arrival*, 52.

40   Volf, *Exclusion and Embrace*, 134.

41   C. S. Lewis, *Mere Christianity* (New York, NY: HarperCollins, 1952), 63.

42   Peterson, *Every Step an Arrival*, 72.

43   Schlossberg, *Idols for Destruction*, 5.

44   Keller, *God's Wisdom*, 93.

45   Keller, *God's Wisdom*, 95.

46   Rev. Casey and Bob Baggott, "On Faith: Your Life Is Your Sermon…What Are You Saying?" VeroNews.com, Vero Beach Media, June 29, 2017, https://veronews.com/2017/06/29/faith-life-sermon-saying/.

47   D. A. Carson, *The Gospel According to John* (Grand Rapids, MI: Wm. B. Eerdmans Publishing Company, 1991), 175.

48   Fr. Soterios Baroody, Untitled (homily, Annunciation Greek Orthodox Church, New York, NY, April 15, 2018).

49   David Foster Wallace, "This Is Water" (commencement speech, Kenyon College, Gambier, OH, May 21, 2005).

50   Keller, *The Songs of Jesus*, 14.

51   Rev. David Bisgrove, "Work and Rest" (sermon, Redeemer Presbyterian Church, New York, NY, April 22, 2018).

52   Bisgrove, "Work and Rest."

53   Tony Ward, "The Wisdom of *Deo Volente*," *Christian Today*, January 17, 2012, https://www.christiantoday.com/amp/the.wisdom.of.deo.volente/29181.htm.

54   Abdu Murray, *Saving Truth: Finding Meaning and Clarity in a Post-Truth World* (Grand Rapids, MI: Zondervan, 2018), 82.

55   Keller, *God's Wisdom*, 122.

56   Lewis, *Mere Christianity*, 134.

57   Young, *Jesus Calling*, 58.

58   C. S. Lewis, *Reflections on the Psalms* (San Francisco, CA: Harcourt Brace, 1958), 94.

59   Young, *Jesus Calling*, 59.

60 John R. W. Stott, *The Message of the Sermon on the Mount* (Downers Grove, IL: InterVarsity Press, 1988), 39.

61 Peterson, *Every Step an Arrival*, 123–24.

62 Keller, *God's Wisdom for Navigating Life*, 129.

63 Young, *Jesus Calling*, 136.

64 Rev. Peter Nicholas, Untitled (sermon, Inspire St. James Church, London, England, May 9, 2018).

65 David B. Calhoun, "'Amazing Grace' John Newton and His Great Hymn," C. S. Lewis Institute, December 1, 2013, https://www.cslewisinstitute.org/resources/amazing-grace-john-newton-and-his-great-hymn/.

66 Patrick Comerford, "Saint Mary Woolnoth: A London Church Celebrated by TS Eliot," Patrick Comerford (blog), May 15, 2018, http://www.patrickcomerford.com/2018/05/saint-mary-woolnoth-london-church.html.

67 C. S. Lewis, *The Four Loves* (Orlando, FL: Harcourt Brace & Company, 1988), 129.

68 Lewis, *The Four Loves*, 126.

69 Rev. Peter Nicholas, Untitled (sermon, Inspire St. James, London, England, May 13, 2018).

70 Young, *Jesus Calling*, 279.

71 Peterson, *Every Step an Arrival*, 143.

72 Thomas Anthony Harris, *I'm OK–You're OK* (New York: NY: Harper & Row Publishers, 1967).

73 Elizabeth Harrison, "9 Things You May Not Know about the Declaration of Independence," History.com, updated April 26, 2023, https://www.history.com/news/9-things-you-may-not-know-about-the-declaration-of-independence.

74 Keller, *God's Wisdom*, 163.

75 Charles Chatput, forward to *From Fire, By Water*, by Sohrab Ahmari (San Francisco, CA: Ignatius Press, 2006), 10.

76 Joshua Brown and Joel Wong, "How Gratitude Changes You and Your Brain," Greater Good Magazine (website), June 6, 2017, https://greatergood.berkeley.edu/article/item/how_gratitude_changes_you_and_your_brain.

77 Alister E. McGrath, *Mere Apologetics: How to Help Seekers and Skeptics Find Faith* (Grand Rapids, MI: Baker Books, 2012), 116.

78   John Stonestreet and G. Shane Morris, "Mopping Up Myths about Masterpiece: The Truth about the Cake Shop Case," Christian Headlines, June 18, 2018, https://www.christianheadlines.com/columnists/breakpoint/mopping-up-myths-about-masterpiece-the-truth-about-the-cake-shop-case.html.

79   McGrath, *Mere Apologetics*, 113.

80   Young, *Jesus Calling*, 101.

81   John Piper, "Total Depravity," Bethlehem Baptist Church, Minneapolis, MN, 1998, https://www.monergism.com/thethreshold/articles/piper/depravity.html.

82   John Piper, "What We Believe about the Five Points of Calvinism," Desiring God (website), March 1, 1985, https://www.desiringgod.org/articles/what-we-believe-about-the-five-points-of-calvinism.

83   Scott Slayton, "Filipino President Says He Will Resign If Someone Proves the Existence of God," Christian Headlines, July 12, 2018, https://www.christianheadlines.com/columnists/scott-slayton/filipino-president-says-he-will-resign-if-someone-proves-the-existence-of-god.html.

84   Chris Loh, "The DC-10 1979 Grounding–What Happened?" Simple Flying, June 7, 2020, https://simpleflying.com/dc-10-1979-grounding/.

85   Rev. David Bisgrove, "Who Is Greater?" (sermon, Redeemer Presbyterian Church, New York, NY, April 7, 2019).

86   J. I. Packer, *A Quest for Godliness: The Puritan Vision of the Christian Life* (Wheaton, IL: Crossway, 990), 144.

87   Dr. Hugh Ross, *Improbable Planet: How Earth Became Humanity's Home* (Grand Rapids, MI: Baking Publishing Group, 2017), 17.

88   Murray, *Saving Truth*, 115.

89   Peterson, *Every Step an Arrival*, 64.

90   Murray, *Saving Truth*, 214.

91   Perry T. Hamalis, "Lent as Liberation," *Public Orthodoxy*, April 22, 2019, https://publicorthodoxy.org/2019/04/22/lent-as-liberation/.

92   Johanna Spyri, *Heidi* (Philadelphia, PA: J.B. Lippincott Company, 1915), 143.

93   Keller, *God's Wisdom*, 212.

94   Keller, *God's Wisdom*, 214.

95   Ross, *Improbable Planet*, 134–35

96 Keller, *The Songs of Jesus*, 108.

97 Mary Fairchild, "What Does '*Christos Anesti*' Mean?," Learn Religions, updated April 12, 2020, https://www.learnreligions.com/meaning-of-christos-anesti-700625.

98 Chris Ciaccia, "'Mysterious Radio Bursts in Outer Space Detected by Alien-hunting Artificial Intelligence," Fox News, September 11, 2018, https://www.foxnews.com/science/mysterious-radio-bursts-in-outer-space-detected-by-alien-hunting-artificial-intelligence.

99 Ross, *Improbable Planet*, 236.

100 Dr. Voddie Baucham Jr., *Expository Apologetics: Answering Objections with the Power of the Word* (Wheaton, IL: Crossway, 2015), 85.

101 *On the Waterfront*, directed by Elia Kazan (Columbia Pictures, 1954).

102 Fr. Chrysostomos Gilbert, No title. (homily, Greek Orthodox Church of the Annunciation, New York, NY, April 21, 2019).

103 Young, *Jesus Calling*, 116.

104 Keller, *The Songs of Jesus*, 112.

105 Keller, *God's Wisdom*, 225.

106 McGrath, *Mere Apologetics*, 24.

107 Blaise Pascal, *Pensees* (Paris: Librairie Generale Francaise, 1972).

108 Peterson, *Every Step an Arrival*, 36.

109 Keller, *The Songs of Jesus*, 118.

110 McGrath, *Mere Apologetics*, 44.

111 Keller, *God's Wisdom*, 223.

112 Norman Doidge, *The Brain That Changes Itself: Stories of Personal Triumph from the Frontiers of Brain Science* (New York: Viking Press, 2017), 63.

113 Keller, *God's Wisdom*, 235.

114 Peter Scheibner, "In My Seat - A Pilot's Story from Sept 10th–11th," Character Health, August 30, 2011, YouTube video, 15:33, https://www.youtube.com/watch?app=desktop&v=cLj4akmncsA.

115 Bob Smietana, "Many Churchgoers Want Sunday Morning Segregated…by Politics," *Christianity Today*, August 23, 2018, https://www.christianitytoday.com/news/2018/august/segregated-sunday-morning-politics-protestant-churches.html.

116 Joe Carter, "Study: Majority of Self-Identified Christians Don't Believe the Holy Spirit Is Real," The Gospel Coalition, September 18, 2021, https://www.thegospelcoalition.org/article/christians-dont-believe-spirit/.

117 McGrath, *Mere Apologetics*, 137–38.

118 C. S. Lewis, "Is Theology Poetry?," in *The Weight of Glory* (New York, NY: HarperCollins Publishers, 2001), 140.

119 Keller, *God's Wisdom*, 252.

120 Keller, *God's Wisdom*, 255.

121 Gerald Schroeder, *Genesis and the Big Bang Theory: The Discovery of Harmony between Modern Science and the Bible* (New York, NY: Bantam Books, 1992), 56.

122 Richard Swinburne, *The Existence of God* (Oxford, England: Oxford University Press, 2004), 93.

123 Peterson, *Every Step an Arrival*, 56.

124 Young, *Jesus Calling*, 131.

125 Stott, *The Message of the Sermon on the Mount*, 134.

126 Samuel Smith, "81 Percent of Family TV Comedies Show Kids Being Exposed to Sexual Dialogue: Report," The Christian Post (website), September 11, 2018, https://www.christianpost.com/amp/81-percent-of-family-tv-comedies-show-kids-being-exposed-sexual-dialogue-report-227281/.

127 Rev. David Bisgrove, "Our Foundation" (sermon, Redeemer Presbyterian Church, New York, NY, September 23, 2018).

128 Anne Lamott, *Bird by Bird: Some Instructions on Writing and Life* (New York, NY: Anchor Books, 1995), 22.

129 For a more comprehensive explanation of this topic, go to https://biblehub.com/commentaries/ephesians/6-5.htm.

130 Peterson, *Every Step an Arrival*, 62.

131 Julie Compton, "'Boy or Girl?' Parents Raising 'Theybies' Let Kids Decide," NBC News (website), July 19, 2018, https://www.nbcnews.com/feature/nbc-out/boy-or-girl-parents-raising-theybies-let-kids-decide-n891836.

132 Keller, *God's Wisdom*, 272.

133 *Independence Day*, directed by Roland Emmerich (20th Century Fox, 1996).

134 Francis A. Schaeffer, *Escape from Reason* (Downers Grove, IL: InterVarsity Press, 2014), 92.

135 Samuel Mills, "The Old Testament Law: Ceremonial, Civil, Moral," Trusting in Jesus, accessed February 24, 2023, https://www.trusting-in-jesus.com/Old-Testament-Law.html.

136 Rev. Bijan Mirtolooi, "Equipping for Movement" (sermon, Redeemer Presbyterian Church, New York, NY, October 7, 2018).

137 Mirtolooi, "Equipping for Movement."

138 Stott, *The Message of the Sermon on the Mount*, 186.

139 Keller, *The Songs of Jesus*, 137.

140 Keller, *God's Wisdom*, 291.

141 Lauren Green, "Dr. Tim Keller's Take on Jonah and Whale…and Lessons for Today's Culture," December 7, 2018, in *Lauren Green's Lighthouse Faith* (podcast), Fox News Radio, https://radio.foxnews.com/2018/12/07/dr-tim-kellers-take-on-jonah-and-whale-and-lessons-for-todays-culture/.

142 Green, "Dr. Tim Keller's Take."

143 *ESV Study Bible* (Wheaton, IL: Crossway, 2008), 2229.

144 Keller, *The Songs of Jesus*, 102.

145 Diogenes Allen, *Christian Belief in a Postmodern World: The Full Wealth of Conviction* (Louisville, KY: Westminster/John Knox Press, 1989), 102.

146 Kayla Koslosky, "Pizza Shop Manager Drives 3 Hours to Bring Dying Man His Favorite Pizza," Christian Headlines, October 24, 2018, https://www.christianheadlines.com/blog/pizza-shop-manager-drives-3-hours-to-bring-dying-man-his-favorite-pizza.html.

147 Allen, *Christian Belief*, 104.

148 Peterson, *Every Step an Arrival*, 80.

149 Erica Nardozzi and Tate Delloye, "Dirty Money: Inside Scandal-ridden Legacy of the Vanderbilt Dynasty," *Daily Mail*, April 9, 2023, https://www.dailymail.co.uk/femail/article-11944115/Inside-scandal-ridden-legacy-Vanderbilt-dynasty.html.

150 Allen, *Christian Belief*, 141.

151 Rev. David Bisgrove, "The Law: Freed to Worship" (sermon, Redeemer Presbyterian Church, New York, NY, May 19, 2019).

152 Piper, *Fifty Reasons*, 58.

153 Young, *Jesus Calling*, 150.

154 Lewis, *Mere Christianity*, 52.

155 Michael Keller, "A Movement of Generosity" (sermon, Redeemer Presbyterian Church, Lincoln Square, New York, NY, October 28, 2018).

156 *The Sound of Music,* directed by Robert Wise, (Los Angeles, CA: Twentieth Century Fox, 1965).

157 Peterson, *A Long Obedience*, 41–42.

158 Timothy Keller, "The Wellspring of Wisdom" (sermon, Redeemer Presbyterian Church, New York, NY, September 26, 2004).

159 N. T. Wright, *For All God's Worth: True Worship and the Calling of the Church* (Grand Rapids, MI: William B. Eerdmans Publishing, 2014), ix.

160 C. S. Lewis, *The Screwtape Letters* (New York, NY: HarperCollins Publishers, 1996), 40.

161 Lewis, *The Four Loves*, 139.

162 Lewis, *The Four Loves*, 126.

163 Raymond C. Van Leeuwen, *Book of Proverbs* (Nashville, TN: Abingdon Press, 1997), 214.

164 Chris Woodford, "Antennas and Transmitters," ExplainThatStuff, October 6, 2021, https://www.explainthatstuff.com/antennas.html.

165 Piper, *Fifty Reasons*, 77.

166 Piper, *Fifty Reasons*, 65.

167 Keller, *The Songs of Jesus*, 47.

168 Keller, *The Songs of Jesus*, 47.

169 Lysa TerKeurst, *It's Not Supposed to Be This Way: Finding Unexpected Strength When Disappointments Leave You Shattered* (Nashville, TN: Nelson Books, 2018), 12.

170 Interview with Pastor Cheryl Anne Kincaid, based on her book: *Hearing the Gospel Through Charles Dickens A Christmas Carol* (Newcastle upon Tyne, England: Cambridge Scholars Publishing, 2011).

171 Keller, *God's Wisdom*, 344.

About the Author

Lauren Green joined Fox News Channel in 1996 and currently serves as the chief religion correspondent based in the New York bureau.

Prior to joining FNC, Green served as a weekend news anchor and correspondent at WBBM-TV in Chicago, Illinois, and as a general assignment reporter at KSTP-TV in St. Paul, Minnesota.

Throughout her career, Green has reported live and on-site for significant religious events, including the beatification of Pope John Paul II, Pope Francis's election to the papacy and first visit to the United States, and both the Retirement and Funeral Masses of Pope Benedict XVI.

Outside of her career at FNC, Green hosts *Fox on Faith*, a weekly series on Fox Radio, as well as the *Lighthouse Faith* podcast, covering all things concerning religion, faith, and beliefs. Interviewees have included Lee Strobel, Eric Metaxas, Richard Land, Anne Graham Lotz, Michael Wear, Joni Eareckson Tada, N. T. Wright, Timothy Keller, Max Lucado, and Ravi Zacharias.

Green's first book, *Lighthouse Faith: God as a Living Reality in a World Immersed in Fog*, released in 2017. It was the culmination of more than a decade of research on the convergence of faith, science, and living.

Green is a concert pianist with a degree in piano performance from the University of Minnesota and released her debut album, *Classic Beauty*, in 2004. She has interviewed some of the most prominent figures in classical music, such as Plácido Domingo, Pierre Boulez, and Joshua Bell, and provided event coverage for the likes of the Van Cliburn International Piano Competition and opening night of The Metropolitan Opera.

A graduate of Northwestern University's Medill School of Journalism, Green was named Miss Minnesota in 1984 and was the third runner-up in the 1985 Miss America contest. She and her husband, Theodore Nikolis, reside in New York City.